T0133083

Grid Application Systems Design

OTHER AUERBACH PUBLICATIONS

Agent-Based Manufacturing and Control Systems: New Agile Manufacturing Solutions for Achieving Peak Performance
Massimo Paolucci and Roberto Sacile
ISBN: 1574443364

Curing the Patch Management Headache
Felicia M. Nicastro
ISBN: 0849328543

Cyber Crime Investigator's Field Guide, Second Edition
Bruce Middleton
ISBN: 0849327687

Disassembly Modeling for Assembly, Maintenance, Reuse and Recycling
A. J. D. Lambert and Surendra M. Gupta
ISBN: 1574443348

The Ethical Hack: A Framework for Business Value Penetration Testing
James S. Tiller
ISBN: 084931609X

Fundamentals of DSL Technology
Philip Golden, Herve Dedieu,
and Krista Jacobsen
ISBN: 0849319137

The HIPAA Program Reference Handbook
Ross Leo
ISBN: 0849322111

Implementing the IT Balanced Scorecard: Aligning IT with Corporate Strategy
Jessica Keyes
ISBN: 0849326214

Information Security Fundamentals
Thomas R. Peltier, Justin Peltier,
and John A. Blackley
ISBN: 0849319579

Information Security Management Handbook, Fifth Edition, Volume 2
Harold F. Tipton and Micki Krause
ISBN: 0849332109

Introduction to Management of Reverse Logistics and Closed Loop Supply Chain Processes
Donald F. Blumberg
ISBN: 1574443607

Maximizing ROI on Software Development
Vijay Sikka
ISBN: 0849323126

Mobile Computing Handbook
Imad Mahgoub and Mohammad Ilyas
ISBN: 0849319714

MPLS for Metropolitan Area Networks
Nam-Kee Tan
ISBN: 084932212X

Multimedia Security Handbook
Borko Furht and Darko Kirovski
ISBN: 0849327733

Network Design: Management and Technical Perspectives, Second Edition
Teresa C. Piliouras
ISBN: 0849316081

Network Security Technologies, Second Edition
Kwok T. Fung
ISBN: 0849330270

Outsourcing Software Development Offshore: Making It Work
Tandy Gold
ISBN: 0849319439

Quality Management Systems: A Handbook for Product Development Organizations
Vivek Nanda
ISBN: 1574443526

A Practical Guide to Security Assessments
Sudhanshu Kairab
ISBN: 0849317061

The Real-Time Enterprise
Dimitris N. Chorafas
ISBN: 0849327776

Software Testing and Continuous Quality Improvement, Second Edition
William E. Lewis
ISBN: 0849325242

Supply Chain Architecture: A Blueprint for Networking the Flow of Material, Information, and Cash
William T. Walker
ISBN: 1574443577

The Windows Serial Port Programming Handbook
Ying Bai
ISBN: 0849322138

AUERBACH PUBLICATIONS

www.auerbach-publications.com
To Order Call: 1-800-272-7737 • Fax: 1-800-374-3401
E-mail: orders@crcpress.com

Grid Application Systems Design

April J. Wells

Auerbach Publications
Taylor & Francis Group
Boca Raton   New York

Auerbach Publications is an imprint of the
Taylor & Francis Group, an **informa** business

CRC Press
Taylor & Francis Group
6000 Broken Sound Parkway NW, Suite 300
Boca Raton, FL 33487-2742

Library of Congress Cataloging-in-Publication Data

Library of Congress Cataloging-in-Publication Data
Wells, April J.
Grid application systems design / April J. Wells.
p. cm.
Includes bibliographical references and index.
ISBN 978-0-8493-2997-5 (hardback : alk. paper)
1. Computational grids (Computer systems) 2. Application
software--Development. 3. System design. I. Title.

QA76.9.C58W43 5 2007
004'.36--dc22
2007024790

Visit the Taylor & Francis Web site at
http://www.taylorandfrancis.com

and the CRC Press Web site at
http://www.crcpress.com

Contents

PART III: APPLICATIONS IN THE GRID

Preface

Computing and computer programming have come a long way since their beginnings. Many of us have seen complete transformations in the technology of computing in our lifetimes. This author is relatively young when one looks at the history of computing, and has seen punch cards, programs stored on cassette tapes, dumb terminals, mainframes, PCs getting smaller and more powerful, and hand-held devices. This author has seen numbered Basic on an Apple IIe, DOS Qbasic, COBOL, highly structured and cryptic C, and Java.

Nearly all of us can remember the rise in popularity of the World Wide Web and how the information superhighway first started to impact our lives. In the beginning, it consisted of loosely connected text files with very few pictures and even fewer sound and video files. In fact, this author can remember being frustrated when using a LYNX browser to search for information for classes, finding graphics in the text, and thinking that they were simply an intrusion. Graphics loaded slowly with the limited bandwidth of the network and often added little or nothing to the content. Look at where we are now. Streaming video, MP3s, games, and chat are daily parts of many millions of lives, along with the convenience of our cellular phones. In preschool, our kids are learning to mouse, type, and interact with mom, dad, and grandma through e-mail and chat. Places where we can reach out and touch our fellow man, such as MySpace, are becoming the new coffee shops and diners. The Web has become such a necessary part of many households and many lives in one way or another that we often take it for granted as much as we do the television or the telephone. This is just another step on the road to utility computing. It is so necessary to doing what we need to do (paying bills in bed, watching movies in the backyard, reading the latest novels with our laptops on our laps) that we miss it greatly when it becomes unavailable for some reason.

Internet cafés have become essential for many tourist locations and we often look for the wireless Internet "Free WiFi" sign on the door before choosing a coffee shop or restaurant (even McDonald's and interstate rest areas have these signs). Housing areas are offering free Internet access or at the very least intranet access, and hotel chains have begun to have to offer free WiFi to attract clientele. In fact, the only place I have seen where there is true escape from the convenience of technology in keeping us connected is at the bottom of the Grand Canyon on a river raft trip.

We are standing now, looking over the precipice into yet another paradigm shift, another breaking technology that promises to completely change how we think about computing: Grid computing. It has been suggested that the Grid may be even bigger than the Web; but when we look at the fact that much of the interaction with the Grid will be through Web interfaces, this is easy to explain.

For most of us, the adventure is just beginning. For those of us who have done our time programming for the mainframe and then for open systems and client–server systems, it is just another new model to learn; for others, it is a very big change. I, for one, look forward to the adventure. I am strapping on my technological parachute and preparing to free-dive off the edge and let the winds of change carry me where they may.

Goals of This Book

The main goal in writing this book, *Grid Application Design*, is to provide the reader with information on the Grid, its beginning, its design, background, and components, and to provide an idea of how these components will impact applications and how those applications can be designed to best fit into this new computing model. Many of the ideas and concepts are not new — far from it; many have been around for decades. These ideas, however, will have to be addressed in the context of the new model, with many different considerations included.

Many people already know about the Grid and the power that it can bring to a computing environment. Many in business, however, are either just beginning to hear rumblings or are afraid to take the first tentative steps. The best medicine for this uncertainty is to understand the new concepts and to start to see the ways that these new concepts can potentially impact their institutions and their ways of computing in the near future.

Audience

The audience for this book consists of people who are starting to look (or who have been looking) at Grid computing as an option, or those who just want to learn more about the emerging technology. When I first started reading about the emerging technology, I shared what I was learning with people with whom I worked. While the future I described was far more quickly emerging and grandiose than reality could hope to keep up with, what I thought would come is slowly coming to pass.

I believe that the ultimate audience for this kind of information is even bigger than I originally thought, however. The audience should include database administrators, security administrators, systems analysts, systems administrators, programmers, and executives — in fact, anyone who is hearing the rumblings and wants to know more is destined to be in the audience of this book and the emerging technology.

The background in Part I is designed as just that — background. A lot of it is simply interesting reading. A lot of it is informational for people who are new to computing — the groundwork if you will of the history that has brought us to where we find ourselves today. If you already know how we got to where we are now, you may want to read it for its entertainment value, a trip down memory lane so to speak, or you may just want to skip large portions of it as irrelevant.

Part II starts cutting into the "meat" of the book, introducing the Grid and its components and important concepts and ideas. Many of these ideas are critical to understanding the underpinnings of the Grid, the underpinnings around which you will build your applications. These concepts have the potential to impact your organization and define the impact of anything that you might bring into, or build within, your Grid environment. A foundational knowledge of this information is vital for those building within the Grid and those administering the Grid and its contents.

Part III delves into the role that application programming will play in this new paradigm and how those applications need to act to "play nicely together."

Structure of the Book

This book is broken down into three sections and eleven chapters as follows.

Part I

Part I lays the groundwork. We discuss some background on computing and how we got to where we are. We are, in many places and many situations, already taking baby steps toward integration of the new paradigm into the existing framework.

Chapter 1

Chapter 1 discusses computer programming paradigm shifts through history, how we got here, the major milestones that we have seen in conceptual programming and the groundwork for the Grid, where we are launching the future today. It includes information on the beginnings of networking and the Internet, as it is the model on which many people are defining the interaction point through which most will work with the Grid.

Chapter 2

Chapter 2 provides a definition of where much of the Grid is now, the major players that have gotten it to where it is, and many of the components that make up the Grid system. Every Grid has components of hardware as well as software. These components work together to create the magic of the whole.

Chapter 3

Chapter 3 is sort of the "proof of the pudding." It provides a partial list of those commercial and academic ventures that have been the early adopters of the Grid and have started to realize its potential. We have a long way to go before anyone can hope to realize anything as ubiquitous as commodity computing, but also we have come a long way from our beginnings. There are more and more organizations beginning to join the growing group that have already adopted the Grid. Some are smaller organizations leveraging inexpensive hardware, and others globally large organizations trying to bring their infrastructures under a single management paradigm.

Part II

Part II goes into the pieces and parts that go into building a Grid. A variety of ideas, concepts, and components are involved in the definition of what one needs to have one's brain around, before stepping off of the precipice and hang-gliding into the future. Not all Grids need to have all components; just as one organization is radically different from another organization, so is one organization's Grid different from that of another organization.

Chapter 4

Chapter 4 looks at the security concerns and some of the means that can be used to address those concerns. As the Grid continues to emerge, so will the security concerns and the security measures developed to address those concerns. With all the different rules and regulations that govern our organizations today, and all the threats (internal as well as external) security is and needs to be uppermost in all of our minds. Security, as it applies to the Grid, has come far in recent years and the implementation has become more flexible and simplified.

Chapter 5

Chapter 5 looks at the underlying hardware on which the Grid runs. Because the Grid can run on nearly anything, from PC to supercomputer, the hardware is difficult to define, but there are emerging components being built today specifically with the goal of enabling the new technology. One of the selling points of a Grid infrastructure is that it can run on nearly anything and that blade servers that are easily snapped into and out of the Grid can add capacity and replace defective components.

Chapter 6

Metadata is important in any large system. Chapter 6 looks at the role that metadata plays and will need to play in the Grid as it continues to evolve. This metadata is used not only to find data, but also to locate resources and to deliver the best possible performance to the programs and applications that run on the infrastructure.

Chapter 7

Many different business and technology drivers are pushing organizations into the features and flexibility that the Grid can offer today and will continue to offer in the future. Chapter 7 looks at not only the technological reasons many organizations have for implementing a Grid environment (and face it, the best reason for many technologists is simply because it is really cool), but also the business drivers that will help the technologists convince business users that the new technology will be the best technology to meet business needs and to allow that technology to make its inroads into the organization. Just as organizations are changing, the drivers for Grid adoption are also changing, but this is simply another layer of flexibility that the Grid can bring.

Part III

Part III goes into deeper details of applications in the Grid environment. Applications have evolved over the past several decades, and continue to redefine themselves depending on the organization in which they find themselves. We have gone from centrally hosted applications on mainframes to client–server applications to widely distributed applications that are accessed via the Internet or intranet. The Grid will add its own environmental impact to the evolution of applications and will help steer the direction that that evolution will take.

Chapter 8

Chapter 8 allows us to look at virtualization as it applies to the organization and to an infrastructure environment. Because the Grid looks at all resources as a generic pool of power from which the computing needs can be met, virtualization of the different components becomes more necessary. While the way that a Windows server works internally differs from the ways that a Linux server or a mainframe works, the ways that an application taps into the power of each server can be very similar. While the I/O performance of an attached disk may differ greatly from the performance of an NAS or a SAN, the access of data from any given device needs to be as seamless as possible and the location of that data must be fluid as well.

Chapter 9

Chapter 9 looks at the strategy and planning needed to create the Grid-enabled applications that we are trying to bring to our organizations or that our organizations are demanding of us. We must look at systems analysis and design in a whole new light because the way we design these applications will have to undergo growing pains.

Chapter 10

Chapter 10 takes programming a step further and looks at the emerging standards of programming that will make the modularization of the Grid applications possible.

Chapter 11

Finally, Chapter 11 puts it all together. We summarize what we already discussed and then discuss where we can go from here. We are standing on the edge of a new era. Let the adventure begin!

Acknowledgments

My heartiest thanks go to everyone who contributed to my ability to bring this book to completion. Thanks, especially, to John Wyzalek from Auerbach Publications for his support and faith that I could do it. His support has been invaluable.

This book is, as are they all, dedicated to my husband Larry, my son Adam, and my daughter Amandya. They are infinitely understanding and patient. And this book has seen its share of pain (both physical and emotional) and tribulation, and for that I am infinitely sorry.

Remember that anything is possible if one works hard enough and wants it badly enough. Make your dreams a reality.

It is also dedicated to our dog Crystal, who died January 17, 2007, just as I was finishing the last chapter of this book. No longer will I work on a chapter and have her warm heavy head resting on my knee. No longer will I have her to keep me company while I read, research, and write. She will be sorely missed. She awaits us at the Rainbow Bridge, her eyes once more clear, her barks echoing in the sunlight as she chases the ducks and the rabbits, the birds, and the prairie dogs. (See www. Rainbows Bridge.com)

Just this side of heaven is a place called Rainbow Bridge.

When an animal dies that has been especially close to someone here, that pet goes to Rainbow Bridge. There are meadows and hills for all of our special friends so they can run and play together. There is plenty of food, water and sunshine, and our friends are warm and comfortable.

All the animals who had been ill and old are restored to health and vigor. Those who were hurt or maimed are made whole and strong again, just as we remember them in our dreams of days and times gone by. The animals are happy and content, except for one small thing; they each miss someone very special to them, who had to be left behind.

They all run and play together, but the day comes when one suddenly stops and looks into the distance. His bright eyes are intent. His eager body quivers. Suddenly he begins to run from the group, flying over the green grass, his legs carrying him faster and faster.

You have been spotted, and when you and your special friend finally meet, you cling together in joyous reunion, never to be parted again. The happy kisses rain upon your face; your hands again caress the beloved head, and you look once more into the trusting eyes of your pet, so long gone from your life but never absent from your heart.

Then you cross Rainbow Bridge together....

—Author unknown

IN THE BEGINNING   1

Every adventure begins at the beginning. If one takes a river raft trip down the Colorado River through the Grand Canyon, one has to start the adventure with a discussion of what will come, of the people who have gone before us down this same river, what one is going to expect from the trip, and what pitfalls one is likely to face along the way.

We will start the adventure with an overview of the evolution of programming paradigms. This section looks at the way programming paradigms have evolved and how programming languages have evolved along with them. Computing itself has, in some fashion, been around as long as man. Programming languages and programming paradigms have been around as long as electronic computing. This section looks at these beginnings and begins to weave the tapestry of where we have been and how we have gotten to this point in the adventure. The adventure winds its way through the bends and curves in the river just as on the river raft trip. There are bumps in the river bottom and rapids along the way, as well as calm easy stretches. We start with mainframes and linear programming. We expand to include different platforms and different paradigms. The way that we approach programming evolves as increased computing resources become available. We have gone from programming of a few kilobytes of memory to the view that "memory and disk space are cheap. We will buy whatever it takes to make the programs run" to make the most of the resources we have.

We start with the advances and begin to look at distributed computing. We look at peer-to-peer processing and then the earliest beginnings of the Grid in all the ways it is becoming defined. We examine the different kids of Grids and how the different definitions can be compared, contrasted, and combined to build the overall picture. Regardless of what one wants to accomplish, a Grid is likely to fill the need. There are even Grids that include the most overlooked resource that a company has — its intellectual capital.

Finally, we look at some of the experiences of others who have stood where many of us stand today, on the edge of deciding whether they really want to take the step off the ledge of the great divide, out of the known and into the future through implementation of the Grid and its new concepts in computing.

This background section brings the reader up to speed. Many will skip or skim the material, while others will enjoy the walk down memory lane, and still others will find walking through these pages of the first section very educational.

Tighten your flotation device, grab onto the ropes lashing the equipment to the raft, and enjoy the adventure.

Chapter 1

History

> In pioneer days they used oxen for heavy pulling, and when one ox
> couldn't budge a log, they didn't try to grow a larger ox. We shouldn't
> be trying for bigger computers, but for more systems of computers.
>
> **— Rear Admiral Grace Murray Hopper**

Computing has become almost synonymous with mechanical computing and PCs
laptops, palmtops, mainframes, midranges, supercomputers, servers, and other modern
devices that are based on this idea of what computing is, but computers and computing
have a rich history. This history has, at its basis, the programs that run the devices and
the programming languages that were used to create them.

Computing

What people think of when they hear the phrase "computer programming"
or "programming languages" often has as much to do with when they became
acquainted with computers and computing as it does with what they do in computing. Many think of assembler language, many others COBOL or FORTRAN, and
still others Visual Basic or Java.

This book has more to do with how the programming is used and the ideas
behind making the programs behave nicely in the Grid environment than it has to
do with how the programs are made or in what programming languages they are
written (although some languages adapt more readily than others).

This chapter, however, provides a general background of programming languages and provides a common starting place.

3

Blaise Pascal, noted mathematician and scientist, in 1642 built a mechanical calculator, called the Pascaline. While Pascal was one of the few to actually make use of his novel device, it did help to lay the foundations for mechanical computing as we know it today. While this was a mechanical adding machine with the capacity for utilizing eight digits, using it meant that the user hand-turned the gear (later, people improved on the design by adding a crank to make turning easier) as the mechanism for carrying out the calculations. In Pascal's system, a one-toothed gear (the one's place) engaged its tooth with the teeth of a gear with ten teeth once every time the single toothed gear revolved. The revolution of the one's place tracker engaging with the ten's place tracker, which in turn engaged the hundreds and thousands, ten thousands, and hundred thousands gears was the same basic principle as the original odometer (the mechanical mechanism used for counting the number of miles, or kilometers that a car has traveled). Of course, this was in the years before odometers were computerized. This Pascaline calculator had its difficulties, however. It had trouble carrying (not an admirable quality in a mathematical machine, but it was a start). The major issue was that its gears tended to jam during use. Pascal was the only person who was able to make repairs to the machine, making broken parts and jammed gears time-consuming conditions to rectify. This was one of the primary reasons for its lack of popularity (that and the fact that the Pascaline would have cost more than the salaries of all the people it could have replaced). The device proved however, that mechanical calculation was possible.

But this was hardware. We are concerned, primarily with software advances that have marked the computer's progress through history. We are going to primarily look at changes in computer programming languages and programming models through history.

Methodology

A programming methodology is a codified set of practices. These practices are often accompanied by either formal training materials or educational programs or, at the very least, diagrams and formal guidelines. Part of the distinction of a methodology is that it is repeatable and carried out over and over in the effort to create software programs or systems. The other part of the distinction is that methodology is centered on software engineering and not simply the method employed in the programming.

Another way to look at methodologies is that they are the assumptions, concepts, values, and practices that constitute a way of viewing reality for the community that shares them, especially in an intellectual discipline.

Paradigm

A programming paradigm, on the other hand, is more relevant to the idea of Grids today.

A programming paradigm is a style of programming (compare this with the methodology which is a style of software engineering) that follows the assumptions, concepts, values, and practices with others who follow the same way of programming. Methodology is the software engineering; the programming paradigm is the way that the programs are constructed.

It takes into account the view that the programmer takes on the execution of the program (is the program a set of interacting objects or simply a sequence of stateless function evaluations?).

Many programming paradigms are as concerned with what they forbid as with what they allow or enable. Do they make use of side effects? Do they allow the GOTO statement? These requirements often are viewed as limiting factors to those who are new to the programming concepts espoused by the paradigm; however, they are typically less limiting in abilities than they are in ways of controlling how a program's flow is understood.

Further, it is important to remember and understand that only rarely does a limitation of a programming language dictate what programming paradigm is chosen. More often, it is true that a given programming language can be used as the language of choice in several paradigms. The paradigm used dictates how the programs are constructed, not the language chosen.

Paradigms often emerge and evolve over time. Many are short lived, while others stand the test of time. The following are the more common paradigms and the programming languages that are most often associated with them.

Data Directed Programming

Data directed programming is not a widely used paradigm, and it is cited first to prove that some paradigms evolve and are widely accepted while others are not. Data directed programming is explained in the textbook *Structure and Interpretation of Computer Programs* (1985, Harold Abelson and Gerald Jay Sussman), typically employs languages such as LISP, but is not widely used in industry.

Procedural Programming

Procedural programming is the programming model based largely on the procedure call. Procedures are also often known as routines, subroutines, functions, or methods. Each of these individual procedures is a series of computational steps to follow. Often, any procedure can be called at any point in a program's execution and can be called by any procedure, including itself, within the running system. Procedural programming is usually very structured and modular.

One of the advantages of procedural programming is that one can reuse code many times in a program without having to copy that code to different places in the program structure. Another advantage is that one can more easily follow procedures beyond GOTO or JUMP statements (which result in what is known as spaghetti code).

One of the features of procedural programming is that it relies on procedures that have strictly defined channels for input and output. Typically, there are clear rules about what types of input and output are allowed or expected. Inputs are usually specified syntactically in the form of *arguments* and the outputs delivered as *return values*.

Another feature is that this paradigm relies extensively on scope. Scope prevents a procedure from accessing the variables of other procedures, and vice versa. This means that even previous instances of a given program unit cannot access these variable values without explicit authorization. Scope helps prevent confusion between variables with the same name that are used in different places or in different ways, and prevents procedures from stepping all over each other.

Because procedural programming helps enforce a simple interface, and self-contained units that can be reused, groups of programmers working independently can write robust pieces of code and store that code in libraries so it can be reused by others in the group and outside the group (meaning that one does not have to continue to reinvent the wheel and that a procedure can be refined over time to be elegant and efficient).

To consider a programming language truly procedural, that programming language must be able to support procedural programming and have an explicit concept of a procedure and a syntax to define it. It should support the specification of argument types, locally scoped variables, recursive procedure calls, and use of procedures in separately built program constructs. Ideally, it should support distinction of input and output arguments. Examples of languages that support this paradigm follow.

The term "procedural programming" is often used as a synonym for imperative programming. Recall that imperative programming specifies the steps the program must take to reach the desired state. It can also refer to a programming paradigm based on the concept of the procedure call.

Procedures (or subroutines, methods, and functions) contain a series of computational steps that should be carried out. These modules allow for flexibility in programming as they can be called multiple times from any point in a program's execution (including recursively from themselves).

Procedural programming is usually a better option than either simple sequential programming or unstructured programming in most situations, particularly in situations where the program requires moderate complexity or s significant ease of maintainability.

In large, complex, and in-depth programs, modularity is usually a desired feature. This modularity can be accomplished through procedure calls that have well-defined input and output channels and clear rules on what types of input and output are allowed or expected. Inputs are typically passed in the form of arguments, and outputs are defined as return values.

Scope (one method that helps keep procedures modular) prevents the procedure from accessing variable values that are not defined in the scope of the module in question, including those defined in other procedures. This scope definition includes limiting the access of variables so that a procedure cannot even access variables from other running instances of themselves. Most procedural programming languages are also imperative languages.

C

The C programming language is a general-purpose, procedural, imperative computer programming language. Typically, it is highly structured and flexible. C was developed in 1972 by Dennis Ritchie, who was employed at Bell Telephone Laboratories. C was intended for use with the UNIX operating system. It did not stay segregated to UNIX, however, but has spread to other operating systems. Today, it is one of the most widely used programming languages and has influenced many other languages (particularly C++ and Java).

C is a cryptic and minimalistic programming language compiled in a relatively simple manner into a runtime program. This makes C highly suitable for many *systems programming* applications.

Despite the fact that C is often used as a low-level programming language and is often used in assembly language programming, the language was designed to encourage machine independence (much like Java). A portable program written in C can be compiled for a wide variety of computer platforms. Unlike Java (discussed later in this chapter), which is interpreted on different platforms, C must be compiled to be effective on the different platforms. By 1973, C had become a powerful enough language that UNIX kernels (which had previously been written in the PDP-11 assembly language) began to be written in C.

In 1978, Ritchie, along with Brian Kernighan, published the first edition of *The C Programming Language*, a book that served as the *de facto* if informal language specification for C. The second edition of the book provides information on the ANSI standard.

C++ (*C plus plus*)

In 1979, Bjarne Stroustrup (also of Bell Laboratories) began to work on a new programming language: C with Classes. Early on, the extension of the classes was added to C itself, bringing the concept of classes, derived classes, type checking, and other features to C with an additional front end. In 1983, the name of the language changed from C with Classes to C++. As the language matured, new features were added. Virtual functions, function naming, operator overloading, user-controlled free store memory control, and additional comment styles were added to make the language more robust and flexible. The first official commercial release of C++ occurred in 1985.

BASIC (Beginner's All-Purpose Symbolic Instruction Code)

The BASIC family of high-level programming languages was originally designed in 1963 by John George Kemeny and Thomas Eugene Kutz at Dartmouth College as a means to provide computer access for students not enrolled in heavily scientific courses (primarily the Dartmouth time-sharing system). At the time, nearly all of the computers required the user to write custom software, and this was typically something only attempted by scientists and mathematicians. This language (or a variant of another) became widespread on home computers in the 1980s and remains popular today in a handful of dialects.

During the 1960s, faster and relatively more affordable computers became increasingly available. With extra processing power, these computers would often sit idle with few or no jobs to run.

Prior to BASIC, programming languages tended to be designed like the machines on which they were designed to run (fast and for a specific purpose, such as scientific formula calculation or business data processing).

The eight design principles of BASIC required that it:

1. Be easy for beginners to use
2. Be a general-purpose programming language
3. Allow for the addition of advanced features for experts and remain simple for beginners
4. Be interactive
5. Provide clear and useful error messages
6. Be able to respond quickly for small programs
7. Not require the programmer to have any understanding of the underlying computer hardware
8. Shield the user from the operating system

BASIC combined the best features of FORTRAN, JOSS, CROC, ALGOL 60, and LISP to make it user friendly, simple to understand, and sufficiently robust to handle the needs of its user community.

While many people tend to make light of BASIC as a programming language, it has historically been both robust and elegant. Initially, it was built to concentrate on mathematical work. It derived its matrix arithmetic support from its early implementation as a batch processing language on the GE-256 mainframe, with string functionality added in 1965. It was efficient enough at mathematical computations that it could beat both FORTRAN II and ALGOL 60 at many computationally intensive programming problems. The GE mainframe supported multiple terminals, which allowed more people access to the environment.

In the early years, BASIC was a compiled language and the decision was made to make the compiler freely available so that the language could become widespread.

Dartmouth provided it to high schools in the local area and provided the compiler to the market free of charge. As a result, knowledge of the language became more widespread (that is, widespread for a computer language).

As BASIC's popularity grew, it began to be implemented more often as an interpreted language rather than a compiled one (or in addition to a compiled one). While these interpreted versions typically perform more slowly than their compiled counterparts one does save on the overhead of having to take the time to compile and distribute a compiled version. Often, these complaints were valid less because of the language itself than because many versions released (especially those released to the public on PCs) left out important features and capabilities.

In 1975, the Altair BASIC developed by Bill Gates and Paul Allen (then Micro-Soft) came to market. Soon after, versions of Microsoft BASIC started to appear on licensed systems and it became even more publicly distributed. It was the standard language of the Apple II systems and was taught in high schools around the country by the early 1980s.

COBOL

COBOL (COmmon Business Oriented Language) was created by the Short Range Committee in 1960 after the committee was tasked with recommending a short-range approach to a common business language. The committee consisted of representatives of six major computer manufacturers and three government agencies. The six computer manufacturers were Burroughs Corporation, IBM, Honeywell Labs, RCA, Sperry Rand, and Sylvania Electric Products. The government agencies were the U.S. Air Force, David Taylor Model Basin, and the National Bureau of Standards.

Early computing meant processing complex numerical and scientific calculations. FORTRAN was very good with numbers. However, as computing started to become more common in business, the programming languages needed to meet more of the needs of business (simple fixed point arithmetic, for example, on a large amount of data rather than extremely complex calculations on a smaller set of data, or character string manipulation, for which FORTRAN is not known).

COBOL (despite the fact that it has been touted as a dead language) has remained successful after 45 years, largely because it is self-documenting and easy to read, and also because it is very good at what it was designed to do.

The original COBOL supported self-modifying code via the ALTER statement (ALTER X to proceed to Y...—much less elegant and understandable than even the GOTO statement because it changes where the GOTO would, depending on the data. The capacity for this feature has since been removed; however, the code containing these statements may still compile and function. COBOL 2002 introduced object-oriented programming support.

FORTRAN

Created in 1957 by John Backus of IBM, FORTRAN (FORmula TRANslator) was the first and is still the most widely used language that concentrates on numerical calculations. The first compiler (for the IBM 704) was released in April 1957. Over time, the language has evolved. Earliest versions did not have the concepts of block IF statements, parameters, SAVE statements, or WHILE statements.

FORTRAN 90 significantly enlarged upon the earlier version to include derived types, array sections, case statements, functions capable of returning arrays module and internal subprograms, dynamic memory allocation, and recursion. FORTRAN 77 did not support recursion.

Many of the basic types of data in use today got their start in FORTRAN, including Boolean variables (TRUE or FALSE), and integer, real, and double-precision numbers. While FORTAN is good at handling numbers, it is not so good at handling input and output.

Perl

Perl is a powerful and dynamic programming language created by Larry Wall and first released to the market in 1987. It borrows many of its features from other languages, including C, LISP, and UNIX languages (shell scripting, SED, and AWK). It is brace delimited and block style in its syntax and has been widely adopted for its string processing abilities.

Ironically, despite the language's power and flexibility, its only documentation in the early years was its main page (which was actually quite lengthy), and it was not until 1991 that *Programming Perl* was published and became the *de facto* book for Perl programmers.

The language grew over the years, and Perl 5 was released in 1994 (and is still supported and remains one of the most widely adopted versions today). This version featured a more robust interpreter (Perl is interpreted rather than compiled) and many new features (objects, packages, and modules, to name a few). Because of the addition of modules, it is possible to extend the language without modifying the interpreter.

In 1995, the Comprehensive Perl Archive Network (CPAN) was established. CPAN (http://www.cpan.org) is often the launching point for a network of Web sites where one can find distributions of Perl source, documentation, scripts, modules, and FAQs that can help a programmer of the language learn and grow. The latest stable release is Perl 5.8.8.

Perl was developed as a text manipulation language but has grown and is now used for many other tasks, including database manipulation, system administration, Web development, network programming, and many others. Perl supports many different programming paradigms (procedural, object oriented, and functional, to name a few), thus making it a robust and elegant choice for many programmers.

Structured Programming

The next programming paradigm is *structured programming*. Conceptually, one can view it as a subset of procedural programming and is arguably the most famous paradigm. It is most famous for reducing (or removing entirely) the reliance on the GOTO statement.

There are two trains of thought when programmers adopt a structured paradigm. The first, often known as Dijkstra's structured programming, reduces the understanding of a program to understanding any given structure on its own and how that structure can be used to build the logic of the program. Conceptually, a given problem can be broken down into a limited number of other problems and each of these subproblems attacked with one of these simple structures. Many programmers who follow this technique tend toward a single point of entry into the program and a single point of exit from it, while others view the single point of entry as the concept to follow but multiple points of exit as the more frequently followed trail.

The other procedure, data structured programming, tends to try to align the data structures with the corresponding program structures and finesse the high-level structure of a program into the model of the underlying data structures processed within the program.

Structured programs consist of simple structures, each typically regarded as a single statement even when made up of multiple lines of code. These statements are the most basic codes units and at the same time are ways of combining even simpler statements (other simple structures or primitive statements such as assignments, procedure calls, or function calls). Traditionally, there are three types of simple structures typified in structured programming:

1. *Flow control* refers to the sequence of statements as they are executed in order.
2. *Selection* occurs when any one of a number of statements occurs, depending on data or the state of the program. This usually occurs in connection with the if-then-else statement, the switch statement, or the case statement.
3. *Repetition* occurs when one statement is repeated either a set number of times, until a certain program state occurs, or until the statement is executed on an entire set of data. The keyword that usually accompanies this type of statement is the WHILE statement, the REPEAT statement, the FOR statement, or the DO UNTIL statement. To adhere to structured programming, each repetition statement usually has one entry point. Depending on the model followed and the business needs of the program, the repetition statement could have one or more than one exit point.

In structured programming, coders break larger pieces of code into shorter subroutines that are often functions, procedures, methods, or blocks and can be either stored within the same body of code or (more typically) in libraries from where one can call them repeatedly and reuse them. These subroutines are small enough to be easily understood and often are localized so that they perform exactly one "job" within the program or within the broader scope of the business logic.

Generally, in structured programming, global variables are used sparingly and use of subroutine local variables is encouraged. These local variables are often passed in, either by reference or by value. This localization of variables also makes isolated pieces of code easier to understand and work with when investigated outside the broader scope of the main or calling program.

Structured programming is often associated with a top-down approach to design, wherein the programmers map out the larger structure of a program in terms of the smaller operations. These smaller operations are then tackled as modules, and implemented and tested individually first and then tied together into the whole program. It is possible to follow a structured programming paradigm with virtually any language; however, it is usually preferable to use a procedural language such as C, Ada, or Pascal.

Ada

A team led by Jean Ichbiah, while working on a contract with the U.S. Department of Defense between 1977 and 1983, designed Ada, a structured programming language. Ada provides the flexibility and elegance of C or C++ but goes a step further by providing one of the best type safety systems (a system that prevents some kinds of unanticipated program behavior called *type errors*) available in a programming language. These type errors occur when a program (or a programmer) performs an operation or calculation on a data type for which it was not designed (such as trying to do math on character strings).

S. Tucker Taft provided a revision to the original programming language, and in Ada 95 added improved support for numerical and financial programming between 1992 and 1995.

Ada has many robust features that make it a versatile language. Exception handling and parallel processing make it very adaptable to changing programming models and paradigms. The Ada 95 revision also added support for object-oriented programming. Ada supports runtime checks as a means to avoid access to unallocated memory, buffer overflows, array access errors, and other avoidable bugs that can be disabled to add further efficiencies. The Ada programming language was named after Ada Lovelace, arguably the first computer programmer.

Pascal

Pascal was developed in 1970 by Niklaus Wirth and is another language that is particularly suitable for structured programming. An offshoot, Object Pascal, was designed to meet more of the needs of object-oriented programming.

Pascal is roughly based on the ALGOL programming language and is named for the mathematician and philosopher Blaise Pascal. The first compiler was designed for the CDC 6000 computer in Zurich, while the first Pascal compiler written in the United States was built at the University of Illinois and was written for the PDP-11. This compiler generated native machine code.

Wirth originally designed Pascal to be used as a teaching language to help students learn structured programming techniques. Many programmers' initial forays into structured programming were with Pascal at the undergraduate level.

Pascal did not remain a strictly instructional language, however. Parts of the original Macintosh operating system used in the Apple Lisa were translated from Pascal code into Motorola 68000 assembly language. While later versions of the operating system incorporated more and more C++ code, the most frequent high-level programming language used for development in early Macintosh computers was Pascal.

Because early work with the language was machine dependent, and as a means to more rapidly distribute the language across platforms and continents, a compiler porting kit was created that included a compiler that generated code for a virtual stack machine (code that lends itself to more efficient interpretation), along with an interpreter for that code (the p code system). The p code was originally intended to be compiled into machine code for the given platform later; however, many implementations allowed it to remain an interpreted language. In 1980, a compiler was developed that brought Pascal to the IBM mainframe.

Unstructured Programming

Unstructured programming is probably the way that many of us learned how to program. Where structured programming is typically concise and tight, unstructured programming is typically more free flowing and often mirrors the thinking process of the programmer.

In unstructured programming, all code is contained in a single continuous block or a single continuous program. Where structured programming breaks a problem into discrete steps or tasks (recall that these are usually functions or subroutines and can be stored and called for program reuse), unstructured programming relies on execution flow statements such as the GOTO statement to force the program logic to follow a specific path based on logic required or data involved.

When reading unstructured code, one often has a difficult time closely following the program logic, and will find that debugging is particularly difficult. For this reason if no other, unstructured programming is usually discouraged in any language that supports structured programming. It is possible to write unstructured code in virtually any language by implementing the logic with a series of combined conditional statements.

Despite the ease of use and the reusability of code sections that come with structured programming, certain scripting languages and older programming languages support the use of GOTO statements.

Although it is true that historically GOTO statements have had a small performance advantage over procedure calls, current hardware architecture has made such advantages virtually nil, and the small processing advantage that may be perceived is negated by the fact that improper use of a GOTO statement (or worse, an ALTER statement in COBOL) can be dangerous programming and may be harmful to data integrity — harmful because obfuscated code can lead a programmer who is maintaining a program to inaccurately read the program logic and make incorrect assumptions.

All of this said, assembly language has always been a predominantly unstructured language due to the very fact that machine language has never been a structured concept.

To see the ultimate in unstructured programming, consider the ALTER statement in earlier versions of COBOL. There was a time when the ALTER statement was much more accepted than it is today. Today, very few people have anything constructive to say on its behalf, and it has long been obsolete from COBOL compilers (however, there are many programs with this code running today).

An ALTER statement in SQL is very useful (necessary even); however, there are insidious side effects to the ALTER statement in COBOL. This statement changes the destination of a GOTO statement to send the logic to another section of the program. It obfuscates the logic of the program and can be very difficult to get rid of even by an experienced programmer trying to follow the logic of a program's statements. Typically, an ALTER can be replaced by a flag, a case statement, or even (to follow the unstructured logic) by other less difficult GOTO statements. Once the ALTERs have been eliminated, work can continue on ridding programs of the GOTOs.

To look at an example, examine the following code snippet:

```
PERFORM 2100-PROCESS-RECORD THRU 2199-EXIT.
*

 2100-PROCESS-RECORD.
   GO TO 2110-PROCESS-HEADER.
*

 2110-PROCESS-HEADER.
* First time, do header processing.
* next time through, change the logic to follow the
code
* so that it processes a detail record
   ALTER 2100-PROCESS-RECORD TO 2200-PROCESS-DETAIL.
   GO TO 2199-EXIT.
*

 2200-PROCESS-DETAIL.
```

```
* Insert the code necessary to process a detail
record
    GO TO 2999-EXIT.
*
 2999-EXIT.
 EXIT.
```

Not messy enough (well, okay, usually there are not that many comments)? Consider a COBOL paragraph that only has one statement, and that statement is an ALTER statement. Logic is routed to the paragraph based on data values, and the changes in values are the keys on which the logic is altered. It soon becomes nearly un-maintainable, and un-debuggable.

Think it cannot possibly get any worse? Guess again. If a GOTO statement has no destination, then it behaves like a CONTINUE statement until an ALTER statement assigns it a destination. Worse yet? You bet.

When ALTER statements were in vogue, so was something known as segmentation (back when resources were much less inexpensive than they are today; that is, the ability to read part of a program into memory, run it, then overlay that segment of program in memory with the next logical segment to avoid having to load the entire program at one time).

Many programs were written to have initialization code, main body code, and then finishing-up code. Once the initialization code was finished running, it was not needed any more, so why keep it around? Overlay it with the main loop. When that finished, overwrite again and load the finishing-up code.

When using ALTER statements in segments of programs, the ALTER can behave in very unexpected ways. If an independent segment contains an altered GOTO, and that segment is overlaid by the next and then for some reason reloaded, the GOTO's logic will be reset to its *original* destination.

These are just a few of the reasons many people do not do unstructured programming, and why many of those who still do, so fail to take it as far as it could be taken.

Imperative Programming

Imperative programming is a paradigm that describes a computational program as statements that change a program's state. Statements, again, are the smallest, stand-alone elements of a program. Programs typically consist of many statements, and each statement can express commands and direct requests and prohibitions.

Often, imperative programming is used synonymously with procedural programming. Many other paradigms define *what* is to be computed. Imperative programming defines *how* the computation is to take place.

Imperative programming is, at its most fundamental, the way that hardware is designed to execute the machine code that is native to that hardware configuration. Program state is, at any given time, defined by the contents in memory that are assigned to that program, along with the statements and instructions on how to execute on the given data.

Real-world examples (rather than programming examples) of imperative programs would be recipes. One starts with a list of things to process, and the recipe tells one how, and in what order, to process those things. Each step in the recipe is a discrete instruction, and the physical world determines the state of the recipe at any given time.

Computerized examples? Nearly any program is, or can be, written in an imperative style. This is partly because that is the way most people think about the world, and computer programs are often nothing more than electronic representations of the physical world. It is also partly because that is the way that the computer processes a program, and it is usually the most efficient means of constructing the program.

Historically, the first imperative languages were the machine languages of the computer on which they were written. They involved setting of switches on circuit boards and the setting of bits at the bit level. In these early programs, the instructions were very simple, by necessity, and this made the hardware manipulation (to some degree) easier to work with. The simplicity of the instructions, however, made it difficult to create complex programs or programs that included branching or data-based decision logic.

FORTRAN was the first (historically) language to remove obstacles that were presented by machine code for complex programs. FORTRAN was not only compiled, but also allowed for the use of named variables, complex expressions, and subprograms. These and other features of imperative languages made FORTRAN a good early language to replace machine languages. It was easier for programmers to learn than machine code and was as powerful at programming logic.

Over the next 20 or so years, there were great strides in other high-level programming languages to fit the imperative paradigm. This new generation of programming languages was developed to better allow expression of mathematical algorithms.

ALGOL

In the mid-1950s, the ALGOL (ALGOrithmic Language) family of imperative computer programming languages was developed. These languages became the *de facto* standards for recording algorithms in print for many years. The inventors of ALGOL were striving to overcome the perceived problems with FORTRAN. ALGOL eventually gave rise to other high-level programming languages, including Pascal and C.

ALGOL consists of bracketed statements laid out in blocks and was the first language to make use of the begin and end pairs to delimit those blocks. It evolved into several main branches, including ALGOL 58, ALGOL 60, and ALGOL 68.

■ ALGOL 58 was the version that first introduced the concept of compound statements. However, these new constructs were originally restricted to controlling the flow of the program only and were not tied in any way to identifier scope. Originally (mid-1958), the name of the language was to be International Algebraic Language (or IAL) but that name was later rejected as pompous and ALGOL was suggested as the name instead. IBM attempted adoption of ALGOL 58, but the language was in direct competition with FORTRAN and in the end FORTRAN won in that environment.

BALGOL evolved as an implementation for the Burroughs 220 and the language evolved along its own lines but it retained ALGOL 58 characteristics. Later, ALGOL was used as the basis of JOVIAL, MAD, NELIAC, and ALGO. In 1960, a division occurred based on unresolved disagreements and ALGOL 60 was born.

- The ALGOL 60 derivative had no official I/O facilities. It was left to implementations people to define their own ways to work with the I/O facilities for the language. These customized facilities were rarely compatible with each other (true customizations rarely are). This version allowed for two evaluation structures for parameter passing: (1) call-by-value and (2) call-by-name. Call-by-name was usually undesirable because it had many limitations and was, therefore, not usually used in program design. One example of this is the fact that, in ALGOL 60, it is impossible to swap the values of two parameters if the parameters that are passed are integer variables and an array is indexed by the same integer variable.

- ALGOL 68 is another version of the same imperative computer programming language that was ALGOL. It was created as the successor to ALGOL 60. ALGOL 68 was designed with the goal of a much wider scope of application and more robust syntax and semantics. ALGOL 68 offered an extensive library of transport (input/output) facilities. Further, it was defined using a two-level grammar formalism that used context-free grammar to generate an innate set of publications that will recognize a given ALGOL 68 program and is able to express requirements that are usually labeled semantics in other languages. These semantics must be expressed in an ambiguity-prone natural language and then later implemented in compilers as nearly natural language ad hoc code parsed in the formal ALGOL language parser.

COBOL (1960) and BASIC (1964) were both attempts to make higher-level programming language syntax appear more English-like and therefore more easily programmed and understood. Later, Pascal and C were designed to follow suit, then Wirth designed Modula 2, Modula 3, and Oberon.

Modula 2

In 1978, Wirth designed a programming language that was sufficiently flexible for systems programming, but was much broader in its application. Modula 2 was developed as an attempt to support separate compilation and data abstraction in a logical and straightforward way.

The syntax for Modula 2 is very similar to Pascal and, in fact, Modula 2 was designed to be very similar to Pascal, with some of the elements of Pascal removed and the module concept added in their place.

One of the most important concepts added to Modula 2 was multitasking, defined as the method by which multiple tasks or processes share common processing resources (memory and CPU). When a computer has only a single CPU, even in a multitask process, only one task is "running" at any point in time. While multiple tasks may in fact be in process, only one can be actively executing its instructions in the CPU. While it is executing, the others are waiting their turn (often round robin) to be the focus of the CPU's attention. Multitasking does this by scheduling the CPU. The act of being able to reassign the CPU from one task to another is known as context switching.

When context switching occurs rapidly enough and frequently enough, it appears that there are parallel processes executing when the single CPU bottleneck has in fact throttled the ability to truly run parallel processes. When a system has more than one CPU, multitasking allows many tasks to run at any given time, many more processes, in fact, than there are CPUs in the system.

Modula 2 can be used to encapsulate a set of related programs and data structures and obfuscate their visibility from other parts of the same program in a very elegant manner.

Each module in a Modula 2 program consists of two parts: (1) a definition module (the interface portion, which contains those parts of the program that will be visible to other modules), and (2) an implementation module (the part of the program that holds the working code that is internal to the given module).

Modula 2 has strict scope control and can be considered a nearly impenetrable wall. No object, other than standard identifiers, is visible inside a module unless it is explicitly imported, and no internal module object is visible from the outside unless it is exported explicitly.

Modula 3

Modula 3 was conceived as a successor to Modula 2 and was designed in the late 1980s. Modula 3 was influenced by work that was in process for Modula 2+ (in use at DESCR at the time) and the language in which the DEC Firefly and the VAX workstation were written.

The main features of Modula 3 were simplicity and safety while allowing the power and flexibility of the system's programming language of Modula 2 to remain. Modula 3 brought with it exception handling, garbage collection, and object orientation. One goal of the project was to bring out a language that implements the most important features of imperative languages in basic forms. It attempted to throttle dangerous features such as multiple inheritance and operator overloading— features that C++ allowed to flourish.

During the 1990s, Modula 3 gained popularity as a teaching language but it was never widely adopted in industry. Modula 3 is no longer taught in most universities, and all textbooks dealing with the subject are out of print. It seems that industry and academia would rather work around the powerful if dangerous features that Modula 3 removed.

Oberon

Oberon (named for the moon of Uranus) was created in 1986 as part of the implementation of the Oberon operating system. The operating system ran on Ceres workstations, which were built around the National Semiconductor 32032 CPU as well as the Chameleon workstation. Oberon (and later Oberon 2) was ported to many other operating systems (including Java platform) where the source code compiles to other source code or bytecode for the Java virtual machine.

This language concentrated on the features essential for the task of creation of the operating system. Oberon is very Modula 2-like but is considerably smaller, allowing for space and coding efficiency for its compilers. It is so small and efficient that one of the early compilers contained only 4000 lines of code. One feature of Oberon that was missing in Modula 2 was garbage collection.

Oberon 2 was created as an extension of the original Oberon programming language. Oberon 2 adds limited reflection, object orientation, and other constructs useful in a programming language (the FOR loop, open arrays, and read-only field export). Because Oberon 2 is a superset of Oberon; it is fully compatible with the earlier version.

Oberon 2 basic types are not objects, classes are not objects, and many operations are not methods. Oberon 2 does not support message passing (although it can be emulated to a limited extent by reflection). Reflection in Oberon 2 reads from a disk file of metadata generated by the compiler.

Declarative Programming

The declarative programming paradigm is a multi-use procedure that has two distinct meanings. To complicate matters, both paradigm meanings are in current use. One definition of this paradigm is that a program is declarative if it describes *what* something is like, rather than the *how* it takes to create it. HTML is a declarative language because it is used to describe what a page should look like (the title, how big it is, where it is, the way the text appears on the page). This is different from imperative programming languages that require the programs to specify the goal and leave the implementation of the algorithm to the software.

The alternative definition is that a program can be considered declarative if it is written as a purely functional program, a purely logic program, or a purely constraint program. The term *declarative language* is often used to cover functional programming languages, logic programming languages, or constraint programming languages and to compare and contrast those languages with languages that are considered imperative.

There is, of course, overlap in these definitions. For example, both constraint programming and logic programming focus on describing the properties of the desired solution (the "what"), leaving unspecified and undefined the actual algorithm that should be used to find that solution (the "how"). Most logic and constraint languages are able to describe algorithms and implementation details.

Further, it is possible to write a declarative program in an imperative programming language (usually through the use of encapsulation). In a declarative program, one simply declares the data structure that needs to be processed by the language's standard algorithms and produces the desired results.

Functional Programming

Functional programming defines computation as the evaluation of mathematical functions, avoiding state data and mutable data. It emphasizes the application of functions rather than changes in state and the execution of sequential commands. A broader definition defines functional programming as a set of common concerns and themes rather than a list of distinctions from other paradigms.

Flow-Driven Programming

Flow-driven programming is used by traditional programmers. Programs that are written in this paradigm follow their own control flow patterns, changing course only at branch points. Flow-driven programs do not typically have their logic influenced by external events. Flow-driven program logic is not in control of when it receives, but rather awaits the input and processes when it comes. Typically, flow-driven programs are written in imperative languages.

Event-Driven Programming

Event-driven programming is a paradigm in which a program's flow is determined by user actions (mouse click, double click, key press, or mouse over) or messages from other programs or program units. This is unlike batch programming where the flow is predetermined by the programmer and the style is taught in any beginning programming class. The concept of event-driven processing is more advanced and the user needs to understand the sequence of events.

Often, event-driven programming includes an event loop that is used to look repeatedly for information to process. This information might be the arrival of a file in the file system, a given sequence of keystrokes on the keyboard, some mouse event, or even a timed event. The event can be polled for in the event loop or event handlers can be programmed to react to hardware-based events. Depending on the program's logic requirements, a mixture of input recognition methods can be used. Once the necessary information arrives, it is simply a matter of writing a code that sets the default for the triggering event.

Event-driven programming stresses flexibility and asynchronicity and is often written as a modeless program. Often, event-driven programming makes use of some form of graphical user interface (GUI). Another widespread use of event-driven programming is in most operating systems. On one level, interrupt handlers are direct event handlers for hardware events and, on another level, software interrupts pass assist with data passing and dispatching software processes. Even command line interfaces (CLIs) are event-driven processes in that their events are key presses at the end of the entered command.

Class-Based Programming

Class-based programming or class orientation is a style of object-oriented programming where inheritance is achieved through the definition of classes of objects rather than the definition of objects themselves. This programming paradigm is the most developed and most popular model, due largely to the fact that objects are defined as entities that combine state, methods, and identity as a combined unit. The structure and behavior of any given object are defined by a class, which is the definition of all objects of a specific type (for example, shape). An object must be explicitly created based on the class, and once created is considered an instance of that class.

Class-based object-oriented programming leverages encapsulation as a means to protect both expressions whose values should not be changed and undesirable type overriding. This is particularly useful because it provides for the implementation of a class of objects that can be changed for aspects not exposed in the interface without impacting user code.

Object-oriented programming languages do not typically offer security restrictions to internal object states and leave the method of access to the programmer as a matter of convention rather than actively preventing the programmers from deliberately implementing such code. It handles inheritance by grouping its objects into classes, defining further classes as extensions of existing classes, extending the concept of classes into trees and lattices, and using that convention as the means to reflect common behaviors.

Language that are commonly used to implement class-based programs include C++, Java, and C#.

Java

Java is a popular object-oriented programming language developed by Sun Microsystems in the early 1990s. First started by James Gosling in June 1991 under the name Oak, the language's goal was to implement a virtual machine and a language that looked similar enough to C and C++ and could be easily learned by existing C programmers. The first public release of Java 1.0 came in 1995. It was originally touted as having *write once, run anywhere code.* This feature provides no cost runtimes on most platforms. The early releases of Java were fairly secure, and its security features were configurable to allow for more or less strict security and restricting of network and file access.

Most Web browser providers were quick to jump on the Java bandwagon and provide for the ability to run Java applets from within Web pages. As Java's popularity grew, so did the Java releases. Java 2 provided multiple configurations that were built for different platforms. J2EE is the enterprise application tool of choice for a large number of organizations.

Java remains a proprietary, if *de facto*, standard that is controlled solely through the Java Community Process (born in 1998, it is a formalized process that allows the involvement of interested parties in the definition of future versions and features of the Java Platform).

Applications written in Java are compiled originally to bytecode, which is later compiled into native machine language at runtime. Sun Microsystems provides GNU general public license implementations of the Java compiler and the Java virtual machine. Increasing numbers of applications or application components are being written in Java as it grows in popularity and efficiency.

Much of the Java language syntax is borrowed from C and C++; however, it has a much simpler object model and far fewer low-level programming facilities.

Sun makes most of its Java implementations publicly available without charge. Revenue for Java is generated by the specialized products such as the Java Enterprise System. In November 2006, Sun released parts of Java as a free/open source under GNU general public license with the release of complete sources under the same license expected early in 2007.

JavaScript, a language that shares similar syntax and a deceptively similar name, is not related.

C#

C# (pronounced C sharp, as in music) is an object-oriented programming language developed by Microsoft as a part of the .NET offering. It was later approved as a standard by the ECMA and ISO organizations. C# has a syntax based on the C++ language and includes aspects of other programming languages (including Visual Basic and Java) but with emphasis on simplification.

C# supports strong type checking, array bounds checking, detection of attempts to use uninitialized variables, and automatic garbage collection, and is intended for use in developing components suitable for distributed environments. In keeping with the growing acceptance for globalization and code portability, C# emphasizes not only source code portability, but also programmer portability.

Prototype-Based Programming

Prototype-based programming is another style of object-oriented programming. Unlike class-based programming, however, in prototype-based programming, classes are not present. Behavior reuse (what we know as inheritance in class-based languages) is accomplished through cloning existing objects that serve as prototypes. This feature makes prototype languages classless programming languages. Classless programming (prototype-based programming) has become increasingly popular recently with the increased use of JavaScript.

In class-based programming, objects come in two general types: (1) classes (which define the basic layout and general functionality of the object) and (2) instances (the usable objects that are loosely based on the particular class). Classes in class-based programming carry the methods (the behaviors of the objects) and instances carry the object's data.

In contrast, prototype-based programming encourages the programmer to focus on the behavior of example objects and worry later about classification of the objects into archetypal objects to be used for no other purpose than to fashion similar classes. This is due, in part, to the fact that many prototype-based systems encourage the alteration of prototypes during runtime (few class-based systems allow, let alone encourage this alteration).

Component-Oriented Programming

Component-oriented programming is a paradigm that provides theories of not only programming, but also software architecture, frameworks, objects, and design patterns. It is an object-oriented design paradigm that suggests that software components can be made as interchangeable and reliable (maybe even more so) as hardware components.

A software component is a single element designed to provide a single defined service that is able to communicate with other services. Software elements should be able to support multiple uses. They should not be context- specific but should be able to be combined easily with other elements and components yet still be deployed or versioned independent of any other element. These components should support encapsulation so that their interfaces are not open to investigation from the outside world.

Simply, a component is an object that is written to a given specification without regard for what that specification is or in what language it is written. By adhering closely to the specification, the given component objects will be reusable in multiple scenarios and robust enough to handle the required flexibility. These components can be objects or collections of objects that can, and often do, exist autonomously on a given server at any point in time. When that computer is accessed, the component is turned into useful code.

UNIX pipes constituted one of the earliest practical uses of this infrastructure concept. Pipes, in software engineering, consist of a chain of processes or processing entities arranged (so to speak) so that the output of one element is the input to the next element. There is usually some buffer (either size or time) between the elements to ensure that one finishes sufficiently before the next one starts to run. Information in the pipeline is usually referred to as a bit stream or a byte stream. Pipes are typically only implemented in multitasking operating systems (where they can be implemented most efficiently) by launching all processes at the same time and allowing data to be automatically serviced when it reaches the next step in the pipeline. This allows the CPU to be naturally switched between processes by a scheduler and idle time to be minimized.

Object-oriented programming (OOP) suggests that objects should be based on real-life modeling (creating objects that are nouns and methods that are verbs). A favorite example of OOP concepts was the one that this author learned in a college class.

I am a vending machine. I have a coin slot. I have product to vend. I have a change-making mechanism. I have a slot through which product is vended. I make change, I collect money, and I vend product. If I am very fancy, I have a bell that dings when product is vended.

Component-based programming, on the other hand, makes no assumptions that objects will be based on anything in the brick-and-mortar world. This paradigm states that software should be created by pasting together sets of prefabricated components, more along the lines of mechanics or electronics. A hard drive is a hard drive whether it is in a Dell, an HP, or a Gateway. Definitions of useful components can often be counter-intuitive to real-world objects, however.

Often, OOP is simpler than component-based programming because, for a component to be truly useful and adopted widely, it needs to be fully documented, thoroughly tested, and its input validity checked and rechecked. For it to be truly useful for end users, administrators, or other component programmers, it needs to have robust error checking and useful error messages. Programmers must be aware that their components can be used in unforeseen ways and attempt to account for that.

A computer that is running several components is often referred to as an application server or participating in distributed computing. These concepts will become increasingly important when we start looking more in depth at Grid computing.

Brad Cox of Stepstone was the father of the formalized concept of the software component (he called them software ICs) and he set about to create the infrastructure that would best support these components. He invented Objective-C (or ObjC) which brings the concept of messaging to the C programming language.

The language today is most often found in the Mac OS X and GNUstep and is the primary language used in the NeXTSTEP architecture. There is not a great deal of practical information available on the ObjC language (particularly for a college student trying to learn how to program in the language) but the concept is broadly understood. NeXTSTEP is the operating system of the brain child of Steve Jobs, the NeXT computer.

Where Cox failed to quite reach the mark he was striving for, IBM with the system object model (SOM) in the early 1990s and Microsoft with its development of component software with the object linking and embedding (OLE) and component object model (COM) was far more successful.

Object Linking and Embedding (OLE)

OLE is a distributed object protocol developed by Microsoft to allow an editor to subcontract parts of a document to another editor and then import that component into the main document. This means that the editors can each do what they do best and the whole of the document is more than just the independent sum of its parts. The word processor will be responsible for the primary body of text, a bitmap editor will handle the creation of pictures, and the spreadsheet editor will take care of mathematical formulas and tables.

When it comes time to assemble the final document, it can be done in a much more compact (size of the final document) way than might otherwise be true, and a single master document can be assembled that pulls in all the final versions of all the components at compilation time. This means that development of the document can occur as parallel streams, and the main document does not have to worry, until it is time to pull it all together, about how many iterations the components took to complete or what the interim steps were, only that the final version of the component is where it is supposed to be when it is supposed to be there.

Component Object Model (COM)

Microsoft introduced its COM in 1993 to help allow inter-process communication and dynamic object creation in any programming language that is set up to support that technology. The COM name was not popularized, however, until several years later.

COM is often used as a global term up into which OLE, ActiveX, and DCOM technologies will roll.

COM is a language-neutral way of implementing objects so that they can be used in any environment, regardless of the architecture of the one on which they were developed. When developers create well-written objects, they can be used easily even in environments where the administrators and programmers have no knowledge of the internal implementation of the object because of its well-defined interfaces that allow it to be used elegantly. While it is true that COM can be implemented on several different platforms, it is also true that it has traditionally been used primarily with Microsoft Windows, although it has to some degree been replaced by the .NET framework.

Concept-Oriented Programming

Whereas object-oriented programming uses objects and classes of objects as the main programming construct, concept-oriented programming uses concepts as the main programming construct. The two concepts that are uppermost in this paradigm are *business methods* (those constructs that are called explicitly in source code) and *representation and access methods* (those called implicitly with the business methods). This means that whenever we call a business method, something is always happening behind the scenes.

For example, if we call a Java method, the Java virtual machine (JVM) needs to resolve the target before it can execute the target. Once the target has been resolved, memory may need to be obtained and the JVM may need to resolve the memory handle into a physical memory address. The methods (both business methods and representation and access methods) can be nested many layers deep and different functions can be executed to check security, application locking, and access accounting. Often, these representation and access methods are well hidden due to the implicit calls that are made on behalf of the business methods.

For this reason (the nesting and implicit calls), the representation and access methods account for most of the system complexity. This means that much effort needs to go into describing the hidden methods, and this effort needs to be an integral part of the program. Much of the elegance of these programs lies in retaining the illusion of instant access to resources while allowing for the complexity of what must go on behind the scenes as efficiently as possible.

Programming Paradigms and Grid

Grid programming, by the very nature of the Grid, will confound definition, likely for years to come. Because the Grid can be many things to many people, the people making the definitions will, by defining what they put on the Grid, play a part in defining the programming paradigm that goes along with that Grid.

One definition, however, is likely to carry through many different threads. Whatever paradigm and whatever programming language or languages rise to meet the Grid challenge, modularity will have to play a large part in the definition.

Modularity, as discussed, leads to smaller programs that are easier to read, write, debug, and maintain. These self-contained functions and procedures can be stored in libraries to be used and reused by other programs and even other languages, depending on how they are written and called.

Modular programs are easier to write and test because each individual component can be written independently and tested thoroughly with minimal effort and time spent on each step. Thought should be given to the logic behind the program and to the way that other programs will interact with it, and concentration can be dedicated to a very discrete problem (often either a business problem or a known programming problem).

Moreover, smaller modules are more easily read and debugged because no extensive sections of code are involved in the overall program as a whole, but rather stored in the smaller subprograms. Reading through discrete amounts of code is simpler and more elegant. Testing the code in each module is quicker, and less code means fewer places that errors can occur. In addition, the testing of the overall program is easier and the programs can be handed off with more confidence because the testing has occurred at many different levels and testing the overall logic may only mean testing the logic of the flow rather than having to test and retest the logic at every step in the code.

The modularity will lead to more robust code modules and function and procedure reuse. Once a module is found to be sound and accurate for computing averages, that code can be used anywhere that a series of numbers needs to be averaged. Another module can be used to compute standard deviation, another return on investment, and another internal rate of return. By making a module that reliably computes a single function, and making it once very well, attention can be paid to less mundane programming challenges. Modular programming does not necessarily have to be associated with object-oriented programming design — however, it often is.

Depending on where the Grid will be implemented, the paradigm may also change.

This book has more to do with how the programming is used and the ideas behind how to make the programs behave efficiently in the Grid environment than it has to do with how the programs are made or in what programming language they are written (although some languages adapt more readily than others).

Chapter 2

Definition and Components

"The least flexible component of any system is the user."

—Lowell Jay Arthur

What better place to start a chapter on the definition of a Grid environment and its components than with a definition of what, in general, are the characteristics of Grid environments?

Definition

A Grid is considered a decentralized system, a spanning system containing multiple administrative domains, that provides a nontrivial quality of service where both the set of users and the total set of resources can (and do) vary dynamically and continuously. It handles large numbers of hardware and software systems to perform functions and computations on large volumes of data. Uniform and transparent access to heterogeneous systems (again hardware and software) is provided to both end users and their applications. However, it is a flexible mechanism in which one can locate resources based on a user's criteria, combined with a set of rules and permissions.

The benefits that a Grid environment is most likely to bring to your organization are, in part:

- A Grid will help with enabling more effective and nearly seamless collaboration of often widely dispersed communities. This is true for both scientific communities and commercial endeavors.
- A Grid will assist with enabling large-scale applications, and the combination of up to tens of thousands of computers.
- A Grid can provide transparent access to high-end resources, power that can approach that found in super-computing environments, from the end users' desktop.
- A Grid can provide a uniform look and feel to a wide range of resources. This will allow users to access files and other resources from a mainframe environment, Windows servers, open systems, and Linux systems without having to be concerned with the syntax and idiosyncrasies involved with each different environment. The front end allows them to manipulate the data and the information in a uniform environment (often a browser-based interface).
- A Grid can allow for location independence. Computational resources can be separated from data, and data can be widely separated (in geography as well as in disparate operating systems) from other pieces of data.

Additionally, Grid computing will allow companies to form partnerships in entirely different ways, allowing them to work more closely and efficiently with colleagues, partners, and suppliers. This can be extended to more than simple partnerships between one core company and its suppliers. The extension can encompass the supplier's suppliers, etc. This collaboration can take on the following characteristics:

- Resource aggregation will allow participating organizations to treat geographically dispersed systems as one virtual supercomputer with efficient resource management.
- Database sharing can allow participants access to any remote database within the Grid. This has proven particularly useful for Grids connected to the life science companies sharing human genome data and for those groups mining data from weather data-gathering databases. While there must be a distinct separation between the data that a company proves willing to share and those pieces of information that it chooses to keep private, the publicly shared data will benefit all parties involved.
- Widely dispersed organizations or groups of organizations using the Grid to allow for collaboration will be able to work together on a project, sharing everything from engineering blueprints to software applications. This can extend to far more than sharing information across what is typically considered a computer system.

The Web has proven, and will continue to prove, to be a good testbed for computing — and in particular, Grid computing. In many ways, peer-to-peer computing (P2P) can be viewed as a small step in the direction of Grid computing. Although P2P does not provide the level of security, authentication, or virtual access to machine architecture that many of the academic, research, and commercial Grids do today, it does allow for working across different platforms and enabling applications and file sharing.

Peer-to-Peer (P2P) Computing

P2P computing is the natural offspring of decentralized software and available technology. Many of the trends in the past decade or more have tended away from huge centralized systems and toward more distributed systems. While management of the decentralized model has historically been more difficult than managing its centralized cousin, and this has stood partly in the way of a far more widespread acceptance of the model. The immense growth of the Internet, the availability of powerful networked computers, more affordable means to acquire larger amounts of bandwidth, and the rise of business-to-business (B2B) transactions, distributed computing in one model or another, have become popular with people interested in file sharing and that is becoming a necessity for more and more corporations.

Peer-to-peer refers to a communication model that includes computing devices (desktops, servers, palm tops) linked directly with each other over a network and includes the associated technology. P2P systems can include any combination of interconnections. Often, people think of P2P as associated with its popular use, enabling users to trade files directly over an Internet connection, without requiring a direct connection to either the central database or file server.

Social issues have also impacted the popularity of P2P computing. When the World Wide Web (WWW) began to emerge, people would put up a page and link to other pages. In turn, those pages would return the link. Without the hyperlink and the WWW, the Internet would likely not be where it is today — good, bad, or indifferent.

The arrival of Napster and other file-sharing environments spawned the development of new and different technologies to allow a user to more easily find those files that he wants to find and others to find those files that he wants to share. Lawsuits aside, the idea is sound and is not likely to die.

Napster

Napster has become, arguably, one of the most infamous P2P models. Trading music from computer to computer, originally free and more recently charging for the songs, Napster provides the means for computers to connect directly to each other and exchange files. Lawsuits pitting P2P file-sharing software companies against the entertainment industry groups threatened not only the company, but could have extended that threat to the model. Courts did find that P2P networks, regardless of what users choose to do to use or abuse the system, has legitimate uses, not the least of which is swapping public domain media and the distribution of open source software.

Gnutella

Since its inception with ARPANET, the Internet's central premise has been file and information sharing. Many people do not realize that this is the underlying history and the underlying premise but only see and understand the WWW as it is today. Gnutella provides the Internet community with a means by which people can use much of the Internet to get back to these basics.

Whereas Napster was based on a centralized network agent, Gnutella is a public and completely decentralized network. No one owns it, and there is no central server available for it. In a true P2P model, every user's computer is a server and every user's computer is a client. Every user contributes to keeping the network alive and healthy.

Gnutella works with two types of clients: (1) leaf (low-capacity users who do not have enough bandwidth CPU power or memory to handle and route general traffic but can process queries and search results and can provide files shared over the network); and (2) ultrapeers who take care of most of the Gnutella traffic, form the core of the network (allowing any leaf the ability to connect close to the core) and protect the leaves from excessive traffic. Ultrapeers may not be sharing files, but may have plenty of bandwidth (512 kbps in both directions). Ultrapeers will typically connect together in groups of five to ten with hundreds of leaves connected to each ultrapeer, making a several hundred- or thousand-computer cluster. In this way, everyone contributes.

The same people who created Winamp at Nullsoft created Gnutella. The protocol was first developed in 1999. When AOL (soon to become AOL Time Warner) acquired Nullsoft, it decided that it could not continue to develop the technology that would become a thread to the parent company's primary industry. While this was likely a gut reaction to the Napster court cases and many saw the entire premise of peer-to-peer as a threat, particularly to the music industry, Gnutella and the peer-to-peer concept are not threats to any industry. Partly in the same way that guns are blamed for killing people, Napster was blamed for being the vehicle used to allow those trading music freely over the Internet to do so. But in the same way that people kill people, people who really want to have access to music covered by copyright law will always find a way if they want to do it badly enough. Technology cannot be blamed for copying a CD to cassette or burning it to another CD or zipping an MP3 file and e-mailing it.

Running Gnutella software and connecting to a node in the Gnutella network allows one to now bring only the information one is willing to make public (and the choice of what to make public is always within one's control), and also allows one to see that information that others have on their computers and decided to also make public.

The Napster ilk of file-sharing software centralize the applications if not the files and they use central servers where it is much easier to snoop traffic and hack one central location. Gnutella allows one to search for information anonymously from a network of independent servers from which one pulls information (information is never pushed) sought independently.

The P2P model feels to this author a lot like the Kevin House (the very first hospitality house in the United States — Mr. and Mrs. Cyril Garvey's (from Sharon, Pennsylvania) memorial to their 13-year-old-son who lost his life battling cancer). The house was a family-like community (or maybe a commune-like community) where guests were given a private room to put their clothes and other personal belongings that they did not want everyone to share.

There was a communal pantry for donated grocery items as well as groceries that guests were willing to share with others staying in the house. Linens, laundry supplies, flatware, and other supplies that people had donated or were willing to share were put into communal locations. Books and magazines for sharing were left in the living room or the library.

P2P works in much the same way. After downloading and installing a software program that allows one to access the system (the keys to the door of the house), connect to the network of other users who have downloaded and installed the same software (other people who visit the cancer hospital). One decides which information on the hard drive that one wants to make public (i.e., what one wants to put into the library and into the pantry) and what one wants to keep private. One can then work with one's own information or access that information that other people have put into their own public locations.

P2P could mean an end to people sending big files as e-mail attachments and their dependence on bandwidth, connection speed, and a central server to process them. However, these attachments can be intercepted, allowing for potential security breaches. Business and e-commerce could both benefit from P2P models providing secure and expedient means of file sharing for its members.

Types

P2P is only one kind of subset of what can be seen as constituting the Grid. There are many views of what the Grid is and what it can be, and each of these views is applicable to a different business issue.

Computational Grid

Word Spy (http://www.wordspy.com/words/computationalgrid.asp) defines a computational grid as "a large collection of computers linked via the Internet so that their combined processing power can be harnessed to work on difficult or time-consuming problems. (Also called *community computation*.)." These Grids provide supercomputing-like power on demand, just as a power grid provides electricity on demand, and frequently the resources and many of the users of those resources are geographically separated.

Typically, when people start talking about Grids and Grid computing, they are most often referring to computational Grids. With the advent of processors that obtain higher and higher performance metrics and the emergence of open system operating systems such as Linux, inexpensive clusters of multiple processor systems for medium- and higher-scale computations and efficiency in utilizing the distributed computing resources are more possible and cost effective. Although a highly significant percentage of personal computers and nearly all servers are powered on and operating virtually all of the time in companies around the globe, much of the time that they are powered on is spent with the CPU sitting idle or nearly idle. Surfing the Web, word processing, spreadsheet manipulation, and other typical day-to-day jobs are not computationally taxing and often only require the memory on the computer with very little use of the actual CPU. The extra horsepower is a benefit when it comes to being able to open several programs at once and seeing quicker response times, but it would be more productive if a way to harness these spare CPU cycles were found.

Enter *computational Grids* that allow one to harness the extra CPU cycles available on network and apply those CPU cycles to other, more resource-intensive purposes. Computational Grids have been built from disparate collections of independent services brought together to achieve a unified environment, allowing for collaboration and cooperation.

Distributed Servers and Computation Sites

Obviously, one of the key components in any computational Grid will be the servers or the sources of CPU cycles. These servers may or may not meet the traditional definition of a server. A mainframe computer, a supercomputer, or another conventional type of server can be the source. However, a PC can also be a source of CPU cycles, as can the newer technology known as a blade server.

Remote Instrumentation

Scientific instruments used to gather data are integral in many computational Grid environments. Because of the historical background (the Grid found its start in particle physics, bioinformatics and the genome projects among other highly scientific endeavors), telescopes, electron microscopes, and other remotely accessible resources are often included as data sources for Grids. In Grids that are in place in the sciences, this instrumentation is often one of the primary sources of data.

One grand vision for remote instrumentation is that data can be captured from arrays of sensors or other data gatherers deployed throughout the environment, and integrated with other data sources. Later, that data is accessed on a global scale in ways that allow it to be visualized, manipulated, and shared from any location. While there may be a need to reevaluate the way we capture and store the measurements from these instruments due to the existing design, there are ways to accomplish the necessary changes.

Remote access of telescopes and satellites has been a reality for quite some time but there are still many types of instrumentation that remain less commonly accessed remotely via a computer network.

Areas that present a lot of possibilities are telemedicine and telecare. With telemedicine, the trend is toward increased growth in the range of locations where advanced medical care must be available and delivered. The goal of telemedicine and telecare is to increase the reliable availability of medical care. Reducing demand on hospital services is one of the primary long-term goals, and another is to improve long-term care and the ultimate quality of life for the patients. Grid technology could go far to facilitate online monitoring of patients and the reliable delivery of the remote data from health-care sites. While ultimately this will be a business decision, this will also mean a higher quality of life for those on the remote ends of the collection devices. If a person can be adequately taken care of in his own home instead of having to be hospitalized far away from where he is comfortable, he will be less reticent to accept the help, and it will be less costly for him and his family to receive quality care.

There remain several technical issues standing in the way of the elegant implementation of these remote medical locations. One of the issues will be to process signals from the remote devices such that significant events can be monitored and data on these events gathered and processed. Communication facilities (wireless and other mobile technology) should be in place to allow for remote access across a variety of bandwidths. These communication channels should be both reliable and not subject to bottlenecks.

Security mechanisms must be in place to allow for the delivery of the information to and from a vast number and types of devices to the collecting areas while maintaining the privacy and anonymity of the patients. While HIPAA (Health Insurance Portability and Accountability Act of 1996) is only a major legal issue in the United States, there will naturally be concerns everywhere. No wants to think his or her medical information is freely accessible to anyone who is dedicated enough to hack the network.

Data Archives

Historically, the data on which researchers have operated has been stored, primarily, in flat files on file systems. These file systems are likely located across many locations in many countries. The digital archival process demands a reliable storage system for digital objects, well-organized information structures for content management, and efficient and accurate information retrieval services for a variety of user needs. This information, hundreds of petabytes of data now based on the continued collection of information at a rate of several petabytes a year, is dispersed all over the Internet, on hundreds of servers. How do researchers turn that information into knowledge? How can they efficiently access that information? How can that information be stored in such a way that it is both stable and accessible to as many people as possible so that the information can be turned into knowledge?

A digital object is defined as something (an image, a sound clip, a text document, a movie clip, astrological data, seismic or map information) that has been digitally encoded and integrated with some form of metadata to support the discovery. It deals with the use and storage of objects with the goals of being able to not only protect the original, but also duplicate that original for longevity. Archival systems must be flexible to facilitate search and retrieval from both heterogeneous and homogeneous sources, and also facilitate the ease of access for resource sharing. Archival systems also must provide lower cost of maintenance and dissemination for the owner as well as for the end user.

Networks

In a system in which several dozen to several thousand computers are linked together to more quickly perform jobs, the interconnection of servers takes on increased importance. Not only is it critical to have a reliable network connecting the pieces, but it is also important to remember that the fastest response time in any system is no faster than slowest piece in the system; and it is important that this network has as low latency as possible. This may be difficult to achieve because of the extreme heterogeneous nature of the components that make up the Grid environment; but in a system that is within the control of a single company or even a multinational organization, the network can be controlled enough so that as much latency as possible can be removed. When and if the Grid becomes true utility computing the way that some suggest, this will be a major hurdle to overcome.

Portal (User Interface)

As in any well-designed system, a user, client, and customer should not need to understand or care about the complexities and intricacies of the system used; they should only see a well-designed interface through which they can accomplish their work. User interfaces can take many forms, and are often application-specific; they can (in a broad sense) be viewed as portals. In fact, they are often portals on a Web page.

Webopedia (http://www.webopedia.com/TERM/W/Web_portal.html) defines a portal as follows:

> Commonly referred to as simply a *portal*, a Web site or service that offers a broad array of resources and services, such as e-mail, forums, search engines, and on-line shopping malls. The first Web portals were online services, such as AOL, that provided access to the Web, but by

now most of the traditional search engines have transformed themselves into Web portals to attract and keep a larger audience.

Many Internet users today understand the concept of a Web portal by which their browser provides a single unified interface through which a user launches applications that will use services and resources but is not required to do anything other than perform his job. From this perspective, the user sees nearly any system as a virtual computing resource. A portal service on the Grid is little different from this conceptual model.

Security

A major requirement for Grid computing is security. At the base of any Grid environment, there must be mechanisms to provide security, including authentication, authorization, data encryption, etc. The Grid security infrastructure (GSI) component of the Globus Toolkit provides robust security mechanisms. The GSI includes an open SSL implementation. It also provides a single sign-on mechanism so that once a user is authenticated, a proxy certificate is created and used in performing actions within the Grid. When designing a Grid environment, one can use the GSI sign-in to grant access to the portal, or have one's own security for the portal. The portal will then be responsible for signing in to the Grid, either using the user's credentials or using a generic set of credentials for all authorized users of the portal.

Security, because it is such a major concern in Grid computing and in database design in general, is addressed more extensively in Chapter 4.

Brokers

A *broker* is a master scheduler. It allows a user or a process to request resources from one or more machines for a job. It can perform load balancing across multiple systems. Brokers discover resources for a job, select appropriate systems, and submit the job. There are meta schedulers, super schedulers, and basic brokers. The meta schedulers take care of load balancing. Super schedulers discover the resources, then select and submit the jobs. Basic brokers quote on resources or discover resources and distribute data and computations based on the determined cost model.

One of the key features of the Grid is the provisioning of work and resources based on both policies and the dynamic needs of the organization. It uses the pool or resources as if they were singular to increase the utilization of any given resource. One can provision more resources at peak times and then re-provision them elsewhere when the peak moves. The larger the pool of resources, the easier it is to reallocate resources dynamically to meet the needs of the business.

Once a user is authenticated to the network, she will be launching one application or another. Based on which application, and potentially on what other parameters are provided by the user, the system then needs to identify appropriate available resources to make use of within the Grid. A broker can carry out the task of identifying resources. The Globus Toolkit does not directly provide the facility for a resource broker, but does provide the framework and tools to add a broker service.

One such service is the Grid resource broker (GRB). One of the current Globus projects of the HPC Lab of the Center for Advanced Computational Technologies at the University of Lecce in Italy (http://www.informatica.unile.it/laboratori/lab-hpc/), GRB is a general framework grid portal that allows those users who are "trusted" or authenticated to access and work within computational grids, making use of a simple GUI.

The user's Web browser must be configured to accept cookies. Authentication to the GRB makes use of MyProxy (a credential repository for the Grid). A user needs to store, inside one of the MyProxy servers, his proxy and authentication information. The GRB will then retrieve the authentication and proxy information based on the user's password and authenticate the user using his (the user's) unique name and information.

User Profiles

When a user starts the GRB, she authenticates herself to the system by means of a login name and her password. This login and all subsequent transactions make use of HTTPS (secure socket layer [SSL] on top of HTTP) to encrypt the user's password, thereby avoiding the transmission of the information over an insecure channel. Once the user is authenticated, she can then start a GRB session. The session will last for a specified number of hours (this number specified at proxy creation time) or until the user logs out. Before the GRB can be used, there must be a user profile containing information about those computational resources on the Grid that a particular user can use. For each machine on which the user has permissions, the profile contains the host name and the path to the user's favorite shell, as well as the conceptual cost per hour for that resource (the weighting factor to assist in the automatic determination of what computer to use for a given job). If a particular computational resource becomes unavailable for an extended period, it should be removed from the profile so that the broker does not attempt vainly to access that resource, wasting time in the contact attempt. Once a profile is set up for a user, the user can view the information stored in the file. Ideally, GRB and other resource brokers will eventually contain additional information to allow for more complex scheduling algorithms.

Searching for Resources

The Grid Index Information Service (GIIS) is an LDAP (lightweight directory access protocol) server that collects the information related to every GRIS (grid resource information service) server available in the organization. This can be seen as a basic broker resource. It allows users or processes to find, if available, those computing resources and their particular features such as memory and number and speed of processors.

GRIS then acts as a super scheduler. Computational resources can be periodically queried about their features and status if a server is running Globus. This is because a GRIS is listening on a port. GRIS is a small LDAP server that stores static (and semi-static) information as well as dynamic information about available Grid hardware and the system software associated with it. GRIS can be looked upon as an active index that allows for the simple central retrieval of a machine's main features. GRB and any other resource broker can tap into this information and make use of it when looking at what resources to schedule for any batch or real time job.

Batch Job Submittal

A user submits a batch job to be worked on by the Grid through the GRB (then acting as a meta scheduler) by entering a machine's host name and the name of the executable to be run (the complete path name if the executable is to be staged from another machine). If needed, we also allow the use of GSI-FTP servers (Globus Security Infrastructure FTP) to copy the executable as well as the input and output files to the machine that the user selected. The job is then submitted to the scheduler and, if the submission is successful, the user can use his browser to verify that the job is in the queue. The GRB stores the information related to the users' jobs automatically. This information can be used later to allow users to check job status.

But what about jobs that the user does not want to run in batch? What about the jobs that need to be run interactively? When dealing with interactive jobs, one uses GSI-FTP to copy both the executable and the input files to the target machine, and the output is sent directly back to the browser for the user to access and act upon.

What happens, then, if one does not know on what machine to run the job on, or if one does not really want to leave that decision entirely up to the end user? The GRB tool is a generic resource broker that allows the user's machine to search the Grid system to find any available computational resources suitable for the submission of the current job, and to submit a batch job on resources that are found to match the specified criteria. If the decision of which machine on which to run is taken out of the user's hands, the GRB automatically performs scheduling, which takes into account the cost information for all nodes found available, and routes the job at hand to the machine or machines that will perform the task in the most cost-effective manner allowed for by the rules.

After submitting a batch job, a user typically finds the need to monitor the job's progress. The GRB allows users to check on the status of any batch jobs previously submitted. This status checking exploits the information saved at job submission time. A job can have any of five statuses: pending, active, suspended, failed, or done. A *pending* job is still sitting in a queue waiting to be executed. *Active* means actively executing. A *suspended* job might be temporarily suspended because a job with a higher priority enters the system and is making use of the required resources.

The suspended job will become either active (when the resource becomes available again) or failed (if something goes wrong in the processing). *Failed* jobs occur for any number of reasons. Normal completion of a job results in a *done* status. When a job receives a done status, the GRB transfers the output file to the selected repository machine using GSI-FTP if this is the action that the user requested.

Sometimes users need to run the same executable with different sets of input. This is true in what-if scenarios or on parameter studies. The GRB allows them elegant means to accomplish this. This resource broker (acting as the basic broker) provides the means for the user to transfer files between machines using GSI-FTP. The GRB supports both single file transfer and whole directory transfer. The GRB service enables the administrator to centrally check the status of the Globus daemons installed on each machine in the Grid.

While most users know that they should always log out of a system when they are finished, this is not always done. There are many reasons why users do not like to log out of a system. Often, the steps needed to log back in feel redundant to the user. Often, users simply feel that if the system is always there when they need it, not logging out will save them time in the end. The GRB allows for automatic logout settings that will take the decision to log out of a system out of the hands of the users after a period of time, and their sessions will expire automatically. This is important for security and for resource management.

Credential Repository

Rather than storing Grid credentials on each machine used to access a Grid, one can store them in a *credential repository*, for example a MyProxy repository, and retrieve the credentials from the repository when needed.

Storing Grid credentials in a repository allows you to retrieve your credentials whenever and from wherever they are needed. A credential repository will allow users to do all this without concern for maintaining local private keys and certificate files locally.

Using any standard Web browser, one can connect to the Grid portal, the portal to retrieve that user's proxy credential to access Grid resources on his behalf. That user can also allow those trusted servers to renew his proxy credentials so that his long-running interactive and batch tasks will not fail simply because of an expired credential. Further, a well-managed credential repository can supply both a more secure and less corruptible storage location for Grid credentials than any typical local end-user systems could hope to supply.

MyProxy, one such credential repository provider, offers a set of flexible authorization mechanisms for controlling access not only to the Grid resources, but also to the repository itself. Server-wide policies allow an administrator to control how end users, programs, and programmers use the repository. Policies can allow users to specify how any credential may be accessed. Certificate-based authentication is required to allow the browser to retrieve credentials from the MyProxy server. If any credential is stored with a passphrase or password, the private key is encrypted with that word or phrase in the repository.

Scheduler

Once the resources have been identified and the permissions on those resources established, the next logical step is to schedule the individual jobs to run on those resources. If users submit stand-alone jobs with no interdependencies, then no specialized scheduler is likely required. If, however, the more likely scenario occurs and a user or set of other processes needs to reserve a specific resource or ensure that the different jobs within the job stream from the application run concurrently (if, for example, there is a need for them to communicate with each other inter-process), then it becomes necessary to use a job scheduler to coordinate the execution of these jobs. A broker may or may not be able to handle complex scheduling.

The Globus Toolkit does not include such a complex scheduler. There are several schedulers currently available. These have been tested with Globus and can be used in a Globus Grid environment. Different levels of schedulers can also be used within the Grid environment. A cluster could be represented as a single resource and have its own scheduler to help manage the nodes it contains. Another higher-level scheduler (the meta scheduler referred to in the "Brokers" section earlier) might be used to schedule work to do on the total cluster, while the cluster's single scheduler would handle the actual scheduling of work on the cluster's individual nodes.

Data Management

If any data — including application modules — must be moved or made accessible to the nodes where an application's jobs will execute, then there must be a secure and reliable method for moving files and data to various nodes within the grid. The Globus Toolkit contains a data management component that provides such services. This component, know as Grid access to secondary storage (GASS), includes facilities such as GridFTP. This feature is built on top of the standard FTP, and adds additional functions and utilizes the GSI for user authentication and authorization. Therefore, once a user has an authenticated proxy certificate, he can use the GridFTP facility to move files without having to go through a login process to every node involved. This facility provides third-party file transfer so that one node can initiate a file transfer between two other nodes.

In a computational Grid, most of the machines are high-performance servers. Figure 2.1 shows a model of a computational grid. The user, in this case in accounting, logs in to the system by means of a portal running on the application server to run his or her application. That application server directs the request to the broker and/or the scheduler, which then distributes the jobs to the available resources that are necessary to complete those jobs. The results are returned to where the user can pick them up, again via the portal interface.

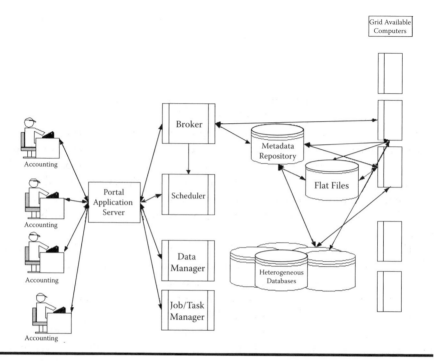

Figure 2.1 Model of a computational grid.

Data Grid

A data grid is typically responsible for housing the access provisions to data across multiple organizations. Users of the data need not ever be concerned with where this data is located as long as they have access to the data that they require. Picture, for example, two universities performing life science research, each passess unique data, that can, through a data grid, share and manage their data, and security issues associated with such sharing, like who has access to what data. Or, two departments within a multinational corporation, one on the United States' West coast and one in the United Kingdom, have a need to access data located in proprietary systems that belong to different departments. Each of these departments could access the other's data across the Grid and still maintain control over their own data.

There are several unique characteristics of data Grids that are not necessarily components of the others.

Storage Mechanism Neutrality

Grid architecture is designed to be as independent as possible because much of the information and data (as well as the metadata) could potentially be stored on low-level devices. This can also apply to lower-level transfer media. Achieving *mechanism neutrality* can be accomplished by defining data access, providing third-party data movement capabilities, allowing for catalog access as well as other interfaces that minimize the peculiarities of the different systems and data transfer algorithms.

Policy Neutrality

Because of the nature of the Grid and the nature of end-user direct interaction with the data, access methods and access paths can less be taken out of the hands of the users and encapsulated in the application. This has significant performance implications, as anyone who has dealt with dynamic query tools (such as Business Objects, Oracle Discoverer, or Cognos' Power Play) can attest. Data movement and the cataloging of replicated information are possible and provided as basic operations for which one can substitute parameters as a user or through application code.

Compatibility with Other Grid Infrastructures

Because data Grids do not necessarily exist in a vacuum and are rarely implemented independent of other Grid components, anything that is configured as a data Grid should be compatible with the other components already in place or destined to be put into place. This compatibility needs to extend as far as possible to enable the adaptation to system conditions at runtime, regardless of when runtime is. This has definite implications for not only the hardware that comprises the system, but also to the data model.

Storage Systems

An administrator may or may not have any control over what kind of storage system the data resides on or what characteristics those storage devices have. While it is important that the end user never have to know or care about storage, it does remain an important feature and something that both the administrators and the programmers have to consider. Storage at the Grid level no longer has physical attributes; rather, it has logical attributes. Physically, how it is implemented is less important (as the data can literally be placed on any storage technology) than its ability to support the required access functions. A distributed file system manages files that are distributed over multiple physical storage devices or multiple sites rather than physically placed on disk.

Files in a data grid represent a conceptual construct, which is a somewhat different from what many people typically consider it. A file, in this instance, is also logical rather than physical, and can be what we typically think of as a file (a flat file stored in a system) or data stored in a database or other means that allow us to store data in an electronically accessible format. A data grid implementation might use a storage resource broker (SRB) system to access data stored within a hierarchical database management system (such as IMS) or a relational database system (such as

DB2, Oracle, or MySQL) or an object-oriented or object-relational database management system that can store data in different kinds of constructs.

Access or Collaboration Grids

An *access grid* is not really something that anyone considers a Grid environment. It is an assembly of resources that support and facilitate group-to-group interaction across a Grid environment. This includes highly distributed meetings, collaborative work sessions with individuals who are geographically distributed, seminars, distance lectures, and training (including lecturer-assisted computer-based training). The primary difference between this and other types of Grids is that the latter focus primarily on computational resources and the access Grid focuses on individuals and communication.

Currently, access grids are in place and in use at more than 150 different institutions around the world. One was in use at Hibbing Community College in Northern Minnesota in the year 2000. I took a manufacturing class and sat with four other students in one of two access grid-enabled classrooms at Hibbing Community College.

The components of an access grid are different.

Large Format Displays

These displays could be wall-mounted LCD panels in a conference room or what could pass for a wide-screen television. These displays allow for face-to-face interactions of participants at different ends of the Earth.

Presentation Environments

Presentation environments include software that one would typically think of, such as PowerPoint, but also include book cameras that allow everyone in a meeting session to look at the same book over the connection. This can save on shipping of materials from one location to another and the need to have a dozen copies of a publication in every location for the purpose of teaching one lesson.

Interfaces to Grid Middleware

Because an access Grid can become an intricate piece in connection with other Grid implementations, interfaces to the Grid middleware are needed to facilitate this interaction. For departmental or enterprise grids, this will be (initially) true. People working on a project who are at different locations can meet face to face rather than over a typical teleconference. They can meet far more frequently than they would be able to if they had to invest in airfare, and in the comfort and familiarity of their own offices.

Other Components

The other components that will be important to an Access Grid implementation depend on the purpose of the Grid and the type of business or research involved. Particle physics will need different components than those needed for a distance education lecture hall.

Scavenging Grid

A scavenging Grid is typically a configuration of a large number of desktop machines. All the machines are scavenged for available CPU cycles and other free resources. The owners or users of the machines are given control of when their resources are and are not available to participate in the Grid environment. If a user does not set up a specified schedule for the scavenging of resources, whenever the machine would become idle, its status would be reported to the central management server and its node would be added to the database of accessible nodes.

Scavenging Grids are in place in many computer labs on university campuses around the world. These desktop systems have periods when they are in heavy use (during programming classes, when term papers are coming due, or when the majority of students are out of classes and are chatting, gaming, or surfing the Internet), but also extended periods when they are idle. During these idle periods, and at times when any given computer is not being accessed, its CPUs could be added to those available resources.

Cycle scavenging has been around for a long time under the SETI@home project without the computer having to be connected to a network or actively registered with a central server's database. SETI (Search for Extra Terrestrial Intelligence) is based at the University of California at Berkeley and creates a virtual supercomputer to analyze the data collected from the Arecibo radio telescope in Puerto Rico. The analysis searches for signs of extraterrestrial intelligence. Using the Internet (to distribute the packets of data for each computer to process and analyze), SETI has managed to bring together the CPUs and processing power of three million or more personal computers around the world.

SETI@home (see Figure 2.2) is simply a screen-saver type of program that works behind the scenes without any deleterious impact on the normal use of the computer. Any PC owner anywhere in the world (PC in this case is a loose definition, as the machine in question can be running MAC, Windows, or Linux) can download the program from the Web and set his computer free to analyze data. These different PCs (the nodes of the loosely defined Grid) with their different speeds and different capabilities all work simultaneously on different parts of the whole problem. When each task is complete, the result set is passed back to the central system and the personal system can then retrieve more chunks of data from the Internet to process. The success of SETI has inspired many other applications of

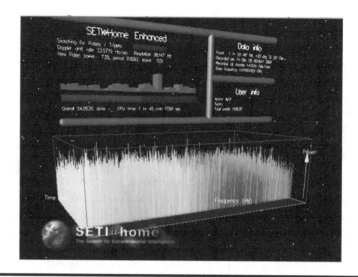

Figure 2.2   SETI@home.

similar type. These include protein-folding simulations (see Figure 2.3) for sifting potential future drugs, filters for astronomical data searching for pulsars, evolutionary programs that attempt to analyze problems in population dynamics, and many others.

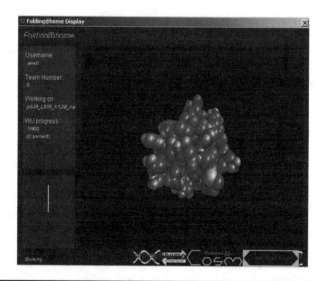

Figure 2.3   Protein-folding simulation.

Grid Scope

Project Grid, Departmental Grid, or Cluster Grid

The simplest and lowest form of Grid environment is typically at the departmental level. Used for multiple projects, a departmental Grid is typically used if a company already has an infrastructure in place.

The major features of a departmental Grid include maximizing the utilization of departmental resources, with allocations based primarily on priorities, with rules and weights assigned to projects and resources to balance out the priorities and allow for the equitable distribution of (and accounting for) the communal resources.

Enterprise Grid or Campus Grid

An enterprise Grid is often what companies foresee when they start looking at implementing a Grid infrastructure. In an enterprise Grid, all major computing resources are shared with every department and project in the entire enterprise. Policies are implemented to ensure computing on demand and allow for the multiple groups' seamless access to the enterprise's resources.

While this may be the ultimate goal of many companies attempting a Grid initiative, it is more typical and realistic for companies to start with a departmental Grid. This allows the company to learn from the experience and build on its start (not only from the technology perspective, but also from the learning curve and people perspectives).

An enterprise Grid consists of several departmental Grids clustered around a central single Grid that should be capable of handling the needs (computing, data, and personal) of multiple departments, each potentially (and quite likely) working on multiple projects, all sharing the same computing resources. The entire enterprise Grid is located inside the corporate firewall and accessible only by those with the authority to access any other information within that firewall.

Global Grid

In a global Grid environment, resources will be shared over the Internet or other widely distributed networking environment. It will provide a unified global view of widely distributed datasets. It may be at an international organizational level (this would likely be made available via an intranet rather than the Internet) or at an interest level or any other level that unifies a group of interested parties. Multiple groups of people in a global Grid environment will be working on multiple projects and sharing a central set of resources. In this phase, companies (if that is the level of globalization) will gain a global view of the distributed databases.

Extending this idea to its penultimate extent, many resources will be made commercially available much in the same way that electricity, water, phone service, and natural gas are currently available to the public. A person, company, or group would subscribe to the service and draw upon the computing resources, as those resources are required.

Chapter 3

Early Adopters

Humans are allergic to change. They love to say, "We've always done it this way." I try to fight that. That's why I have a clock on my wall that runs counter-clockwise.

—Rear Admiral Grace Murray Hopper

The Grid can be a core business competency to anyone who learns that he or she faces periods of shortages of CPU cycles, or approaches that point. Certain industries are inherently more apt to make early use of emerging technology.

Computational and Experimental Scientists

Computational scientists are frequently dispersed but also have a preexisting need to interact either with each other or with remote resources. These resources can be computers, telescopes, particle accelerators, or electron microscopes. Computational scientists (those who are more directly connected to theory) will be interested in making use of the ability to visualize applications in real-time, and experimental scientists (the more numerous group connected to the observations) will make even more extensive use of the remote instrumentation in gathering data and large-scale CPU power and visualization devices such as the CAVE virtual reality modeler.

Bioinformatics

Bioinformatics involves applying considerable computer technology to biology and medicine. It seeks to integrate genomic, post-genomic (the genome mapping projects), and proteomic disciplines in an attempt to use these as tools to cure cancer. There are several organizations around the world that seek to implement Grid systems, often on a series of supercomputer systems, to make these resources available to bioinformatics users. These supercomputers will likely play a very large role in providing the "glue" and shared memory structures for Grid-enabled distributed computing applications.

One major site of life science applications is the North Carolina Bioinformatics Grid Project in Research Triangle Park, North Carolina. While its projects did not start out with the defined goal of building a Grid, the Grid architecture grew out of a natural need by several organizations for significant amounts of computing resources. Based on their requirements for high-performance computing and extensive scalability, and also on a simple model providing a single unified user interface, the Grid system spans a number of computers at three universities, several large commercial and government research facilities, and the North Carolina Supercomputing Center.

Corporations

Corporations have become increasingly more global. The World Wide Web has allowed the extensive adoption of corporate intranets for even modest-sized companies. These two facts make corporations targets for Grid technologies. Portals allow for the presentation of interfaces through the intranet browser, and the global nature of many organizations means that the wide distribution could make extensive use of the underlying technology.

These are the kinds of groups that will make extensive use of the grid in the future, but who made the decision to be on the cutting edge and become the first companies and groups to adopt the Grid infrastructure?

Academia

As with many of the major advances in technology, academia is where Grid gathered its earliest adopters. There is a deep and impressive amount of research and data connected with Grid implementations waiting to be found.

University of Houston, Texas, United States

The University of Houston's high performance computing group was formed in 1999 to provide the faculty and students with a centralized parallel computing environment more powerful than any of the resources that would have been available to individual departments. Previously, the university had relied on a conventional infrastructure but the total cost of ownership was becoming prohibitive and the infrastructure was not providing the performance and scalability needed. Thus, it installed several Sun Fire servers, blade servers, and StorEdge storage arrays, and also installed the Sun Open Net Environment (Sun ONE) grid engine and the Solaris operating system to better meet its needs.

The impact of the Grid at the University of Houston will have a far-reaching impact all over the state of Texas. The institution is a part of High-Performance Computing Across Texas (HiPCAT), a consortium of Texas institutions dedicated to using advanced computing, visualization, data storage, and networking technologies to enhance research and educational activities. It is through HiPCAT that the university is involved with the Texas Internet Grid for Research and Education (TIGRE) project. The project will allow for the sharing of computing resources, instruments, and data that will allow the creation of massive scientific simulations and analyses.

It will also collaborate with Texas A&M's weather experts to work on developing an accurate air quality model for the Houston region. This new infrastructure will foster partnerships rather than competitions within the university systems of the state.

University of Ulm, Germany

The University of Ulm is one of Germany's premier medical, scientific, and mathematical institutions and demands a tremendous amount of computing power. To help support such intensive computing, in 2001 the University of Ulm partnered with Stuttgart University to implement Sun Fire 6800 server clusters running the Sun One Grid Engine as a batch system for workload management. This allows researchers throughout the region from different universities as well as industrial partners to experiment using the high-performance distributed computing capabilities. The project was aptly named the Sun Center for Excellence for Computational Chemistry.

The White Rose University Consortium, United Kingdom

The White Rose University Consortium comprises the University of Leeds, the University of York, and the University of Sheffield for the purpose of sharing technological resources. These resources include computers, data, applications, and storage and network resources. To facilitate this sharing, the consortium turned to Sun Microsystems to build the joint infrastructure for scientific computing. The project, called the White Rose Grid, utilized Sun Fire 6800, Sun Fire V880, Sun StorEdge array, and Sun Blade 100 servers at each of the three locations, and utilized Grid computing technology to allow for on-demand computational capacity available to participating universities and also to an even wider commercial and academic market. The White Rose Grid has contributed extensively to the development of business and commercial use of Grid technology in the United Kingdom.

Science

Particle Physics

As recently as 1990, CERN, in combination with a few other particle physics laboratories comprised the entire World Wide Web. The Web was designed at CERN to help facilitate the exchange of information among scientists who were working on separate computers often at widely dispersed sites. The United Kingdom has always played a significant role in revolutionary developments.

The Grid is no exception. The Web is aimed at an efficient and effective exchange of information. Grid is concerned with the exchange of computing power, storage of data, and access to very large databases without the users having to deliberately search manually for the resources. Once connected to the Grid, the users see the computing resources as one huge system. It is a viable and practical solution to data-intensive problems that scientists must overcome if they are to continue to make historic advancements over the coming years.

Still among the leaders, U.K. physicists are currently preparing themselves for the Large Hadron Collider (LHC) that will be turned on in 2007 at CERN. It will produce an enormous stream of data (to the tune of millions of gigabytes per year). That stream of data must be stored and processed. The processing could utilize the computing power of nearly 100,000 processors, a scale that no single computer center has or will be able to provide to the dedication of both the storage and computing requirements of the entire LHC operation. This is where Grid computing can thrive. The distribution of computation and data via the Grid for a project of this magnitude is essential. The United Kingdom expects to continue to play a significant role in the emerging technology and the analysis of data from the LHC. Many new and exciting discoveries are anticipated.

U.K. physicists are also participating in a number of projects, although not on the scale of the LHC, using Grid developments to hone their skills and learn through experience how to use the Grid as a tool for day-to-day analysis.

The cartoons available at http://www.gridpp.ac.uk/cartoon.html depict excellent examples of what this Grid will mean to scientists in the United Kingdom. While these distributed resources are available, they must be negotiated and manipulated by each individual scientist as needed, and each scientist requires a separate account on each system, as well as an account for every system, making the management of accounts almost a full-time occupation. Once the accounts are managed, the jobs must be submitted individually and the results of those jobs collected manually by the scientist. The Grid will enable the scientists to treat these resources as a single integrated computer system, with single sign-on and middleware handling all the details and allowing the scientists to concentrate on science.

Industry

Many industries are currently primed for participating in the Grid. These industries are computational and data intensive and ready to make a change from the conventional to something that passes for cutting edge.

Gaming

The online gaming industry is one of the first businesses in which a new technology is going to start making commercial inroads in order to succeed. Ironically, through the gaming industry, the emerging technology will touch many millions of people who will have no idea what hardware they are using. Millions of dedicated game console platforms are already in homes worldwide, including play stations, X-boxes, and game cubes, as well as the PC. These dedicated consoles, together with the PC gaming market, form a multi-billion dollar industry. Games have become a serious business, and the Grid has become one of the means by which provider companies have started to flesh out the games and ensure that the game field is not only wide and diverse, but always available worldwide whenever any of the millions of subscribers want to play.

However, online gaming, faces several hurdles. The computer systems, the game systems, and environments are very complex, not only to create and manage, but also to play. Not only are they complex, but they have notoriously been very expensive to create and operate because a game publisher must invest in new systems (hardware, operating systems, and supporting software) for every new game launched. Another drawback to buying gaming services is that they are frequently taken offline, often for several hours at a time, for server maintenance. Conventional technology dictates that game providers must run several identical copies of the virtual world, each copy called a shard or server, to segment different players onto separate servers (a player can typically choose the shard on which he or she wants to interact), or separate shards, thereby limiting much of the possible inter-character interaction (by forcing a player's character to exist on exactly one server at any one time) and further exacerbating reliability and support problems because of the additional hardware and server maintenance downtime. While this copying of the system allows for load balancing of users (each server environment allows only a certain number of concurrent users), it severely limits what those users can do while online, because it limits the number of other players with whom they can interact.

A prime example of what a huge phenomenon online gaming is EverQuest. EverQuest is notorious for dedicated players who play seriously, and also use online auction sites such as Ebay to sell characters, secrets, and equipment from the virtual game world. They are reported to have a virtual economy that makes its setting one of the largest economies in the world — real or virtual.

The Grid has begun to prove that it can overcome many of these issues and provide added flexibility, reliability, and depth to gaming world features.

The Butterfly.net Grid is the first commercial Grid system that has the capability of processing online virtual video games across a network of server farms, thus allowing the most efficient utilization of computing resources for extremely high-performance, three-dimensional, immersive game worlds.

One of the expenses game developers incur is when they spend more than $3 million for the development of a game and its underlying infrastructure, anticipating 100,000 people turning out, and then only a tenth of that number play. While not as much of a problem from the accounting perspective, but more of a problem from the player's perspective is when the same game is anticipated to draw 100,000 players and it draws 500,000 players, and the servers are not scaled to handle the load. With Butterfly.net, these issues are not part of the picture. Because it is a service provider and its infrastructure is always available and almost infinitely scalable, the game developers making use of the service can concentrate on developing robust games and organizing and orienting people within the game as the how to scale the game so that it will be rich enough to hold their attention. This challenge is more fun and interesting than trying to determine how to support exactly the number of players who decide to subscribe.

The Butterfly.net hardware consists of low-cost, commodity-type systems. Cost savings lie in standardization. Launching multiple games on one Grid can allow for the scaling back of games that are unpopular, while allowing the computing and communications resources to divert to games with more popularity. Operating all games together with no mirror universes, the less popular as well as the big hits, becomes much easier and profitable. What is more, it allows all administrators to learn one platform, thus limiting the learning curve.

In the Grid configuration, a three-tiered architecture utilizes a gateway to switch people between servers when necessary. Because the model is entirely on the server, many different kinds of interfaces to the game can be created, allowing people with many different kinds of gaming platforms to interact with the same game, together. With such a small footprint on the client machine, and the vast majority of the processing occurring on the servers, from a network perspective, this configuration is extremely efficient, with much smaller packets being sent and received and very low latency, meaning that narrowband dial-up works just as efficiently as broadband connections. Any computer regardless of connection speed can allow its user to enjoy a very rich and exciting gaming experience.

Extend this concept and its findings to the corporate environment and consider what this could mean. Where, with conventional configurations, high volumes of data are transferred across a network and a single server or small cluster is responsible for all of the processing, with this new configuration, each of the servers can handle a smaller chunk of the problem and return a result set in a much more efficient manner.

Financial

The Grid is a wonderful platform on which to perform high-intensity financial market calculations. Typically, these calculations include considerable numbers of what-if scenarios, and are means by which the suggestions provided to the customer are based.

Wachovia

The fixed-income derivative trading unit at Wachovia received a computing boost when it installed its Grid computing solution designed by DataSynapse. Before the implementation of the new environment, it took 15 hours to run simulations. Since installing the Grid environment, and taking advantage of the underutilized servers and desktops, those same simulations now take 15 minutes. Wachovia is putting it to work in areas such as financial derivatives, wherein large corporate customers can hedge their risks on foreign exchange transactions or stock index futures.

Wachovia's trading volumes under the new system increased several hundred percent, and the number of simulations that it was able to run increased over 2000 percent. As a result of these improvements, Wachovia can make larger, less risky, and more complex trades than ever before, making both its clients and the company more money. Its Grid computing adoption has been driven by the need for the company to optimize resources, lower its computing costs, and implement disaster prevention and disaster recovery systems.

RBC Insurance

RBC Insurance, one of North America's largest diversified financial services companies, took an existing application and Grid-enabled it. It now runs this application on a Grid platform based on the IBM eServer xSeries. This new computing solution has allowed RBC Insurance to reduce time spent on job scheduling by nearly 75 percent, and the time spent processing an actuarial application by as much as 97 percent (again, performing jobs that once took several hours in mere minutes). Based on the stellar performance seen in initial trials, RBC Insurance is looking forward to expanding the Grid computing environment to take advantage of these kinds of savings with even more applications and business units. Being able to virtualize its applications and its infrastructure, RBC Insurance will be able to deliver higher quality services to its clients faster than ever, making the Grid system a significant component in its competitive edge. (See http://www-1.ibm.com/grid/grid_success_stories.shtml.)

Charles Schwab

Computer World (http://www.computerworld.com/), on December 19, 2003, reported the Charles Schwab–IBM partnership in the Schwab Grid venture. Schwab and IBM worked together to connect twelve Intel processor servers in the Phoenix data center to launch the Schwab Grid system to improve the performance of an investment management application. It has already shown improvements in the short time that it has been operational.

It took Schwab's 15-member team working with IBM nearly a year to build the system that utilizes the Globus Toolkit 2.0 running on servers with the Red Hat Linux operating system (leveraging an open source in an effort to improve the total quality of customer service) and the DB2 database, WebSphere (IBM's application server), along with the BEA Systems' WebLogic application server.

Schwab anticipates ramping up its Grid presence by rolling out even more applications on Grid technology by combining well over 1000 commodity servers providing the spare CPU cycles to speed up even more of Schwab's computationally intensive applications, thereby speeding up processing and also lowering the total cost of ownership. Thus the Grid provides one of the competitive advantages for the company. While hard numbers are not revealed because Schwab wants to keep its competitive edge, it has been suggested that it has been able to provide times for customer planning that are now seconds to minutes — and used to range up to several days. The retirement planning tool now running successfully on the Grid can calculate portfolio scenarios based on retirement goals and take into account risk tolerances and a client's preference in investment plans. These what-if scenarios are historically computationally intensive and can take a long time on a traditional architecture.

Prior to adopting this new architecture, Schwab had to scale its computing capacity up to twice or more of the average required load so that it had the ability to handle the peak loads without missing processing windows. This meant that it often had significant excess capacity laying nearly idle on a less than peak trading day. With Grid computing, it is possible to funnel this unused capacity in a far more efficient manner.

The master server breaks up the computationally intensive processes into a series of smaller jobs that run in parallel and sends those smaller jobs to the other resources on the Grid for processing. When all the result sets are in, the master node reassembles all the pieces and presents the unified result set to the requesting manager to fulfill clients' requirements.

Life Sciences

American Diabetes Association

One of the initial forays into a somewhat commercial use of Grid technology that impacts the lives of many thousands of people every day is the use of Gateway Inc.'s Grid (backed by United Device's Grid MP Alliance platform) by the American Diabetes Association (ADA). Making use of this platform to run computationally intensive applications designed to accelerate diabetes-related research, the ADA can create a robust environment in which it can run analysis on several variables at once when researching the different aspects of diabetes care and clinical studies. Cross-correlations between patients with high blood pressure and diabetes or other co-occurring conditions can be drawn with an analysis of the pros and cons of administering different dosages of medicines on patients based on age, weight, and other variables far faster than if the same analysis was done using a traditional architecture.

Using processing on demand, the ADA has already experienced dramatic improvements in the time it takes to process a single component of diabetes-related research — from nearly two days down to one hour (less than $0.25 in computing expense), and is expecting even further reductions in time through this improved efficiency. Previously, these calculations would have stretched the limits of a normal computing environment, causing delays in calculations and in finding potential new treatments.

Gateway Inc. has begun linking thousands of PCs nationwide to create a Grid computing environment that is capable of scaling to nearly 11 teraflops in performance (ranking the Gateway Processing on Demand Grid among the top ten largest supercomputers in the world based on raw processing power). Its processing on demand initiative made available the computing power of over 6000 PCs to research institutions (ADA) as well as to universities, government agencies, and businesses. This initiative allowed companies to concentrate on the core competencies while allowing those with excess computing power to provide those cycles at a charge that would be less than it would cost to create that excess capacity and knowledge base in-house (less than $0.25 per hour for unlimited computing power and one trillion floating point operations per second). Compare this cost to the hundreds of thousands of dollars that it would cost to perform similar computations and calculations on rented supercomputer time, and one can easily see the cost benefit to making use of a Grid environment. This is the ultimate *utility computing* model that the Grid stands poised to eventually become.

North Carolina Genomics and Bioinformatics Consortium

Members of the North Carolina Genomics and Bioinformatics Consortium, a group of more than 70 academic and commercial organizations, created the NC BioGrid using Avaki's technology and Grid software.

Avaki's technology will allow researchers and educators to use a unified research environment that will not only simplify their ability to share computing and data resources, but will also improve their ability to perform data mining as well as analysis and modeling of biological data.

The NC BioGrid combines genetic mapping information, information on protein folding and protein synthesis as it relates to genetic transcription and other related protein and genetic related data worldwide with software and hardware provided by the North Carolina Supercomputing Center, the North Carolina Research and Education Network, and the NC Network Applications Center, along with the Avaki Grid software. This allows researchers to utilize a unified environment that will allow them to focus on their research because it masks the complicity of managing the data stored at different locations and on different types of hardware protected by a variety of security models.

This production Grid will likely become one of the cornerstone research resources for the researchers involved, although they will remain unaware of its inner workings — that is the beauty of the system.

Spain's Institute of Cancer Research

The Institute of Cancer Research at the University of Salamanca, Spain installed a Grid system based on technology developed by GridSystems, a Majorcan company that works to optimize the computer resources available at customer sites. The Institute of Cancer Research is using this infrastructure change to help investigate the genes that may be involved in the development of tumors. In future phases, researchers will use the distributed computing infrastructure to analyze protein folding.

Petroleum

Royal Dutch Shell

IBM has been working with Royal Dutch Shell to build Grid-enabled software that will run on a Grid infrastructure for applications that interpret seismic data. Royal Dutch Shell, running Linux on IBM xSeries servers with Globus Toolkit, cut its processing time of seismic data while improving the quality of the resulting data. This allows employees to focus on key scientific problems rather than double-checking the validity of data and waiting for computations to complete.

Utilities

Kansai Electric Power Co., Inc.

Kansai Electric Power Co., Inc. (KEPCO), Japan's second largest electric utility, has been working with IBM to develop an information-based Grid that will allow it to federate various data sources and virtualize these sources across the enterprise. The KEPCO IBM Grid solution will integrate the information traditionally distributed across departments and other affiliated companies to enable information sharing. This Grid will allow KEPCO to not only use its existing systems (thereby cutting time for implementation), but also to develop new businesses and business processes more rapidly at minimum cost.

Manufacturing

Ford Motor Company

Ford Motor's Engine and Transmission Groups, when requested to cut information technology costs, invested in nearly 500 dual-processor Sun Blade workstations from Sun Microsystems, Inc., for use by its designers and engineers. The dual-processor configuration might initially seem overkill as workstations for typical individual users, but engineers often need considerable power at their disposal to complete their jobs. The cost of these scaled-up workstations was less expensive than two single-processor workstations would have been. Also, when the investment in these workstations was made, they were bought with key components in a Grid computing environment in mind. During the day, when engineers are hard at work, one of the processors is dedicated for the user's local computer-aided design jobs (typically interactive mechanical computer aided design, or MCAD jobs), while the second processor is made available to the Grid for mechanical computer-aided engineering (MCAE) jobs. When users leave for the day, Ford effectively has a thousand CPUs to run MCAE batch jobs in the Grid.

Grid computing was a low-cost way that allowed Ford to harness the spare CPU cycles from the group of workstations. Grid computing put to work all the available CPUs at idle workstations, while virtually doing away with the need for powerful servers and, in many cases, for supercomputers.

Saab Automobile

Since the middle of 1999, Saab Automobile AB has been using Sun's One Grid Engine to create a pool of 100 Sun workstations for use in external aerodynamics and other simulations. Saab now uses this Grid environment in essence as an inexpensive virtual supercomputer 24 hours a day, 365 days a year. Originally built for Solaris and Linux, One has grown to encompass open-source versions for nearly all operations of UNIX and also for the Mac OS X operating system.

Motorola Semiconductor

Motorola Semiconductor uses Grid-enabled software to allocate additional CPU cycles to individual projects as deadlines approach. The company had nearly 400 workstations in a heterogeneous environment plus several servers that could be clustered into a server farm, with each server powered with anywhere from two to ten processors and upward of a half dozen to a dozen gigabytes of memory. Seeing these resources lying idle at night and on weekends, as they are in thousands of offices around the world, officials decided that it might be worthwhile to try to borrow some extra computing power. They found a way, Sun's Grid Software (Sun One), to maximize the resources they already had and share it among different groups.

Engineers now send their computationally intensive engineering jobs to the One Grid Engine and let it find the most appropriate systems on which to run them, thereby allowing them to run more regression tests in a shorter amount of time and making the risk of poor quality far lower than thought easily achievable.

Project MegaGrid

Oracle, Dell, EMC, and Intel partnered to form Project MegaGrid in an effort to develop a standardized approach to building and deploying enterprise Grid infrastructures. This alliance combines the technologies from multiple vendors into a single unified deployment of best practices that reduce the customer integration burden. This venture allows customers to achieve the benefits of low-cost Grid infrastructure.

Project MegaGrid brings solutions to many businesses and IT challenges, including:

- *Reducing cost.* Bringing together predefined and pretested technology combinations helps other businesses save money by helping them minimize the downtime necessary for a Grid implementation and simplifying the deployment and management of Grid infrastructure. By working together to perfect the implementation, these organizations bring their experience and strengths to the implementation for other organizations to benefit from and to assist in their own implementation of Grid infrastructures.
- *Improved quality of service.* Access to information on the end-to-end testing, validation, and clustering (with its load balancing and its high-availability configurations) set the expectations of reliable service levels for the business. Access to information on other organizations' reliable performance allows not only the MegaGrid organization, but also other organizations leveraging their models, to rely on service levels for their businesses that will meet or exceed business needs coupled with the flexibility of fast response times.
- *Reduced risk.* The MegaGrid partnership has validated solutions and cooperates in the engineering necessary to minimize downtime and expedite maintenance and support processes.
- *Managing growth.* The Grid solutions provided by this alliance revolve greatly around scalability and centralized management to accommodate growth in both hardware and number of users and achieves the lowest possible cost.
- *Accelerating time to value.* Because these solutions are pretested and the best practices validated and simplified, they accelerate deployment time for the end customers.

This group's vision is to provide a reliable, repeatable, low-cost methodology of deploying Grid computing. The solutions devised by this partnership help other organizations reduce management complexity and provide highly available solutions. By leveraging what these organizations have joined together to produce, they ease their own adoption of an overall solution. And if any organization already has one or more of the components provided by this partnership, the implementation is even easier.

What the group provide is anything but theoretical. Dell has implemented a solution internally and runs the majority of its internal systems via its Grid infrastructure and leverages the power and flexibility that it proposes to other organizations.

Dell helped to perfect the phased approach that allows the organization to continue working as it has always worked while building advancements into the environment in phases, each phase building on the lessons learned and the advancements of the previous phases. This is the way that the Grid grew organically in most environments where it has thrived and this approach mimics the way that Grid made its way into production environment infrastructures. Dell grew its production environments from a few beginning clusters to a fully supported data center.

Because each of the organizations in the partnership brings its own strengths and flexibly configured product bundles, it brings additional flexibility to an organization seeking to deploy Grid infrastructure. Because any organization can choose the products and pricing models to employ, it can further control costs and add components.

This arrangement will help any company in any industry that wants to reduce operation costs and brings to the organization a reliable, high-performance, highly available environment.

Dell put its own experiences into the partnership. Several years ago, this computer manufacturer was experiencing signs of aging in its European offline order management system. These signs pointed to the potential of system failure for line manufacturing, thereby impacting the fulfillment of orders of potentially tens of thousands of computers at any given time. Dell's volume was also growing. This growth was pushing the limits of the European system. To avoid potential disruption that could cause millions of dollars of missed revenue, Dell chose to standardize on Grid technology. It wanted to stabilize its environment, but also wanted faster performance, lower cost, and the flexibility to apply the technology in other places within the organization. This choice meant that Dell could scale its business with lower costs. To further limit the impact of cost, Dell chose to run Dell-on-Dell hardware.

Southern Partnership for Advanced Computational Infrastructure (SPACI)

SPACI was created to promote the applied research on Grid computing. This partnership helps transfer technology and research to the business community. Intel, MSC Software, and HP Italia are strategic and founding partners of the project. They bring their own varied applications and situations to add value to the overall organization.

SPACI works with climatology and atmospheric physics for applications of meteorology and dispersion of the uppermost atmospheric layer. The motor industry is involved in the partnership, where there are Grids for fluid dynamic applications and flow simulations in the combustion chambers of the internal combustion engine system. Nanotechnology organizations use Grids for the calculation of structural electronic and optical properties of organic molecules.

Chicago Stock Exchange

The Chicago Stock Exchange (CHX) trades more than 3500 issues and competes with NYSE, NASDAQ, AMEX, and smaller regional stock exchanges by combining the benefits of a regulated auction market with traditional cutting-edge technology. CHX was the first floor-based stock exchange that fully automated order execution. This meant that orders sent to the trading floor could be routed, executed, and confirmed in less than one second. This made it easier for investors to buy and sell. It also set the bar high for meeting or exceeding customer expectations.

CHX furthered its results-oriented vision by implementing its Grid environment in 2002, leveraging high availability and lower total cost of ownership. This laid the groundwork for the establishment of a services-based architecture that will continue to allow CHX to excel as a technology leader.

Ohio Savings Bank

Ohio Savings Bank was founded in 1889 and has grown from a single Cleveland-based branch office with $20,000 in assets to one of the nation's most prominent mortgage lenders. Today, it has over 50 branches and nearly $13 billion in assets.

Growth for Ohio Savings Bank led to the need for increased performance and stability of the bank's computer systems. The Grid system provided the option of altering its mix of offerings more easily and focus resources where they would provide the best mix of technology. This would boost availability, lower costs, and raise service levels. It would allow for enhanced cross-selling and lay the groundwork for services-based architecture by consolidating the bank's call center, mortgage application processing, and data warehouse into a single virtual architecture.

Governmental Agencies

Governmental agencies have computationally complex requirements too. Are they making use of this emerging technology? Of course they are.

The U.S. government's great demand for high-performance computing resources. Teams of scientists and researchers seek access to computers powerful enough to execute their large-scale projects, and Grid computing is a powerful operation concept that will allow them to find greater efficiencies and better leverage existing computing resources.

NASA

NASA acquired the information power Grid to help manage its combined scientific computing and engineering computing workloads. Applications that simulate wing design can now be easily linked with engine simulation software in another part of the country, and the results of the simulations and analysis can then be delivered back to one computer. The Grid lets scientists create tests that had not been practical or possible before the Grid.

The Grid solution extends the distributed resource management capabilities by coordinating the scheduling of the computing resources among the different NASA centers without requiring NASA to purchase additional hardware and without the users and programmers having to learn or implement any new job submission language or queuing system.

Before implementing the new Grid environment, users at NASA centers were constrained by the limited capacity of their local server farms. While these resources were optimized, users often required more processors or access to processors that had different performance characteristics. This was particularly true for structural analysis applications used in aerodynamics and propulsion projects requiring prompt access to highly intensive computing resources. The implemented Grid system and the accompanying Linux clusters have helped in resolving these issues. NASA is now considering new inter-agency opportunities for additional uses of Grid computing.

U.S. Department of Defense

IBM, United Devices, and Accelrys have all joined efforts to help the U.S. Department of Defense in the fight against bioterrorism by searching for a smallpox cure, linking the power of more than two million computers to assist in the effort. The project will scavenge otherwise idle spare CPU cycles that will be donated by millions of computer owners around the world in a massive research Grid, looking for new drugs. Results from the smallpox research Grid project will be used by hospitals in the event of a smallpox outbreak, and will also be delivered to the Secretary of Defense.

Smallpox, once considered eradicated, currently has no specific treatment and the only prevention has been vaccination. Many people in the United States were required to be vaccinated prior to entering elementary school. Routine vaccination was discontinued several years ago.

The smallpox research Grid project will allow researchers at facilities around the world to access the computing power needed to identify the new anti-viral drugs necessary to fight this disease.

Individuals can participate in the project by downloading a screensaver at www. grid.org. Similar to the SETI project's screensaver, the smallpox research Grid screen saver will patiently wait for slack periods of time when a computer is able to donate idle processing power and link it into a worldwide Grid. The connected computers will act as a virtual supercomputer capable of analyzing billions of molecules in a fraction of the time it would ordinarily take in a laboratory. Once a piece of the processing is complete the resident program will send results back to the central data center and will request new data to analyze and the cycle will begins again.

European Union

Europe has decided that the Grid is a competitive advantage and is now utilizing that advantage. While American universities often lead in technology, it is often difficult to put these new technologies into widespread general use, partly because the government has a hands-off policy related to implementing industrial policies.

Because European governments have traditionally been effective in the deployment of unified standards and concentrating on technologies that offer a significant economic advantage, the Europeans working have the advantage of having a clearer road map than their counterparts in the United States, where any planning for large-scale computing and networking infrastructures is scattered throughout the federal government. They see the Grid as such a serious advance in computing that they have a ten-year strategic plan.

In early 2004, the European Union was preparing to launch two major Grid initiatives. The first one, called Enabling Grids for E-Science in Europe, attempts to build the largest international grid infrastructure to date. It will operate in more than 70 institutions throughout Europe, and will provide 24/7 Grid services and a computing capacity roughly comparable to nearly 20,000 of the most powerful existing personal computers. The other project is a distributed supercomputing project being led by France's National Center for Scientific Research. This project will connect seven supercomputers throughout Europe on an optical network (high-speed interconnects).

Furthermore, the British government is taking the lead by supporting several different projects, not the least of which is the Diagnostic Mammography National Database project, which is using Grid computing to store, scan, and analyze mammograms. Because it has governmental backing, the project is more likely to achieve integration with the national health care system.

The United States is making strides in the deployment of computing Grids for computationally intensive scientific applications (e.g., studying earthquake risks and analyzing weather patterns).

Flemish Government

In a December 2003 article, *Primeur Monthly* (http://www.hoise.com/primeur/04/articles/monthly/AE-PR-01-04-84.html) discusses the emerging Flemish Grid that is being assisted by the Flemish Government.

The Flemish government is helping fund the BEGrid computational Grid initiative to assist researchers in gaining experience with Grid technologies and working to connect to other international Grids. With applications such as astronomy, astrophysics, bioinformatics, chemistry, climatology, genomics, and high-energy physics, it will not take long for this Grid to join other computational Grids to make even more strides in the research community.

BEGrid will become a part of the pan-European computing and data Grids and thus join with the Enabling Grids for E-Science and Industry in Europe's Integrated Infrastructure Initiative (a project designed to create and deploy Grid technologies throughout the European research area to enable e-science applications).

Ironically, when the Flemish government surveyed potential users in universities and other educational institutions, fewer than half the respondents did not know what the Grid and Grid computing were, although most believed that the Grid was important for them and for the future of computing.

Suggested barriers to Grid implementation include shortage of personnel, lack of required hardware and software, and the lack of an existing knowledge base.

Benefits

The benefits provided by the to these early adopters are broad. As with research universities, commercial ventures that adopt the Grid as a central technology solution can hope to find business virtualization, added flexibility in infrastructure, instant access to data resources, and leveraging their capital investments.

Virtualization

In servers as in storage area networks (SANs) or network attached storage (NAS), virtualization is the key concept, with large arrays of individual physical devices working together on a high-speed network and, under control of clever software, acting as a single, powerful, and highly flexible resource.

Virtualization enables a company or other organization to balance the supply and demand of computing cycles, and other computing and electronic resources, by providing users with what appears to be a single, transparent, aggregated source of computing power. It provides the ability for the organization to lower the total cost of computing by providing access to on-demand, reliable, and transparent access to available computer resources.

This means that these organizations can leverage investments in current existing heterogeneous resources, increasing return on investment and return on assets, and enabling them to do more with less. It can mean reduced infrastructure and other operational costs, including spending for hardware and software resources. The single interface can lead to improved user productivity with faster response time, faster time to answer, and more reliable results, often leading to not only a time benefit to the company, but also often increasing revenues and profits.

THE PARTS AND PIECES

Let us be patient with one another, And even patient with ourselves. We have a long, long way to go. So let us hasten along the road, the road of human tenderness and generosity. Groping, we may find one another's hands in the dark.

—Emily Greene Balch (1867–1961),

Nobel Peace Prize Winner in 1946

Just what is involved in building a Grid system? Grids will support different sets of user communities. Each of the systems, based on the user requirements, will be built with different components. There is not likely going to be a one-size-fits-all, off-the-shelf product that will be dropped into place. However, some basic pieces will be included in most configurations.

Scale

Two of the most differential pieces of any Grid project are the scope and scale of the project and the resulting Grid. Many companies look at implementing an entire Grid system. This is not likely to be the end product, unless there is no existing infrastructure.

What is more likely is that smaller projects will spring up, introducing Grid systems in pockets inside organizations and, as those projects succeed, they will expand to fill the vacuums and will prove to be successful in many applications.

Section 2 provides a description of what is entailed in defining a Grid environment. New paradigms must be looked through when defining a Grid environment and a different kind of mind is required.

The replication of processing and data across resources requires the Grid to have a few basic characteristics.

Robustness

Each file must be successfully and confidently replicated in at least two sites. While one of these sites must have read/write/update access, so that one or more processes can make alterations to the data, the others may be read-only versions.

Data must be able to be replicated and multiple sites on the Grid System must be available to process any required application, while this is not a big concern for an open source, certain applications in the Grid system will be operating system-dependent or hardware-dependent, and resources must be available to process these requirements.

Efficiency

To increase the efficiency of the Grid environment, files (database files, replication members, flat files, and other resources) should be located as closely as possible to where they are to be used. High-powered telescopes and other remote instrumentation should be located in places where they can most efficiently perform their functions. Data should be located where it can be easily accessible to the applications that are acting upon it.

Transparency

It is important that that the users not have to know or care where or how the data is stored or where or how the application is running. They should not have to worry about how the Grid is constructed, where the components are located, or on what operating system the processes are running.

Fault Tolerance

One of the most important features of a Grid environment is its fault tolerance. It should have no single point of failure and no need for one central controlling thread to make sure that all the nodes are working. A thread should be able to run on virtually every system, each checking for the others to determine that they are available.

If a node does fail, an e-mail can be sent to the administrators of the Grid system, and the control threads can start to redistribute the processing, applications, and information located on the failed node to others in the system so that even in fault conditions, transparency is maintained. These threads need to be maintainable so that a node can be disabled if maintenance needs to take place without the control thread attempting to redistribute existing load based on that resource's unavailability.

The replicas of the central control thread can back up the meta data and configuration files as well as providing alternative paths into the Grid for the purpose of assuring availability and maintenance load balancing and ease of control.

Centralized Distributed Control

Because much of the Grid and its processing rely on a Web interface into the system — not only for application access from the users, but also by the administrators to maintain the system — the Web (intranet, Internet, and extranet) is a key component in the system. These interfaces allow one to administer or access the Grid from virtually anywhere on the planet that has Internet access and that access extends to being able to access the interface.

This distributed control allows users to access the Grid and its processing in ways that might be difficult in other circumstances (mobile technology, highly remote access, administrators on the road without direct access to the network) and can provide more flexible avenues for access to match the more flexible infrastructure. It also means that a thin client or other Web-enabled front end can process requests, limiting the need to invest in as many high-end components just to provide disk space necessary to complete the typical processing (making even more components available over which distribution of CPU cycles can be farmed and pushing data access out to those components).

This means that the Grid will become even more flexible as time passes and applications are built to be accessed in the ultimate distributed mechanism, the Web browser. More applications are being built to take advantage of this architecture (Oracle E-Business Suite, for example) and that will continued.

Onward

The Grid has been prevalent in academia for several years and has also started to make its presence felt in the business community as more companies are being asked to do more with less. Budgets are tight, and in many cases getting tighter. Resources are thin, particularly skilled human capital that can be scarce, undertrained, or expensive. Many companies have an overall over abundance of idle computing power, often utilizing only 10 to 20 percent of their available capacity, but having pockets of time or areas where processing is on the thin side (Monday night processing of accumulated data, month-end accounting closing processes, or a four-hour job to calculate the what-if scenario for a client). Companies are looking at the free and idle cycles that are going unused in some areas and determining that it might be possible to reallocate those cycles elsewhere, rather than having to invest in still more hardware to get those taxed resources over their difficult moments.

The companies with taxed resources do not need more power connected to those resources; what they need is more equitable distribution of the existing processing, more efficient processing with what they already have that is sitting idle. There should be a way to tie these machines together into a single pool of available labor that can be drawn against during tight times. If one can accomplish this, work will get done faster, more efficiently, and often with fewer errors and can become a competitive advantage while cutting expenses.

Open standards and protocols have become essential parts of the backbone of the Grid, with services enabling users to get their job done and for those services to interact seamlessly together to accomplish the following:

- Information queries
- Network bandwidth allocation
- Data extraction
- Data management
- Request processing
- Session management
- Workload balancing
- Processing distribution

A good service, however, is not just limited to what tasks it can accomplish for the user (whether a human or another Grid component) but also it can help enable virtualization, or the appearance that the Grid system is simply one big system and not a sum of its parts. It is this ability that many see as the ultimate future of the Grid, the future that will take it to the level where computing resources are as available and purchasable as water, gas, and electric utilities are in many parts of the world today. One will no more care from where the CPU cycles originate than one cares now where the electricity that runs the toaster comes from. One only cares that it works. If Grid computing is taken to its ultimate end, and many people believe that it will, it will be taken just as much for granted as the other utilities in our lives are today.

Chapter 4

Security

Life was simple before World War II. After that, we had systems.

—Rear Admiral Grace Murray Hopper

Security, at its highest level, simply prevents unauthorized disclosure of or modification to data and ensures continued operation of the system. This is a difficult enough feat when one is looking at a simple network configuration.

Security

When one looks at a configuration that allows access to a large number of computers, data, and other resources in multiple location, security takes on increased significance. In a world that faces new virus threats nearly every month and hackers are able to get into almost any system, it is important to have an understanding of the security issues and potential solutions.

Computer and network security can be broken down into significant chunks that have their own sets of issues. Security deals with authentication, access control, accounting, and data integrity.

Authentication

Answers.com (http://www.answers.com/authentication&r=67) defines *authentication* as follows:

> Verifying the identity of a user logging onto a network. Passwords, digital certificates, smart cards and biometrics can be used to prove

the identity of the client to the network. Passwords and digital certificates can also be used to identify the network to the client. The latter is important in wireless networks to ensure that the desired network is being accessed.

Authentication deals with one party gaining the assurance that the identity of another is declared and true, preventing impersonation. Entity authentication is the process of one party in the communication process being assured through quantitative evidence that the identity of a second party in the communication process is correct and allowed. Identification or authentication can be accepted or terminated without being accepted (or rejected).

Authentication, at its root, is the process of confirming an identity. This identity can be attributed to the user of the system but in a Grid environment, the identity can be attributed to any component accessing any other component. In the context of any network interactions, authentication involves the ability of one party to confidently identify another party. Authentication over networks (and nearly all communication today takes place over networks) can take many forms. Certificates are one way of supporting authentication, and are discussed later in this chapter.

Authentication includes not only identification of a user to the network, but also the verification that a message or request is accurate in its integrity (through the use of MAC addresses or e-mail authentication, for example). Human authentication includes challenge-response authentication. Challenge–response authentication is often used in a computerized version in password checking and resetting. Often when an account is set up, a challenge question is registered along with the correct answer to that question as it relates to that user. When this is the case, if a password request comes in or a user attempts to log in to the server, the challenge question must be correctly answered. It is important that this challenge question not be something that is either easily guessable or easily researchable (for example, your mother's maiden name) because that would be simple enough for someone who really wanted to gain a user's access to the system to determine.

There are several different tools and methodologies one can use to authenticate user identity, to include the following.

Passwords and Personal Identification Numbers

Passwords and personal identification numbers (PIN numbers) are examples of authentication based on something that the user (and in theory only the user) should know. It is the lowest level and least secure method of authentication.

Password security is usually one of the first levels of security that a user comes into contact with when accessing a computer or the network. The combination of user ID (or bank account number, for example) and password or PIN number will allow someone to access a network or a bank account to some degree.

In many organizations, this is where security often stops. Once the user is authenticated to the network, that user can do anything that he is permitted to do without any further authentication or with minimal other authentication (more user IDs and passwords) necessary.

However, passwords are often easily compromised. Users are notorious for using weak passwords (passwords that are children's or spouse's names, anniversary dates, or simply an easily guessed string of numbers).

Some security models require strong passwords. This means that rules in place govern when passwords expire, whether the word can be a dictionary-recognizable word, whether uppercase letters are allowed, numbers and special characters are necessary, and how often a password can be reused. While this does not preclude a user from circumventing the system (using @pple instead of apple, for example), it does make guessing passwords less simple for someone trying to access a system as someone else.

But strong passwords have their own issues. Often, users will create a password that will be secure enough for the filters but then write it on a sticky note or tape it to the monitor or the underside of the keyboard. In this case, the user has defeated the whole purpose of using difficult-to-guess passwords by providing easy access.

Public Key Infrastructure and Digital Certificates

Public key infrastructure (PKI) and digital certificate security is more secure than password authentication alone. These security measures are examples of what the user must use to authenticate them to the network or the application.

Tokens

Another example by which security can be implemented in an organization is through tokens (hardware or software tokens). These tokens can be physical devices that an authorized user of computer services is given to aid with user authentication.

Security Tokens

Security tokens, hardware tokens, authentication tokens, or cryptographic tokens can be physical devices an authorized user of a given computer system is issued to aid in authentication.

These tokens are small enough to fit in a pocket, purse, or on a keychain. Some of these tokens store cryptographic keys, digital signatures, biometric data, or other uniquely identifiable information. Typically these tokens are tamper-resistant and many even include small keypads that will allow the user to enter a PIN into the device before the information it contains can be accessed.

Some tokens work very simply internally, while others are more complex and can contain information necessary for multiple authentication levels. Some token vendors use their own proprietary approaches to tokens and these are patented.

Many tokens contain information necessary for digital signature (making them even more important to guard against loss). They allow secure on-board (on the token) generation and storage of private keys to enable the digital signatures that can double for user authentication. To do all this, the token must have a unique number. It is important to note, however, that not all tokens are created equal, not all approaches fully qualify for digital signatures, and any key that does not have some kind of user interface (keyboard or otherwise) cannot be used in many signing scenarios (bank transactions, for example).

Tokens can be used to store information necessary for some single sign-on solutions. The passwords are stored on the token so that users do not need to remember the complex passwords assigned to them. This can lead to more secure password use in organizations. Also connected to passwords, a token can facilitate one-time passwords that change after every log-on or that expire after a given time interval (often multiple times even in a given session).

Strong passwords, for certain applications or organizations, are still not sufficiently strong and complex. If an organization uses tokens, it can use one-time passwords that are based on complex mathematical algorithms such as cryptographic hashes as a means to generate a password that is completely unlike the previous one by starting from a secret shared key as the seed material. Some algorithms are standardized, while others are covered by patents.

Biometric information can be stored on and retrieved from tokens to add additional layers of security. When these are inserted into a computer's USB port, a software program resident on the computer is launched that allows the user to access the system. The software associated often allows the user to generate one-time and time-sensitive passwords and digital signatures based on the biometric information stored on the token such that broader access can be accomplished and more granularities in security can be used.

Some tokens are equipped with a cryptocard button that generates a new, one-time-use password every time a button is pressed. The computer and token combination typically have an agreed-upon algorithm that allows the computer to accept a password that can be generated several values ahead of where it should be because there are often inadvertent or accidental button clicks that advance the password past where it is "supposed" to be or a client fails for some reason to authenticate.

Some token types are meant to be a disconnected — they do not need any kind of input device other than what ordinarily comes with the computer. Some types need input devices. Often hidden costs are associated with special input devices.

Some are either USB tokens or Bluetooth tokens. USB tokens are considered connected because they need USB ports to be available for them to use, but they do not need any proprietary input devices — only what comes with most computers. Bluetooth devices are meant to be used when there is a Bluetooth-enabled device for use and can be used within 30 or so feet of the device. When a Bluetooth–USB combination token is used, it provides more flexibility and security.

Disconnected tokens are much more common than connected tokens. Remember that there are good sides and bad sides to any choices that one makes. The upside of disconnected tokens is that they need no readers or input devices to allow them to be useful. The downside, however, is that they have relatively short battery lives (three to five years typically). Some USB tokens have lifetimes of ten years or more. As a way around this, some tokens allow for changing batteries, thereby reducing the total cost of ownership but allowing for the potential compromise (regardless of how remote) of the token.

One other kind of reader-reliant token is the PC card meant for use with a laptop. By carrying the PC card independently of the laptop, security can be better assured, but again, there are downsides to the technology such as additional wear-and-tear on the cards because they are meant to be inserted into and removed from the port.

Smart Cards

Smart cards serve as another example of having a user tied to a token. A smart card roughly resembles a credit card in appearance and cards can be mistaken for a credit card. The added thickness is due to an embedded microprocessor that is often found under a contact pad on one end of the card rather than in a magnetic strip on the card's back.

These smart cards have been used in European countries for many years but are only recently starting to become more popular in the Americas. The card carries all the embedded intelligence necessary to verify that it is authorized to access a given network or service. What it does not necessarily do is verify that the person who is trying to use it to access the network is who that person claims to be by virtue of having the card.

The host computer has a card reader that "talks" to the microprocessor embedded in the smart card, accesses the information that the card contains, and views that data as read-only information to be used for authentication. These cards receive their information from an independent source and contain a limited instruction set that can be used for applications such as PKI cryptography.

Smart cards are used for credit cards, electronic cash, wireless communication access, computer system access, frequent flyer or other loyalty programs, banking, access to broadband computer or other communication channels, and even government identification.

Smart cards or tokens can be used with personal computers, laptops, or terminals to authenticate a user, or they can be tied to a Web browser on a computer to supplement secure socket layers (SSLs) (discussed later in this chapter) to improve the security of Internet or intranet (or in our case Grid) transactions.

Biometrics

Biometric security has everything to do with identity. It utilizes a uniquely measurable characteristic of a human being that can be used to identify him or her. Primary areas of biometric technology are face recognition, fingerprints, iris recognition, total hand geometry, palm prints, retina mapping, signature, and voice. Other areas have been used, including body odors, ear shapes, and even keystroke dynamics.

Biometric access, to be truly effective, should operate in real-time (as in retinal scanners, fingerprint readers, or voice scanners). This means that storage of the information is less secure. However, it is important to note that one can often accomplish the same or similar access control using biometric information stored in a secure manner.

There are mobile biometric data readers currently available that a user can carry and plug into appropriate devices. These devices launch an application that reads the biometric data from the device, verifies the accuracy of the data and the relevance to the security that is in place, and lets the user in — or not.

Geography

Geography-based authentication combines location with other methods to provide the user with unique access to data. While it is not always simple to allow the computer system to know where the user is when she logs in, it is possible to determine from what IP address the user is accessing the system and from that IP address infer from what portion of the network the user is logging in. This kind of authentication can direct a user's request to the proper resources, or limit access to local resources, thereby limiting the potential for intercepting the message in transit over the network.

Depending on the security necessary for the organization and the level of privacy needed for the data involved, security measures to this level are sometimes necessary.

When making authentication decisions for the organization, it is best to take into account the level of security necessary and mandated by the organization, as well as the nature of the data involved before making decisions that affect the overall system.

Network interactions typically take place between a client (for example, browser software running on a personal computer) and a server, the software and hardware used to host a Web site. Remember that in a Grid environment, a computer in the system can be acting at any time as either a client, a server, or both. Client authentication is identification of a client by a server such that the server is then confident that the client is who it claims. Server authentication is identification of a server by a client such that the client is then certain that the identity of the server is what it claims.

Verifying the identity of a participant to an operation or request constitutes authentication in a Grid environment. A principal or claimant is the participant under whose authority an operation is performed or authorized. This principal can be a user logged on to a remote system on whose behalf the application is running; a local user logged directly into the server; or the server itself.

The basis of the identification can be something known (PINs or secret keys whose knowledge is demonstrated in a challenge–response protocol); or something possessed (physical accessory, passport-like in function). Other bases could be magnetic-striped cards like a credit card, chip cards or smart cards containing physically embedded microprocessor or password generators providing time-variant passwords) or something that is inherent to a human or an electronic entity (signatures, fingerprints, iris or retinal patterns). Identification protocols differ significantly, but they do have several common properties.

Reciprocity of Identification

One of these common properties is reciprocity of identification. This means that one or both parties can (and may have to) corroborate their identity using either unilateral or mutual identification techniques. These can be fixed password schemes; however, this system may be susceptible to another entity posing as the principal, having gained access to the password by illicit means.

Computational Efficiency

Computational efficiency is another potentially common identification protocol property that specifies the number of operations required to execute the protocol.

Communication Efficiency

Communication efficiency involves the number of passes that a message might have to exchange and the total bandwidth (total number of bits, required to be transmitted.

Third-Party Real-Time Involvement

The real-time involvement of a third party may constitute a necessary property in many identification protocols. The third party could be an online trusted entity that acts to distribute symmetric keys to all the communicating parties for the purpose of authentication. An online untrusted directory service could also be used to distribute public key certificates or offline certification authority. More details on the two different means of keys are discussed later in thus chapter in the section on cryptography.

Further, the nature of trust required of a third party is another potential protocol property. It may involve trusting the third party to correctly authenticate each of the parties and bind each entity's name to a public key. This third entity could be also trusted with the private keys of the entities.

Nature of Security Guarantees

The nature of security guarantees is yet another property that can be included in the protocol definition. Provable and zero knowledge properties are the common example.

Secret Storage

Finally, the storage of secrets, including the location and method used to guarantee the storage of critical key material and information may be necessary in the different security protocols used. But what methods are used to ensure that only authenticated users and servers access resources?

Passwords

Historically, one of the most common and conventional schemes used for authentication is the password. Passwords provide weak authentication, with one password tied to each user or entity in the communication link. Typically, passwords are strings of four to ten characters (the more characters, the less easily appropriated). that a user can memorize. If a password is sufficiently complicated as to not be easily guessable, it then becomes difficult to remember.

A better way is required.

Private Key Cryptography

Cryptography is a process associated with scrambling plain text into cipher text (encryption) and back into plain text again (decryption). Cryptography concerns itself with (1) confidentiality, keeping the information known only to those for whom it was intended; (2) integrity, keeping the information unaltered or unalterable while it is stored or while it is transmitted without that alteration being apparent; (3) non-repudiation, making sure that the creator or sender of the information is unable to deny later that the data was deliberately sent or created; and (4) authentication, the sender and the receiver can verify each other's identity as well as the origin and the destination of the information. One of the basic problems in cryptography is allowing for secure communication over an insecure channel.

User A wants to send a secret or sensitive message to User B over what may be an insecure communication channel (a tapped line, a channel open to packet sniffing). Traditionally, the common solution to this situation is private key encryption. Users A and B agree on both an encryption and a decryption algorithm and a secret key to the algorithm. While an intruder may be able to figure out the algorithm, the unavailable secret key allows the encoded message to remain secret. Private key algorithms are also referred to as symmetric or synchronous algorithms (communication events that are coordinated in time).

Traditionally in private key cryptography, the sender and the receiver of any message know, and use, the same private (secret) key. The sender uses the private key to encrypt the message and the receiver uses the same key to decrypt the message. This is known as symmetric cryptography or secret key cryptography. One of the main challenges is getting both the sender and the receiver to agree on the secret key without anyone else being able to learn the key. If they are in separate physical locations, a courier must be trusted (phone system or other transmission medium) to prevent the disclosure of the key. If anyone were to intercept the key, he could later use that key to read, modify or forge other messages that are encrypted or authenticated. The generation, transmission, and storage of these keys is called key management, and cryptosystems must deal with these key management issues. This is particularly true with a large number of users or in an open system.

There are advantages and disadvantages to private key cryptography. Table 4.1 lists these advantages and disadvantages.

Table 4.1   Advantages and Disadvantages of Private Key Cryptography

Advantages:

Symmetric algorithms can be designed to facilitate high rates of data throughput.

Keys for symmetric algorithms are typically relatively short.

Symmetric algorithms can be employed as primitives (or building blocks) to construct various other cryptographic mechanisms. The more advanced constructs include stronger ciphers, pseudorandom number generators, hash functions, and computationally highly efficient digital signature schemes. Simple transformations are typically easy to analyze, and by extension break, but grouped together they can be used to build much stronger end products.

Disadvantages:

The key must remain secret at both ends of every communication channel.

As the number of connections in the network increases, so does the number of key pairs that must be managed. As a result of this increase, management is often accomplished through the use of an unconditionally trusted third party (TTP). Any time one adds an extra person to the mixture, the result is a increased risk of discovery.

To ensure that private key security in networks remains viable, the key must be changed frequently, possibly with every communication session. This adds further management issues and complexity. In a two-party communication, sound cryptographic practice dictates that the key be changed frequently and perhaps for each communication session.

Digital signatures that arise as a result of symmetric algorithms require large keys (often prohibitively long in comparison to the amount of data associated with each message packet) or (again) the use of a TTP.

Block Ciphers

A block cipher is a symmetric key encryption algorithm that is applied to a fixed-length block of data (for example, 64 or 128 contiguous bits) at one time, taking the group as a single unit rather than one bit at a time. The resulting cipher text is identical in length to the plain text version of the message. To ensure that identical blocks of text are not encrypted the same way every time, making the cipher easier to break, it is common to use the text in one block as a part of the key for the encryption of subsequent blocks. A random number is used, combined with the text of the first block along with the key to ensure that the subsequent block's encrypting bears no resemblance to the previous blocks. This is called block chaining.

Stream Ciphers

The main alternative to a block cipher, although used less frequently, is a stream cipher. Stream ciphers encrypt each individual character of a plain text message or individual bits (or bytes) of a data stream, one at a time, using the encryption transformation. The transformation algorithm varies over time. Stream ciphers are typically faster than block ciphers at the hardware level and are also more appropriate in some telecommunications applications, when buffering space is limited or when individual characters must be processed, rather than allowing blocks of data to be decrypted at one time. Stream ciphers have little or no error propagation, so they may also be advantageous in situations where transmission errors are highly likely. Stream ciphers are sometimes referred to as state ciphers, as the encryption of any particular bit depends on the system's and the bit's current state. Most of the ciphers used in this type of encryption consist of a pseudorandom number generator. XORing each plain text bit with the corresponding key bit in the key stream accomplishes encryption. This means that if a single bit of error is introduced to the data, it results in a single bit of error in the decrypted message, not the entire block or the remainder of the message. This also means, however, that stream ciphers are more prone to a type of attack known as bit fiddling, where causing a bit to be dropped can result (depending on the bit) in complete garbling. (This is particularly true in self-synchronizing stream ciphers where the encryption of the current bit depends on the encryption of the previous several cipher text bits. Fortunately, the garbling caused by the interference lasts only as long as that bit's influence on the message remains.

Synchronous stream ciphers encrypt each bit independently of every other bit.

Public Key Cryptography

Public key cryptography, first described by Diffe and Hellman in 1976, is another cipher. The encryption and decryption keys are different. Private keys have to be the same, and the knowledge of the encryption method lends no clue to the decryption method. Public key cryptography is based on a one-way or trapdoor function. This kind of function is a transformation of text that is simple to implement and simple to apply; however, it is less easy to reverse. If one looks at a simple example mathematically, it is easy to multiply two very large prime numbers together and come up with the product; however, given the product, it is not as easy to arrive at the original factors.

Public key cryptography answers the problem encountered when one person has a message that he wants only certain friends to be able to read. If he were to use private key cryptography, all of his friends would have to know the key; and that would necessitate a secure channel over which to distribute the key. However, if he had a secure channel, he would not need cryptography to ensure the secrecy of the message. In public key cryptography, he only has to publish the public key and the security is not in doubt.

Utilizing a public key infrastructure enables an organization to provide authentication as well as access control, confidentiality, and non-repudiation to its networked applications. The infrastructure along with its related standards and techniques, underlies the security features of many products, including Netscape and Apache with single sign-on and the secure socket layer (SSL) protocol.

All Internet and intranet communications use TCP/IP (the *de facto* standard), which allows information to be sent from one computer to another over often-separated networks and through a variety of intermediate computers before it reaches its ultimate destination. Under normal circumstances, these computers allow messages to pass without interfering with the transmission in any way. While the ability for a message or data packet to hop from network to network and computer to computer to get from its source to its destination is a flexibility feature of TCP/IP, it also means that information sent from one computer *will* travel over disparate networks and through several to hundreds of computers, any one of which has the potential for someone to interfere with the communication in any of the following ways:

■ *Eavesdropping.* The information remains intact, and *only* its privacy is compromised. In this way, nefarious individuals can learn credit card numbers, bank account numbers, or other classified or sensitive information.

■ *Tampering.* Information in transit is changed (or replaced) and then allowed to proceed to the intended recipient. In this way, someone could alter an order for goods (either changing what was ordered or the shipping address) or change information in a contract before allowing that contract to reach its destination.

■ *Impersonation.* As information passes through the network, it passes to a person who is pretending to be the intended recipient. This can, itself, take two forms:

— *Spoofing.* A person simply pretends to be someone else. A person can pretend to have a spoofed e-mail address (highly common in the ever-popular spam and virus mailing) or a computer can spoofingly identify itself as another site or computer.

— *Misrepresentation*. As with any organizational misrepresentation, one person or one organization can make a claim to be one thing (a legitimate business, a low-price retailer, or something else that is perfectly aboveboard) while processing credit card payments without actually providing the service advertised. This would be similar to someone on a street corner selling fake Rolex watches.

Public key cryptography makes it relatively easy to take precautions with messages and information that may be sensitive in nature while allowing it to travel freely over TCP/IP or other protocol networks. Encryption and decryption are easily addressed with public key cryptography. It allows both of the communicating parties (regardless of how many pairs or how many people are communicating with a single resource) to disguise the information that they are sending to each other. While the sender can encrypt the information and the receiver decrypts it, during the time that the message is in transit, the information is completely unintelligible to an intruder. If someone were able to tamper with the information and modify it in any way, the attempt at modification or substitution would be easily detected. But public key cryptography goes further than just making sure that the information gets from point A to point B without interruption. It also allows the recipient to determine where the information originated (the identity of the sender) and prevents the sender from later claiming that the information received was never actually sent.

Whereas private key cryptography is called symmetric encryption, public key encryption is called asymmetric and involves a pair of keys, one of which is a private key but the other is a public key. Both of these keys are associated with an entity that needs the ability to digitally sign and encrypt its data. The public keys are published, and the private keys of both the sender and the receiver (not the same secret key as in private key encryption) are kept secret and serve as the means by which the receiver decrypts the message.

If one compares the computational effort required for public versus private key, asymmetric public key encryption requires more computational effort, and is therefore not always the best solution for large amounts of data. It is possible to use public key encryption and send an additional symmetric key, which can then be used to encrypt additional data. This is the approach used by the SSL (secure sockets layer) protocol.

This still may not be a desirable way to encrypt sensitive data, however, because anyone with your public key, which is by definition published, could decrypt the data. In general, the strength of the encryption is directly related to the difficulty in discovering the key. Discovering the key, in turn, depends on both the cipher that is chosen and the length of the key. The difficulty in discovering the key for one of the most commonly used ciphers for public key encryption depends on the difficulty in factoring large numbers, a well-known mathematical problem. This is one of the reasons that encryption strength is often described in terms of the sizes of the keys (in number of bits) used in the encryption of the data (with the longer keys providing the stronger encryption algorithm). Different ciphers use different key lengths to achieve the same level of encryption, based on the mathematics used in the algorithm. This is another reason that private key cryptography is considered stronger; it can use all possible values for a given key length rather than a subset of the values.

What is currently considered sufficiently strong encryption is strong only relative to the time used. Formerly 64-bit encryption was considered sufficiently strong for asymmetric cryptography (public key cryptography) and now, for many purposes, 512 bits are required, and that may soon not be strong enough. The advantages of public key cryptography include:

1. The public key is published, although authenticity must be guaranteed. The private key part must, however, still be kept secret.
2. Network key administration can be accomplished through trusted third parties but they do not have to be unconditionally trusted and may be able to be utilized in an offline manner rather than in real-time.
3. Depending on how they are used, the key pairs can remain unchanged for long periods of time. This can mean an extended number of sessions or even several years.
4. Public keys can typically be fewer (depending on the size of the network, this can be significant) than the private keys in a symmetric algorithm.

The disadvantages of public key encryption include:

1. Throughput rates are significantly slower than simple private key encryption.
2. Key sizes are often significantly larger than those in private key encryption.
3. Public key algorithms have not been found to be unbreakably secure. Because they are based on a finite set of mathematical functions and computers are good at math, the encryption, given enough computing resources, can still in theory be broken.

A digital certificate is an attachment to an electronic packet, similar to an attachment to an e-mail. Where e-mail attachments are designed to carry additional information that one wants the receiving party to know, the certificate carries additional information that one wants the receiver's computer to know, information that is used for security purposes. The certificates are based on a combination of public key and private key encryption. Each key is like its own unique encryption device, as no two keys are ever identical. This is why a digital certificate can be used as a digital signature as a means to identify its owner (http://developer.netscape.com/docs/manuals/security/pkin/contents.htm#1041271).

Encryption and decryption together address the problems of network snooping and eavesdropping.

Eavesdropping on the contents of network packets is one of the main security issues that must be addressed, but encryption and decryption alone do not address tampering or impersonation. Public key encryption and cryptography address the issues of eavesdropping and tampering, as well as impersonation. Tamper detection relies on a mathematical function called a one-way hash, a fixed-length number, that has a unique value for a given set of hashed data. Any change in the data, even the deletion or alteration of a single character, would result in a completely different value. Moreover, the contents cannot be deduced from the hashed data (this is why it is called one-way).

Digital Signature

Digital certificates help automate the process of distributing public keys as well as exchanging the resulting security information. Once one has installed the digital certificate either on a computer or on a server, the machine on which it is installed or the Web site on the server through which people are accessing the information will have its own private key. While it is possible to use one's private key for encryption of data and one's public key for decryption, it would not be desirable to follow this scheme for the encryption of really sensitive data; it is one of the main pieces for digitally signing any data. Rather than encrypting the data itself, signing software creates a one-way hash of the data, and then uses the private key to encrypt the hash. This encrypted hash, along with other information (including hashing algorithms), is what is known as a digital signature.

Items are transferred from the source to the recipient. The messages that are moving from one to the other consist of signed data, and contain both the original data (a one-way hash of the original data) and the digital signature encrypted with the signer's private key. To validate the data's integrity, the receiving computer's software first uses the original signer's public key to decrypt the hash, resulting in an unencrypted and easily readable set of data. The receiver's computer then uses the same hashing algorithm that was used to generate the original hash to then generate yet another new version of the one-way hash of the same data. This rehashing is possible because information about the original hashing algorithm used is sent along with the digital signature. The receiving computer's software, once the new hash has been calculated, compares the new hash value against the original hashed dataset. If the two hashes match identically, there can be absolute certainty that data has not been changed since it was signed and sent. If they do not match, the data may have been tampered with since it was signed, corruption may have occurred in transit, or the signature may have been created with a private key that does not correspond directly to the public key presented by the signer.

If the hashes match identically, the recipient can have confidence that the public key used to decrypt the digital signature corresponds to the private key used to create the digital signature. This directly confirms the identity of the signer. This also, however, requires some way of confirming that the original public key belonged to a particular person or entity.

In this way, the significance of the digital signature is comparable to a handwritten signature. Once one has signed data, it is difficult, if not nearly impossible, to later deny having any part in the creation and signing. Assuming that the private key was in no way compromised or that it never was outside the signer's control, this same certainty has crossed to the computer and other digital devices. A digital signature is often as legally binding as a handwritten signature, enabling it to provide a high degree of non-repudiation.

To exchange information using a digital certificate, the sender accesses the certificate that contains the public key. That user's computer or server then validates the identity of the owner of the certificate and (if the user is verified) encrypts the data that the sender wants to share with the owner of the public key using SSL utilizing the receiver's public key. Only the receiver's private key can then decrypt that message.

The X.509 standard is the most widely used and the *de facto* for digital certificates. Because X.509 is not officially sanctioned by the International Telecommunications Union (ITU), only recommended, the standards are not always followed in the same way by all vendors over all platforms; there are occasions when idiosyncrasies occur. This means that a certificate that is created by one application may or may not be strictly understood or readable by other kinds or brands of applications.

A digital certificate is an electronic document, similar to a driver's license, a passport, or other identification, that is used not only to identify an individual, but also to uniquely identify a server, a company, or any other entity and to associate that unique identity with a unique public key. In this way, public key cryptography is used in certificates to address the problem of impersonation.

To get a driver's license, passport, or voter's registration card, one needs to apply to a government agency, which verifies identity, ability to drive, address, and other information before issuing the identification. Certificates work a lot like these more familiar forms of identification. Certificate authorities (CAs) are the entities that validate identities and issue the certificates (similar to the government entities but not affiliated with any agency for any government). These CAs can be either independent trusted third parties or internal organizations running their own certificate-issuing software. The methods used to validate an identity can vary, depending on the particular policies of the given CA. Before issuing a certificate, the CA uses its published verification procedures to ensure that the entity requesting a certificate is who or what it claims to be.

Because a digital certificate binds a particular public key to the name of the entity (person, server, or other entity), the certificate can help prevent the attempted use of fraudulent public keys for the purpose of impersonation. Only the certified public key will encrypt a message that can be decrypted by that person's private key. Moreover, the public key and certificate always include the name of the entity that they identify, as well as an expiration date and the name of the CA that issued the certificate, and a serial number so that the entity with whom one is sharing information is the correct party. This allows the certificate to be the official introduction for users who know and trust the CA but who do not necessarily know or trust the entity identified by the certificate.

Certification authorities will create valid and reliable certificates as required by legal agreements. There are several commercially available CAs, including VeriSign (one of the most popular and common 40-bit and 128-bit encryption CAs) as well as Thawte (128-bit encryption) and Entrust (128-bit encryption).

X.509 is the most widely used digital certificate definition standard. It describes how to write the data format. An X.509 certificate contains the following components:

- The version identifies which version of the X.509 standard applies to contents of the certificate. The version affects what information can be contained within it. There have been three versions to date.
  — *Version 1* first became available in 1988. It is widely deployed and is the most generic version.
  — *Version 2* introduced the concept of unique subject name and issuer identifiers to handle the possibility of reuse of subject or issuer names over time. Version 2 certificates are not widely used.
  — *Version 3* became available in 1996 and supports the idea of extensions (additional security inclusions in a certificate).
- The serial number assigned by the entity that created the certificate distinguishes it from other certificates that entity has issued. One of the most useful features of a serial number is when a certificate is revoked, the number is placed on a certificate revocation list (CRL).
- The signature algorithm identifier identifies the algorithm used by the certificate authority to sign the certificate.
- The issuer name is the name of the entity that signed the certificate. This issuer is typically a certificate authority. Using the certificate implies that one trusts the entity that signed the certificate.
- Because each certificate is valid only for a limited amount of time, the validity period is described by a start date and time and by an end date and time. The difference in this time period can be as short as a few seconds or as long as several decades. The validity period chosen depends on several factors, such as the strength of the private key used to sign the certificate and the amount that the person contracting with the authority is willing to pay for a certificate. The validity period is the amount of time that entities can expect to be able to rely on the public value, and is trustable as long as the certificate's associated private key has not been compromised.

- The subject name is the name of the entity that the public key certificate identifies. This name is intended to uniquely identify an entity across the Internet or any other network.
- The subject public key information is the public key of the entity named, as well as an algorithm identifier that specifies to which public key cryptography system this specific key belongs and any associated key parameters required by the certificate.

The goal in a Grid environment is to prevent unauthorized access and to protect itself from the users (intended inappropriate access as well as accidental). It is also just as important that mutual authentication of servers to each other occurs. This is critical in ensuring that the resources and the data provided by any given server are not provided by a hacker, attacker, or an intruder.

The users and the servers must be authenticated, and users must also be reasonably comfortable that the data on which they are working is clean and secure. Data origin authentication is how this is accomplished. It is the assurance that any given message, data item, or executable object actually originated with a particular principal. To accomplish this, information is used to determine whether a program was modified by or sent by an attacker with the intent to compromise the resource that the program was accessing. This, alone does not ensure that the data sent by a principal is intact and unaltered, only that at some point in its lifetime, it was generated by the principal.

Packet interception, alteration to the data, and forwarding of that data to the intended destination could potentially occur. This is one of the challenges of data security in a Grid.

In a Grid environment, remote authentication is accomplished by verification of a cryptographic identity in a way that establishes trust that there has been an unbroken chain from the relying party to a named human, system, or service identity and from that named entity back to the relying party. This trust is accomplished through an essential sequence of steps, each of which occurs in an essential order to achieve acceptance of a remote user on a Grid resource and return to the named entity in question.

Delegation is accomplished by generating and sending a proxy certificate along with its private key to any remote Grid system so that the remote system may be allowed to act on behalf of the user. This is the basis for what single sign-on accomplishes in a Grid; the user or entity proves its identity once, when it signs in, and then proceeds to delegate its authority to the remote systems for any subsequent processing steps. The trust establishment process involves:

1. Binding an entity identity to a distinguished name or the subject name in an X.509 identity certificate
2. Binding a public key to the distinguished name (generating an X.509 certificate)

3. Assuring that the public key that is presented to the system actually represents the user that it is supposed to be representing. This is accomplished through the cryptography algorithms and the protocols of public key infrastructure
4. Ensuring that messages originating from an entity and therefore tied to the entity maintaining the distinguished name could only have originated with that entity
5. Mutual authentication, accomplished when the two ends of a communication channel agree on each other's identity
6. Delegation of identity to the remote Grid systems through the cryptographic techniques and protocols used for generating and managing the proxy certificates (directly derived from the CA-issued identity certificates)

Authorization

Authorization in a computer network is the permission for a user or system to access a particular object (computer, resource, data, or program). Authorized users should, in practice, be the only ones allowed to access specific data or resources. Details of who is or is not authorized perform certain task are usually maintained in special access control lists (ACLs).

Traditionally, authorization is based on authenticated identity of the requesting user and on information that is local to the server. Individuals are identified as authorized to perform an operation after identity and permissions associated with the particular files, services, directories, and operations are requested. The authorization mechanisms in the Grid will be similar to those in any other arena except for more options for access permissions.

Access to a file in a data repository, access to reserve network bandwidth, and access to allow for running a task on a given node are examples of accesses granted via ACLs. The ability to run a task on a certain machine can be based on the identity of the user (the principal) and also on the identity of the task or the application to be run and the machine on which it has been requested to run. ACLs may contain the names or checksums of those authorized programs, together with the names of principals authorized to invoke the programs and the machines on which a function is requested to run.

Delegation of Authority

Delegation of authority is the means by which a user process that is authorized to perform operations on given machines can grant that authority to perform operations to another process on its behalf. Delegation of authority is more restrictive than delegation of identity, and it is an important service for tasks that will run remotely on the Grid, but must make calls to read or write remotely stored data.

Accounting

Accounting is the tracking, limiting, and charging for consumption of resources. This is critical for fair allocation of resources. Accounting is tied closely with authorization. It is important, particularly in a Grid environment and its fluid form, to have a means of payment for the use of resources and that the usage of these resources can be tracked carefully and accurately so that a user is charged accurately for the resources. Accounting is not punitive; it is an attempt to ensure that computing resources are available, an incentive to make judicious use of the resources.

There should be a distributed mechanism to maintain the prescribed quotas across all systems in the Grid environment to ensure that users are not exceeding the resource limits simply by spreading the access over different pieces of the system.

Accounting, in the Grid computing paradigm, is an emerging field; and only a few rules are currently in place to make sure that users do not overstep their authority even inadvertently.

Audit

While the word "audit" conjures up thoughts of the Internal Revenue Service, audit is also not punitive in a computing context and serves as more of a record-keeping mechanism. True, it is a way to determine what went wrong but it can be much more. If there is a problem in the system, auditing is a means to determine what may have gone wrong; and if there is an intrusion into the system, it can assist with its detection and tracking.

Again, because of the nature of the Grid environment, audit must be a distributed mechanism. One of the challenges with auditing in the Grid environment concerns the scope of intrusion detection. One needs to maintain a record or log of all access and all log-able events so that analysis can be done later, but also in such a manner that, if necessary, analysis can be undertaken concurrently with the logging. This record must be protected to ensure the confidentiality of audited data, make sure that the record is in no way open to modification by any means other than the audit mechanism, and that deletion of records is impossible. Also, the record must be protected in such a way to prevent a denial-of-service attack spawned from its contents. The primary difficulty with auditing in the Grid environment is inherent with the type of applications and connections that go along with the Grid because many normal Grid activities may appear similar to network attacks.

Access Control

Access control deals with the configuration of users and those actions that they should be allowed to do. Within the database, access control involves creation of uses and granting them the roles and privileges to do what they need to do to accomplish their jobs.

Access control technology has evolved from research and development efforts that were originally supported by the Department of Defense (DoD) and resulted in two fundamental types of access control: (1) discretionary access control (DAC) and (2) mandatory access control (MAC). Because of its Defense Department background, the initial research and resulting applications addressed primarily the prevention of unauthorized access to classified information. Recent applications, however, have begun applying many of these policies to commercial environments.

DAC allows individual users to permit or revoke access control to any of the objects over which they have direct control. These users are considered the owners of the objects that they control. In corporations whose users do not have this level of authority to objects, the corporation or agency is the owner of the system, all objects within the system, and all programs and operations that act upon these objects and systems. Access authority and priorities are controlled by the organization typically through systems administrators and are typically based on employee function rather than ownership of the data.

MAC is defined in the DoD's Trusted Computer Security Evaluation Criteria (TCSEC), and is loosely defined as a means of restricting the access to objects based on the sensitivity of the information (principle of least privilege) and the formal authorization to those objects (often gained through different levels of clearance).

Policies such as these for access control are not always well suited to the requirements of organizations that process unclassified information, but rather information that may be sensitive to their industry. In these secure but not critically secure environments, the security objectives are often used to support the higher-level organizational policies derived from the existing laws, business rules, and business practices, ethics, regulations, or generally accepted practices within the organization. Organizations and their resulting environments usually require the ability to control the actions of individuals within the organization beyond simply controlling their ability to access information based on its sensitivity.

Frequently, an organization may want to have a way to let people access a system based on something other than who they are. This restriction of access based on something other than identity is known as *access control* and it is a critical piece of Grid access security.

"Allow and Deny"

There are certain directives, typically used in conjunction with a Web server and its software (for example, Apache), that allow or deny certain access based on IP or based on the directory structure accessed. These directives provide the means to allow or deny access based on host name or the host IP address of the machine requesting the document.

The usage of these directives is as follows:

- Allow from <address>. Address is replaced by an IP address or partial IP address, or by a fully qualified domain name (or partial domain name) or by multiples of any combination of these. One can also replace address by the word "all" (for public place) or "none" (if one does not want anyone to have direct access).
- Deny from <address>. Again, address is replaced by any component applicable to "allow from all." "Deny from none" is equivalent to "allow from all," and "deny from all" is equivalent to "allow from none."

Combining "Order" with these other two directives can give one some certainty that one is restricting access in the way that one thinks. "Order Deny, Allow" tells the server that you want to apply the deny directive first and then apply the allow directive. The following example will deny access to everyone but will then allow access from a host named myhost.mycompany.com.

```
Order Deny, Allow

Deny from all

Allow from myhost.mycompany.com
```

The idea of allow and deny is particularly good if one has a well-segmented network. If the accounting department is segmented to a particular series of IP addresses, and they are the only employees permitted to use one segment of a server or perform one kind of job on the Grid, limiting access to those IP addresses would be a simple way to do this.

"Satisfy"

There is also a means by which one can specify that any of several criteria can be taken into account and be considered when the server is trying to determine whether a particular user's server will be granted admission. The selectivity of "satisfy" is either "any" or "all." The default is to assume that the entity attempting access is "all," meaning that (if there is several criteria) all of the different criteria need to be met to allow someone access to the given portions. If "any" is the specified selectivity, all anyone has to do is meet one of the criteria to gain access.

Role-Based Access

Access is the ability to use a computer resource, make changes to either the resource or contents of the resource, or view settings or contents of the resource; and access control is the means by which the ability to accomplish these tasks is granted or denied. Computer-based access control can allow one to determine what user or server processes can access a specific resource as well as the type of access permitted.

Role-based access allows the computers to make these access decisions based on the roles that either individual users have as a part of the organization or the roles that a Grid component has within the Grid. The determination of appropriate roles must be carefully addressed based on business rules within the organization. Access rights are then grouped based on who is allowed to perform what action on these resources, and the rights are granted to the role that a group of individuals is given. Any individual can be put into one or more than one role, based on the actual role he or she undertakes within the organization. Again, the premise of least privilege needs to play a part, and groupins to allow a person with more organizational authority to have more Grid resource authority.

Usage Control

The freedom gained with the advent of the Internet and the World Wide Web to use and transmit data by any number of unspecified users has led to a lack of usage control over what information is transferred via the network. This is a growing problem.

Usage control should be aimed at managing the use of software, data, and other resources at the point and place of use so that no matter how the user or entity arrives at that point, there will be equitable management of those resources.

This idea is not new; it has been around for decades with pay-per-use software and copy-free software, both concepts that are related to usage-based revenue collection in industries such as cable video. In this model, software could be freely copied and distributed anywhere without charge but with revenue collection based solely on usage. A usage control scheme expands on this notion by incorporating a mechanism for assigning usage of rights on a per-user basis. By applying usage control programs. A far more flexible and user-friendly system of usage control can be obtained by using simple revenue collection and password-based user approval.

Usage control can be used for not only software distribution, but also for any resources scattered on one's own network. In a Grid environment, this can extend to anything within the Grid. Usage control can be brought to the level of the virtualized storage files, databases, CPU—resources, anything that can be used can have the usage control mechanism applied to it to more equitably to distribute these resources.

Cryptography

Cryptography, derived from the Greek words *kryptos* (hidden) and *grafo* (write), is the study of message secrecy or the techniques of secret writing. In recent years it has become a branch of security administration in information theory — the mathematical study of information and its transmission from one point to another. It deals with a combination of authentication and access control, and contributes to the primary techniques of computer and network security.

Block Cipher

A block cipher is a method of encrypting text to produce cipher text or the cryptographic key, and the algorithms are applied to a block of data, for example, 64 contiguous bits at once as a group rather than one bit at a time. So that identical blocks of text do not get encrypted in exactly the same way in a message, even if those groups of texts are identical, it is common to apply the cipher text from the previously encrypted block to the next block in the sequence. This makes it more difficult to decipher the site for text should someone happen upon it, so that identical messages encrypted on the same day do not produce the same site for text. An initialization vector derived from a random number generator is typically combined with the text in the first block and the key. This ensures that all subsequent blocks resulting in the site for text do not match that of the first encrypting.

A block cipher is a symmetric key encryption algorithm that transforms a fixed-length block of plain text into cipher text of exactly the same length. That transformation takes place under the action of the user-provided secret key and decryption is performed by applying the reverse transformation to the cipher text using the exact same secret key. The fixed line is called the block size; and for many block ciphers, this is 64 bits. In the near future, the block size will increase to 128 bits as processors become more sophisticated.

It is possible to make block ciphers even more robust by creating an iterative block cipher. This is accomplished by encrypting a plain text block by processes that have several rounds of the same transformation also known as a round function applied to the data using a sub-key. The set of sub-keys is derived from the user-provided secret key by special function, and the set of sub-keys is called the keys schedule. The number of rounds in any one iterated cipher depends solely on the desired security level. However, it is important to remember the trade-off between security and performance. In most cases, an increased number of rounds will improve the security offered by the block cipher; but for some ciphers, the sheer number of rounds required to achieve adequate security will be entirely too large for the site to be practical or desirable.

Stream Ciphers

Another encryption algorithm, much less used alternative to block ciphers is the stream cipher. A stream cipher is a symmetric encryption algorithm (symmetric because the message is encrypted and decrypted using the same key). Stream ciphers can be exceptionally fast algorithms, even faster than block ciphers, partly because they operate on smaller units of plain text data, usually at the bit level.

A stream cipher generates a keystream; combining that keystream with the text, typically using a bitwise XOR operation, provides the encryption. Generation of the keystream can be a synchronous stream cipher, where the keystream is generated independently of the plain text original or the cipher text, or self-synchronizing, where the keystream can depend on the data and its encryption. A synchronous stream cipher is the most common type. As yet, there has been little attempt at standardization of deriving a stream cipher, although there are modes of block ciphers that can be effectively transformed into a keystream generation algorithm, making a block cipher also double as a stream cipher. This could be used to combine the best points of both means of encryption although stream ciphers are likely to remain faster.

Many different types of stream ciphers have been proposed in the cryptographic literature, and at least as many appear in implementations and products worldwide. Many are based on the use of linear feedback shift registers (LFSRs), as this type of cipher tends to be more amenable to analysis and it is easier to assess the security offered.

There are four different approaches to stream cipher design: (1) the information-theoretic approach, (2) the system-theoretic design, (3) the complexity-theoretic approach, and (4) a randomized cipher. In essence, the cryptographer designs the cipher along established guidelines that ensure that the cipher is resistant to all known attacks.

Linear Feedback Shift Register

A linear feedback shift register (LFSR) is one of the mechanisms used for generating a keystream sequence of bits. The register, whose behavior is regulated by a clock and clocking instances, consists of cells set by an initialization vector. The vector is, typically, the secret key. The contents of the register's cells are right shifted in position, and a bitwise XOR of the resulting cell's contents is placed in the leftmost cell.

LFSRs are fast and easy to implement at both the hardware and the software levels. However, sequences generated by a single register are not completely secure because any reasonably powerful mathematical framework allows for their straightforward analysis and decryption. LFSRs are most useful when used as building blocks in even more secure systems.

One-Time Pad

A one-time pad (OTP), or its alternative name, the Vernam cipher, uses a string of bits generated completely at random. The keystream is exactly the same length as the plain text message that it is intended to encrypt. The random string is combined with the plain text using a bitwise XOR and, as a result, produces the cipher text. Because the entire encryption keystream is random, an opponent with even an infinite amount of computational resources can only guess at the content of the plain text if he sees the cipher text. Such a cipher is said to offer perfect secrecy. The analysis of the one-time pad is one of the cornerstones of modern cryptography.

OTPs saw high use during wartime when messages over diplomatic channels required exceptionally high security. The primary drawback to the OTP is that the secret key, which can only be used once, is exactly as long as the message and therefore difficult to manage. While an OTP is perfectly secure, it is highly impractical.

Stream ciphers were originally developed as close approximations to the OTP. While contemporary stream ciphers are unable to provide the satisfying, theoretically perfect security of the OTP, they are far more practical.

Shift Register Cascades

A shift register cascade is an entire set of LFSRs interconnected so that the behavior of any given register depends directly on the behavior of the previous register in the cascade. This interconnection is achieved using one register to control the clock of the following register. Because many different configurations are possible, and many different parameter choices are available, this is one of the methods that takes the simple LFSR to a more secure level.

Shrinking Generators

Shrinking generators, developed originally by Coppersmith, Krawczyk, and Mansour, are stream ciphers based on the simple interaction between the outputs from two linear feedback shift registers. The bits from one output are used to determine whether the corresponding bits of the second output will be used as a part of the keystream. It is simple and scalable, and has good security properties. A drawback of the shrinking generator is that the output rate of the overall keystream will not be consistent or constant unless precautions are taken.

A variation of the shrinking generator is the self-shrinking generator whose output is a single LFSR used to extract bits from the same output, rather than the output of another LFSR. We have little data on effects and results from tests on the cryptanalysis of the technique.

Part of the interest in stream ciphers is their commonality with the one-time pad. An OTP is an encryption algorithm in which the plain text of a message is combined with a random key that is the same length as the message and can potentially be unbreakable. It is truly random, never reused, and secret.

OTP encryption is touted as the closest to unbreakable ever achieved. If (and only if) the key is truly perfectly random, a bitwise XOR-based is perfectly secure.

This means that an attacker cannot simply compute (or un-compute) the plain text from the cipher text without explicit knowledge of the key. This is true even for a brute-force search of all the keys. Trying every possible key combination does not help because any possible combination of plain text is equally likely from the cipher text. In this symmetric encryption, random bits of a pad are bitwise XOR-ed with the other bits of the message to produce a cipher that can only be decrypted by re-XOR-ing the message with a copy of the *same* pad. While the decryption depends on the safe transmittal of the exact key used for encryption to facilitate decryption, the main drawback to a one-time pad as a security measure is that there are exactly as many bits in the key as are in the original plain text message, and no portion of the key sequence is ever to be used (or reused) in another encryption.

Accountability

Problems and resource allocation arise continuously in computer services, and these issues are usually solved by making users accountable for their use of resources. In a Grid environment, this takes planning and discipline. Traditional file systems and communication media use accountability to maintain centralized control over the resources for which they are responsible. Typically, these controls are implemented by way of constructs known, ironically, as user accounts. File systems use quotas to restrict the amount of data that any user can store on the system. ISPs (Internet service providers) measure the bandwidth their clients and their clients' Web traffic use and often charge fees in proportion to this amount. Even Web hosting is often based on a combination of the amount of bandwidth allocated to an account, coupled with the amount of space and number of e-mail accounts allocated to that host's site. Without these limits and controls, any user has the incentive to squeeze resources to maximize personal gain. However, all users on a system appear to have the same incentive. It will soon become impossible for anyone to do any work on a server without strict controls and strict accountability because all resources will be exhausted.

The overloading of a system's bandwidth or processing ability and the ultimate cause of a loss in service or of all network connectivity is a called denial-of-service (DoS) attack. A DoS attack, while typically wreaked upon a network by an outside entity, can also be caused by legitimate internal clients using the available resources on the network. One simple way to maintain data availability is to mirror it. Instead of storing data on just one machine, it is stored on several different machines. Because of the inherent underlying architecture of the Grid, this is simple. When one machine becomes congested or when there is a DoS situation because of resource unavailability or extremely heavy network traffic, no one server goes down entirely and all others in the network that have access to the data are still available for connection.

The exploitation of a system by storing a disproportionately large amount of data, a large number of files, or otherwise overloading the storage capabilities of that resource, thereby disallowing other users' ability to have a proportionally equitable amount of space is considered a storage flooding attack.

Accountability can be enforced, in part, by restricting access, wherein each computer system tries to limit its users to a certain number of connections, a certain quantity of data storage, or a certain amount of data that can be either uploaded to or downloaded from the system. Favored users are often granted extended resource allowances. The determination of these favored users is normally done by maintaining a reputation for each user with which the system communicates. Those users viewed as having low reputations are typically allowed fewer resources or are mistrusted entirely, and find that their transactions are either rejected or given significantly lower priority. Favored users are granted more access to resources such as storage and bandwidth and also CPUs and other resources.

In relatively simple distributed systems, rudimentary accountability measures are typically sufficient, particularly if the list of accounts is somewhat static and all of its account members are known to each hostname or address; then any misbehavior on any one user's part can lead to a permanent bad reputation. Moreover, if all the operators of the system are known, then preexisting legal methods such as legal contracts for nondisclosure agreements can help ensure that system administration abides by protocol.

However, by definition, the Grid environment is not an inherently simple distributed system. The technology makes it difficult to uniquely and permanently identify Grid users, their operators, and their contributing resources. Even if these users have identified handles on the Grid, they have no idea on what resource they are connected, on what resource their jobs are going to run, and therefore they have no good way to access centrally their usage history or predict performance. Furthermore, individuals using the Grid environment are rarely bound by any kind of contract and would likely not be charged for breaching contracts because of the cost–benefit analysis and time delays involved in attempting to enforce them.

The main goal of accountability is to maximize the server's utility to the overall system while minimizing the potential threats that either the server or access to the Grid through that server could pose. There are two primary ways to minimize the threat. The first approach is to limit the risk and bandwidth use or whatever resources were improperly used to an amount roughly equal to the benefit from the transaction. The other approach is to make the risk proportional to the trust that one has in the other parties also on the Grid.

Data Integrity

Data integrity refers to the validity of the data. It is a term that often encompasses many other ideas. It often refers to the consistency of the data, its accuracy, the preservation of the data for its intended use, and its condition of being maintained during any operations (transfer, storage, and retrieval). In data communication, it refers to the condition when data is transferred from the source to the destination and has not been accidentally or maliciously modified, altered, or destroyed.

Data (singularly or as a chunk or set) means different things to different people. It consists distinct pieces of information, usually formatted in a particular way. Data can exist in a wide variety of forms. It can be numbers or letters and words on a piece of paper. It can be bits and bytes that are stored in electronic memory (working memory or stored to disk), in an electronic system, or it can be individual facts and memories that are stored in a person's brain. In a computing context is the binary, machine-readable information that is stored and read. While there are often distinctions made between plain text ASCII files and what are considered data files, both are stored as binary bits and bytes at the machine level, and are therefore both within the realm of what we are discussing. These distinctions blur even further when database management systems and their files enter the equation and the amount of information and data that must be maintained with integrity expands.

Data integrity can be compromised in a number of ways. One of the most common is simply human error when the data is entered. This is the garbage in-garbage out GIGO scenario. Controlling this type of integrity involves the interfaces that are created, through which users can add or alter data. Another alternative is to add constraints to the database and the data tables to ensure that only appropriate data is entered.

Errors occur when data is transmitted from one computer to another. Sometimes these errors are introduced accidentally; and sometimes the error introduction is deliberate. The deliberate introduction of errors can be controlled in the manner already discussed. Accidental introduction can occur during transmission, through attenuation, impulse noise, crosstalk, jitter, and delay distortion. Details of these different error-introducing situations follow.

Attenuation

Attenuation is the weakening of the transmitted signal over increasing distances. Attenuation occurs in both analog (voice over phone lines) and digital (data over transmission media) signals, and the loss of signal is expressed in either decibels or voltage loss per unit of distance (this distance depends on the media over which the signal travels). The lower the attenuation amount, the greater the efficiency of the media (fiber optics are more efficient than twisted-pair phone lines) is considered. Repeaters can be used to re-boost the signal to allow it to travel with less attenuation over far greater distances.

Impulse Noise

Noise or undesired disturbances within the frequency band of interest (the band through which the signal is traveling), consists of random occurrences of spikes caused by a short surge of electrical, magnetic, or electromagnetic energy, each spike having random amplitude and spectral content. Noise in data transmission is considered the random variations of one or more of the characteristics of any entity such as voltage, current, or data, amplitude, or frequency.

Crosstalk

Crosstalk is the disturbance along a circuit caused by electromagnetic interference. This occurs when one signal disrupts a signal in an adjacent circuit and causes one or both signals to become confused and cross over each other. In a telephone circuit, the phenomenon of crosstalk can result in someone hearing part of a voice conversation from another circuit. It can occur in microcircuits within computers and audio equipment as well as within network circuits. The term is also applied to optical signals that interfere with each other (a much bigger problem before the advent of cable TV and satellite TV). Shielding the different circuits from each other and separating them with distance are both effective ways of controlling crosstalk.

Jitter

Jitter is an abrupt and unwanted variation in one or more signal characteristics (amplitude, phase, pulse width, and position). It can include the interval between successive pulses, the amplitude of successive cycles, or the frequency or phase of successive cycles. It is a significant factor in nearly all communication links.

Phase jitter is the unintended phase modulation of a primary signal by one or more other signals somewhere through the transmission process. Phase jitter is expressed in degrees relating to the peak-to-peak deviation over the specified frequency ranges. When jitter becomes excessive, it can cause errors and result in the need for data recovery. Jitter measurements are typically made in conjunction with noise measurements, because noise and jitter can have a high impact on one another.

Phase jitter may be transient or periodic in nature and may be caused by noise in the transmission media.

Amplitude jitter is the measure of incidental amplitude modulation of the transmitted holding tone. It can be caused by many of the same sources as phase jitter, and can be caused indirectly by attenuation distortion and envelope delay. Amplitude jitter can be caused by phase jitter, and vice versa. Noise can also have a deleterious effect on amplitude jitter measurements. Because there are several possible contributors to this situation, it is often necessary to measure these parameters as well to determine the true cause of the impairment. Amplitude jitter is evaluated over the same frequency ranges as phase jitter, and is expressed in percent.

Delay Distortion

Delay distortion describes a condition in which various frequency components of a transmitted signal exhibit different propagation delays, with the greatest delays occurring near the upper and lower limits of the circuit band due to reactance. Reactance is the property of resisting or impeding the flow of a current.

Delay distortion is the difference in delay between the frequency tested and a reference frequency near the center of the circuit band, which is the point of minimum delay. When delays between various frequency components of the data transmission become large enough, interference can result and is expressed in microseconds.

Software bugs and viruses are other causes of disruption in data integrity. Software bugs can cause corrupt or invalid data. A program may not take into account the fact that leap years will occasionally end on a Sunday, causing a month-end closing to be unable to occur on an appropriate schedule. That can cause incorrect reports because of the timing of the recognition of revenues.

But the corruption can be far worse. Bugs also cause data to become invalid and unreadable. Viruses are also the cause of data integrity issues. Viruses have become more of a means of flooding servers with mail volume in recent years than in becoming truly destructive, but this trend may not continue. Destructive and invasive viruses can be the cause of extreme corruption and devastation.

Hardware malfunction can be another data integrity issues. Disks crash, controllers malfunction and other hardware components can cause corruption. Hardware redundancy can help with this.

Natural disasters, such as fires, floods, tornadoes, and hurricanes, can also have a devastating effect on data integrity. Disasters cause outages and they also can affect the power that is available to the network. Floods can cause damage to computer components. Fire can destroy components beyond repair and beyond recovery. Disaster recovery practices, that have been practiced and found adequate can assist in the mitigation of the damages caused by disasters.

Capability Resource Management

Capability is all about access. *Preventing* access means making sure that Person A can either not access or not damage Person B's data or resources. Person A should not be able to read Person B's medical records, for example, unless Person B has a valid reason to do so. If Person A can access those records, she should definitely not be able to delete them unless she owns them. *Limiting* access means ensuring that a program cannot do more than one intends it to do. This is something that is often seen as concerning spyware, pop-ups, and viruses. *Granting* access means that a user wants to allow another user or another group of users the ability to work together on a project, a particular file, or set of files, but wants to be selective in who can work on the given files. *Revoking* access is undoing access; when the group is done working on the project, access for them to read, alter, and update the files that the group had been working on previously can be removed.

The term "capability" was first introduced in computing by Dennis and Van Horn in 1966 in an article entitled "Programming Semantics for Multiprogrammed Computations," suggesting that one can design a computer system in such a way that in order to access any given object, a program must have a special token. The token designates a particular object and gives an accessing program the authority to perform a certain specific set of actions (read or write or update) on that object. This token is known as a capability.

The capabilities of a system specify can be compared to the keys on a typical key ring. The car key has the purpose of providing access to one specific car; the actions that one can perform on that car are the capabilities of that car (opening the doors, opening the trunk, starting the car). The house key's purpose is to open the door on one specific house; the mailbox key is the means by which one can open a single specific mail box. The keys do not care who has them or who uses them. If a neighbor wants you to water his plants while he is out of town, he hands you his key (delegates his authority to access his house to you). Car keys often include a primary key or valet key, or a door and ignition key. The valet key can start the car and unlock the door, but cannot lock or unlock the glove box, demonstrating how two capabilities can be designated for the same object (in this example, a car; but in a computing scenario, particularly the Grid example, two capabilities can be designated for the same computing resource) but allow (authorize) different actions to be taken on that object. Just as with keys, capabilities can be copied. Moreover, one could go further than simply copying the capabilities; one could make variants of the initial capability accomplished through the copy.

The term "resource" refers to software, servers, network segments, or circuits. A client is anyone, human or computer or other component or a data packet sent though a network; and condition specifies how the resource can be used. Capability consists of rules determining what a client's prerogatives are, what rights that client holds, and under what condition a resource can be used by that client.

In a capability-based computer system, a system that can have significant ramifications on a Grid system, all access to all objects in the system is accomplished through capabilities. Capabilities provide the *only* means a client has of accessing the system's objects. Every program holds a set of capabilities, its set of keys to the system. If Program A has been given the capability to talk to Program B, then these two programs can grant their capabilities to each other. In most capability systems, a program can (although it may not be practical to do so) have an infinite number of capabilities. Systems that have programs with large numbers of capabilities often tend to be slow. A better design idea allows each program to hold only a fixed small number of capabilities (usually less than 50) but allows a means for storing additional capabilities if they are needed. Capabilities must be granted. Because the optimum goal is to make the set of capabilities held by each program as specific and as small as possible, to optimize performance, and prevent abuse of authority it does not have. So that it cannot pass on, unintentionally, this authority to other programs that it can communicate to, the system uses a premise known as the principle of least privilege.

Capabilities are often implemented using ACLs (access control lists), or a special file listing all programs and the users allowed to run them, via the operating system's security mechanisms, the programs running under the authority of the user can access those files to which the user running the program has access. The programs have the authority to do virtually anything. The user under whom they run serves as the limiting factor.

Capability systems have historically not had widespread acceptance, in part because of the fact that early capability systems were built into the hardware before we knew a lot about hardware architecture. This made them prohibitively slow and often incredibly complex. While with today's more open and flexible operating systems, capability is considerably less complex and more efficient than it used to be, the bad reputation often remains. In a Grid system, it may be an optimum solution to a new problem.

Database Security

This chapter has described the different ways to secure a network and the different encryption methods that can be used to implement security, but what about securing the data and the databases and the files that can be accessed along with the databases?

Inference

Databases are typically designed to promote open and flexible access to data. This design feature is particularly useful for end users who are not typically highly technical people, yet require the ability to access the data, often in real-time with tools that allow them almost direct access to the structures. This is also one of the characteristic that make databases particularly susceptible to less than honorable activity.

One of the design decisions that many database administrators and designers make is naming things so that they are able to be logically accessed by end users through a query tool without the need to map information through an external means or making the users find their own means to remember what data is stored in what table. This usually means naming a table for the grouping of data that is stored in it and also naming columns within the table logically. Ordinarily, this is a design decision that works well for the end users and the programmers who are accessing the data. Unfortunately, it can also work very well for someone searching through a system for information to which he should not have access.

This problem, from a security perspective, is known as inference. Inference means that someone can piece together or infer information at one level of security and use that information to determine a fact that should be protected by a higher security level.

Table 4.2   Claim Table

Claim Number	Claimant SSN	Claim Date
12345	111111111	2/29/2004
13456	111111111	3/2/2004
14567	222222222	6/2/2003
15678	333333333	5/5/1998
16789	222222222	4/24/1985
17890	555555555	7/27/2004

Tables 4.2, 4.3 and 4.4 consist of a health insurance claim table, the claimant table to go along with the claims, and the diagnosis table. It does not take much work to infer that Joe W. Smith has been diagnosed with tuberculosis and that Bill Jones has been diagnosed with hepatitis A. With current laws governing what information can be freely available, or even less than freely available, the ability to make these kinds of inferences is undesirable.

Database security can be looked at from four perspectives: (1) server security, (2) database connections, (3) table access control, and (4) database access control.

Application Security

When looking at application security, consider the threat classifications that are directly related to the situation in which the application will be housed.

A brute-force attack is an automated process of trial and error that can be used to guess a person's username and password, credit card number, PIN, or cryptographic

Table 4.3   Claimant Table

Claimant SSN	Claimant Last Name	Claimant FName	Claimant M I	Claimant Street Address1	Claimant Street Address2	Claimant Zip	Phone
111111111	Smith	Joe	W	123 Any street	Apartment 23	79124	8005551212
222222222	Jones	William	J	321 Leftmost road		16127	8885551212

Table 4.4　Diagnosis Table

Claim No.	Physician No.	Appt_Date	Diagnosis	Xray-bfile	Test-Results-bfiles	Physician Notes bfile
12345	123098	3/2/2004	Tuberculosis		Blood work results 12345	Notes 12345
14567	9870654	6/13/2003	Hepatitis A		Test results 14567	Notes 14567

key. Once the process is successful, the attacker is able to access an account. While it is difficult for a programmer or application designer to prevent the attempt at brute-force attacks or their success, an acknowledgment of the risk of these attacks will provide awareness that it could pose problems. The use of strong passwords or cryptographic keys with a larger key length can help foil such an attack. A reverse brute-force attack tries multiple usernames against a single password. This can be particularly effective in systems containing thousands or millions of user accounts because with each additional username, the chance that more than one user account has the same password increases. Brute-force attacks are popular and often successful but can take days, weeks, or even years to be effective.

Insufficient authentication occurs whenever a Web site permits an attacker to access sensitive content or functionality without having to properly authenticate. The use of Web-based administration tools is often an effective place for this type of attack to occur. It is, therefore, important that these not be readily or directly accessible without demanding accurate authentication of the user attempting to access these applications. These tools should not be directly linked to any location that is readily accessible but rather should demand that the user know the URL location of the tools.

Weak password recovery validation permits an attacker to illegally obtain, recover, or change another user's password. More Web sites require users to enter user IDs and passwords and require the user to remember the combination of user IDs and passwords precisely. Over time, particularly if the Web site is not frequently accessed, the user's ability to remember the combination is difficult. For this reason, password recovery is important for those sites to provide a mechanism for the retrieval of this information. Often, this is accomplished through the use of "key questions," the answers to which presumably only the user knows. Another mechanism is for the user to provide a hint during registration and that hint is used later to retrieve the user ID and password combination. Still other sites use information that is only relevant to the given user (social security number, telephone number, zip code, or address, for example) as proof of user identity. Password retrieval is often used in combination with password recovery validation to gain ultimate access to information.

Insufficient authorization is when a Web site permits access to sensitive or protected content or functionality that should ordinarily require increased access control restrictions. Recall that when a user accesses a system, she should have only the ability to access the information that she is authorized to access. After authentication, authorization is performed.

Insufficient session expiration occurs when a Web site permits an attacker or intruder to reuse old session credentials or session IDs for authorization. This attack is used to steal the identity of a user or impersonate the other user. HTTP is, notoriously, a stateless protocol. For this reason, Web sites often use session IDs to uniquely identify one user from another. This means that the session IDs must be maintained (ostensibly confidentially) to keep multiple users from using the same log-in account. If a session ID is stolen from another user's session, that ID can be used to perform fraudulent transactions. This can be mitigated by the use of proper session expiration. If system administrators implement short session expiration times, it is more difficult to gain nefarious access except in cases where the ID is used nearly immediately after hijacking. Network sniffers or cross-site scripting attacks can be used to hijack the session ID. Library computers or work environments are other places where session expiration (or lack thereof) can allow the next user to access the previous user's information. Longer expiration times increase the likelihood of successful access by the attacker.

Session fixation occurs when an attack technique forces a user session ID to an explicit value. A number of techniques can be used to deliberately set a session to a given ID value. There are two ways that sessions can be managed with respect to the ID values. Permissive systems allow browsers to specify any ID, and these session IDs are maintained with no contact to the Web site; strict systems that only accept server-side generated values require the attacker to maintain the trap session with periodic Web site contact so that inactivity timeouts do not occur. Web sites that use session IDs ordinarily are fixation cookie based and are the easiest to attack. Cross-site scripting can be used to pepper a Web site with pervious HTTP session requests and, after another user logs on to the Web site and that user's session ID is fixed, the attacker will wait log in; and once this is accomplished, the attacker uses the peppered session ID value to force her way into the user's online identity.

Content spoofing occurs when the attacker tricks an authorized user into believing that certain content appearing in a Web site is legitimate and not from an external source. Spoofing is often accomplished using an e-mail or instant message that suggests that users visit a Web site designated by a malicious URL. The link appears to be legitimate in the text of the message but the underlying URL misdirects the user to a copy of the actual Web site but with a malicious URL underlying the actual code. Because the URL in the browser bar appears to be legitimate, users believe they are where they should be and enter their account information into the hijacked Web pages. This attack takes advantage of the trusting nature of many users and the relationship of those users and their frequently used Web sites.

Cross-site scripting forces a Web site to echo attacker-supplied executable code, which loads into a user's browser. The code itself can be written in virtually any browser-supported language. When the browser executes the code, it executes within the security context of the hosting Web site. Because of the level of privilege being leveraged, the code can modify, transmit, or remove sensitive data that is accessible through that browser. The account can be hijacked through cookie theft and redirect the browser session to another location or fraudulent content. Again, these attacks prey on the trust relationship between users and their frequented Web sites.

Buffer overflow attacks alter the flow of the application's code by overwriting parts of memory and altering the flow or the logic of the code. These attacks are often leveraged against databases. Buffer overflow errors take advantage of common software flaws that result in error conditions. The error occurs when data is written to memory and that data exceeds the allocated size of the buffer. As the overflow occurs, adjacent memory addresses are overwritten. This causes the software to fault or crash. When software is written in such a way that properly crafted input can be used to overflow buffers, security issues result. This kind of overflow can be used to cause denial of service (DoS) attacks. DoS attacks occur when memory is corrupted and software fails, often entire systems of software. Buffer overflow vulnerabilities can be used to overwrite stack pointers and redirect programs to execute malicious instructions and change program variables. These attacks have become more frequent as they are easily leveraged against Web servers although far less frequently in the application layer itself because the attacker would need to exploit custom code on remote systems and blind attacks are rarely successful.

Format string attacks alter the flow of the application using string formatting library features that allow it to access unauthorized memory space. This takes advantage of programming languages' vulnerability that occurs when user-supplied data is used directly as formatting string input.

LDAP injection is an attack technique used to exploit Web sites that reconstruct LDAP statements from user-supplied input. It is used to circumvent the security that is put into place and can be used to hijack not only on one application, but the overall system in general. Lightweight directory access protocol (LDAP) is an open standard protocol used for querying and manipulating X.500 directory services. LDAP runs over TCP and Web applications often use the user-supplied input as a means to create custom LDAP statements that are used by dynamic Web page requests. Web applications that fail to properly sanitize user-supplied input make it possible for attackers to alter the construction of an LDAP statement. By modifying this LDAP statement, the process will run with the same permissions as the original component that executed the command. This can cause serious security problems when the permissions grant the rights to query, modify, or remove anything inside the LDAP tree. Similar techniques can be used to exploit vulnerabilities in SQL injection.

Operating system commanding occurs when a Web site is used to execute operating system commands through manipulation of application input. Again, if a Web application does not take adequate measures to sanitize user-supplied input before using it in the application, an attacker that tricks the application into executing operating system commands will have those commands run, at the operating system level, with the same privileges as the component that executed the command. This means that nefarious code can run within the database server, application server, or Web server with more authority than should ordinarily be possible.

SQL injection occurs when database access and unauthorized database access occur, through a Web site, based on user-supplied input. Most database applications, from the small to the enterprise sized, can be accessed using SQL statements. SQL is an ANSI as well as ISO standard. Many databases customize the user of SQL by adding their own extensions; however, most will also accept standard SQL statements. Many Web applications use user-supplied input as a means to create dynamically custom SQL statements and dynamic Web page requests. Again, any Web application that fails to sanitize the user-supplied input allows an attacker to alter the construction of the back-end SQL statements. The process will run with the same permissions as the hijacked component, thereby allowing attackers to potentially gain control of the database or execute commands on the system. Blind SQL injection is used to return a user-friendly error page that explicitly states what mistake the attacker has made. Blind SQL injection is easily detected by putting a Boolean statement into the parameter.

Server side include injection occurs when an attacker is able to send code into a Web-based application and that code will later execute locally on the Web server. Before serving a Web page, the Web server can parse and execute server side include statements that are legitimate before returning the page to the user. Message boards, content management systems, and guest books typically use these server side includes to provide valued content to the user. An attacker who submits a server side include may have the ability to execute arbitrary operating system commands or provide protected file contents to the attacker when that attacker accesses the page.

Information leakage occurs when a Web site is allowed to reveal sensitive data that can be used by an attacker to assist in exploiting the system. This information can include code itself, code comments, error messages, or other information. The information can be presented within HTML comments, error messages, source code, or simply plain text. Many Web sites can be coaxed into revealing this kind of information. While this may or may not breach security, it can provide useful information to the attacker that can be used for future attacks. The potential leakage should be limited to the greatest extent possible. This means that any debugging information that might be left in the code by developers should be removed, as should any contextual information such as directory structures, SQL query structures, or names of key processes used by the overall Web site. Code should be scrubbed for any hardcoded usernames and passwords, and any logical locations for these usernames and passwords should be examined as well. Information leakage can also apply to data that would ordinarily be deemed confidential (account numbers, driver's license numbers, passport numbers, social security information, or credit card information, for example) yet is improperly protected by the Web site.

Abuse of functionality uses a Web site's own features and functionality as a means to consume, defraud, or circumvent access control mechanisms. Some functionality is open to abuse and causes unexpected behavior in functionality, often including security functionality. While some functionality, if usurped, would simply annoy or inconvenience users, others could potentially allow for the defrauding of the system or the organization as a whole. The level of potential abuse varies from application to application and organization to organization. These attacks are often intertwined with other types of attacks, and abuse of functionality attacks are commonly used as a force multiplier.

DoS is a technique with the intent of preventing a Web site from serving normal user activity. DoS attacks are often launched as an annoyance to a target, preventing users from accessing the desired applications. DoS attacks are typically centered in the network layer, although application layer attacks are not unheard of. The attacks succeed by starving a system of critical resources.

Server Security

Server security deals with physically limiting access to the database server itself. This is one of the most important security issues for both external threats and internal accidents. Therefore, it must be one of the most carefully planned and one of the earliest dealt with aspects of the security setup. Basically, the idea behind server security is that what one cannot see, one cannot access, or one cannot know that one might want to access. This is one of the primary issues with inference. If one can see what might be there, then one is more apt to try to see what one can find.

What about internally? Many people in a company know that the financials database resides on the UNIX box and is in Oracle, that the HR system resides on a Windows server in SQL, that the purchasing system resides partly in IMS on the mainframe and partly on DB2 on the mainframe, and that client data resides in several different databases on different platforms and servers but is all accessed via a Web interface with the Web server sitting on a Linux platform. One person with the incorrect access or one person with just enough access and a little too much time and creativity could find information that is inappropriate.

One premise of server access is *least privileges*. The principle of least privilege has been seen as important for meeting integrity objectives. A person should be given exactly the amount of privilege necessary to perform a job. This means that administrators need to identify exactly what that user's job is, and determine the minimum set of privileges required to perform that job. Restriction of the user to a domain with exactly those privileges and nothing more is critical. In this way, denied privileges cannot be used to circumvent organizational security policy, even in boredom or inadvertently.

The principle of least privilege is applicable not only to internal users, but also to people who are permitted to access the server from the outside. Only trusted IP addresses should be able to access a database server (or any other servers, for that matter). If only trusted IP addresses can access the servers and users access the information through an interface, the least privileges principle is upheld and only servers not end users can access a database server.

Database Connections

Unauthorized database connections represent another are where caution should be exercised. With many of the Grid interfaces taking place via an Internet or intranet site, one needs to ensure validation of all updates to the database and thus ensure that they are warranted and also make sure that with dynamic SQL, one is removing any possible SQL that might be embedded from a user within the interface.

This extends also to allowing everyone to use the same user ID to access the database. While it is true that it makes for easier administration if one has fewer user IDs, it is also true that it is less likely that one will be able to discover who has caused something to happen to a database and it makes it much easier for someone to find out the user ID. Furthermore, it is important to look very carefully at exactly what rights and privileges the user who is connecting needs to have. It is better to have twenty different user IDs than ten if one can divide the security requirements among those who have read access and users who need the ability to update, insert, or delete information.

Table Access Control

Again, following the principle of least privilege, table access must be restricted to only that access needed to perform a job. If a person has a need to update a table, that is the level of access that he should have. If, however, a user only needs to retrieve data from a table or set of tables, he should have only read access to the information. While it is much easier to simply grant unlimited access to anyone, or (worse) allow everyone to log in as the same user, the owner of the tables and objects, this poses not only security hazards, but it is asking for trouble. Allowing these connections can lead to dropped objects and altered definitions of the objects. Any set of tables or any system should have three different classes of users: the owner of the tables and other objects (this user should be the owner and the only one who is able to alter the physical definition for the objects and access to this user should be closely guarded), an update class or role (this class of user is the one who can insert information and update information in the tables), and a read-only user who can query the tables and alter nothing. There can be a derivation in the update user. There may be some situations where one has users who should be allowed to update information that is already in the table, and other people who can insert new information into the table. While it will add another layer of complexity to user administration in the database, it is better in the long run for security purposes to allow for the added complexity.

Further, columns within the table may contain information that only certain people should be able to see. If all access to the information is strictly limited through an application interface, the interface can provide a lot of security to this end. Based on login, IP, or other criteria, certain selective information can be kept from access by the wrong people; and in fact, a programmer could keep those users who should not know about the data from even knowing of its existence. However, it is difficult to limit access through an interface, especially when many users may be given a tool like Business Objects, Oracle Discoverer, or other GUI (graphical user interface) through which they can select tables and columns and provide limiting criteria to bring back the data for which they are looking. If their access is not limited at either the tool level or at the report level within the tool, it must be limited at the database or schema level by the administrator.

By way of an example, it may be necessary for a user to be able to see all the employee information except salaries and commission amounts. It becomes necessary, either programmatically or through views or other mechanisms within the database, to limit that particular class of user to the ability to see only the information that is necessary and to not have access to columns to which they should not have access. They may, for example, see the salary table (or an aliased version of the salary table so even the table's purpose is hidden) as in Table 4.5.

Table 4.5   Limited Version of Salary Table

Client_ID	Employee_SSN	Employee_Type	Employee_ID
a43094	111111111	Manager	989898
a45902	888888888	Salary	876542
a74235	777777777	Hourly	434343
a74235	900000000	Hourly	242424
a74235	800000000	Salary	131313
b74235	999999999	Hourly	123456
b34562	999999999	Salary	234567
b34562	700000000	Salary	111222
b34562	600000000	Hourly	222334
b34562	500000000	Consulting	444665

Table 4.6   Salary Table Limited to One Client ID

Client_ID	Employee_ SSN	Employee_ Type	Employee_ Salary	Employee_ Commission	Employee_ID
b34562	999999999	Salary	36000		234567
b34562	700000000	Salary	36000		111222
b34562	600000000	Hourly	36		222334
b34562	500000000	Consulting	56		444665

There is still another consideration when looking at access to tables. With more and more data being stored, the database and tables are getting bigger, particularly with the application service provider model. If the data from many different end users and many different user companies is stored together in the same tables, it is important to be able to limit access only to data that is applicable to the end user. This is true for a read-only user as well as for those able to insert, update, and delete information. Different database management systems provide different means to accomplish this.

Again, by way of example, drawing upon the information in Table 4.5, one can see in both Tables 4.6 and 4.7, the information as if it existed in two different tables based on who is accessing the information. In this way one can create a virtually private database for each of the users logging on. In this way, a database accessible from the Grid will likely need to be created for ease of access and security at the data level.

Restricting Database Access

Because a database does not exist in a vacuum and rarely without the supporting access of a network, it is important to look at the network access of the database

Table 4.7   Salary Table as Seen by Another Client

Client_ID	Employee_ SSN	Employee_ Type	Employee_ Salary	Employee_ Commission	Employee_ID
a74235	999999999	Hourly	18	0.1	434343
a74235	900000000	Hourly	18	0.1	242424
a74235	800000000	Salary	42000		131313

system. While this has been primarily accessed through the Internet or through an intranet, similar ideas should be considered at for a database that will be accessed via a Grid interface.

Because it is usually important to restrict most access to the database to that accomplished through an interface, and to make sure that any access is through verified locations, steps need to be taken to ensure this level of security. There are many ways to prevent open access from the network, regardless of the size and complexity of the network, and every database management system has its own set of unique features, as does each operating system on which each database management system resides. What follows are some of the most common methods:

- *Trusted IP addresses.* UNIX servers are typically configured to answer only those pings that originate from a list of trusted hosts. This is usually accomplished by configuring the contents of the host file (a file whose purpose is to restrict server access to only a list of specific users).
- *Server account disabling.* Causing a login ID to be locked after three failed password attempts will thwart hacker. Without this simple security feature, anyone could run a password generation program, a program that generates millions of passwords until it "guesses" a given user ID password combination.
- *Special tools.* Products exist that will alert systems administration when they detect what they perceive as an external server attempting to breach the system's security.
- *Kerberos security.* Kerberos is a network authentication protocol designed to provide strong authentication for client–server applications using secret-key cryptography. Kerberos, named after the three-headed dog, Cerberus, that guarded the passage to the underworld, is available as a free implementation from the Massachusetts Institute of Technology as well as through many commercial products.
- *Port access security.* Oracle, as well as other database applications, listens to a specific port number on the server. If someone is attempting to access the database over a port that the database has not been instructed to listen to, no connection will be made.

There are also differences in the ways different database management engines handle their own security. The database user query stores and analyzes many millions of rows of information, ranging from information that is safely public to the data that needs to be kept extremely private. DBAs (database administrators) grant and restrict access appropriately. However, the DBMS must also offer ways to keep unauthorized users from accessing classified data

DBMS

Every DBMS has its own methods of implementing various levels of security. It is important for the database administrator to work with the rest of a security team in implementing the database-specific features that allow each database to limit within itself what each user can do. It is important that those administrators know what the security features are and how to effectively implement those features in a widespread system.

Chapter 5

Hardware

If it draws blood, it's hardware.

—Author Unknown

Typically, when thinking about a Grid, what one most naturally starts considering is, quite naturally, the hardware. The Grid is all about sharing hardware resources, scavenging for CPU cycles, and making the most efficient use of the hardware resources at an organization's disposal. But exactly what hardware are we talking about?

Computers

One of the most interesting things about computers and the Grid is that nearly any computer and operating system can quickly and easily be connected to the Grid and become a Grid server and member. Because of the nature of the Grid and the fact that as an operating paradigm it works well with heterogeneous hardware and operating systems, it is flexible enough to adapt easily to having mainframe components along with Intel-based Linux machines, midrange open systems, and Windows servers as components of the environment.

Some systems of supercomputers are linked together in an extremely high-performance Grid system; computer labs at colleges and universities allow the computers during their downtime to be linked together through the network, and CPU resources are scavenged and used to perform scientific computations. Entire organizations can utilize the same or similar concepts. Every computer in the organization could have its CPUs accessed during off-hours to assist in performing daily batch processing. Think this is stretching it? How many computers are in your office? How taxed are they, even when they are at their busiest — 10 percent on average, even 50 percent for the busiest administrator or programmer? While hard drives are always getting bigger and faster, it is still surprising how much computing power is sitting on the typical desktop of an employee today. If one wants to give a PC something taxing to do, recalculate the values in the spreadsheet, spell-check a Word document, or retrieve information from a database. It is unlikely, even if one does all of these at once, that the operations will push the limits of capability of the common desktop computer that basically sits around doing very little, waiting for some important job to come along. Now consider what these computers are doing at night. Even the computers that get logged off of at night are left turned on so that software updates can be pushed out over the network. But realistically, how often is the software updated? Now consider how many companies do batch processing overnight because the network is less busy and online customers are not as active. How many companies base their IT budgets on being able to scale their systems to they take advantage of the computing power during the day when online customers are hitting the system hard (but in transactional mode that is not a heavy CPU hitter, typically) and buy capacity so that they can make sure that the batch processing that occurs overnight can successfully finish during the batch window? What would happen if these companies were able to take advantage of the CPU power sitting idle on the desktops of all the employees to assist with the batch processing?

Many companies see CPU loads like that in Figure 5.1 during a day, or like that in Figure 5.2 during a month. Considerable extra processing is done on the server in Figure 5.2 during the beginning of the month, when the company closes its books in accounting, and the processing load falls off considerably after that. Historically, the company would need to buy enough computing power to meet the needs of the 90+ percent CPU usage, and the excess capacity would go on use of the majority of the day. If the company did not have the CPU power at the point where needed, batch processing would suffer and it would probably miss the batch window. Now consider if this same company were to scavenge the network for CPU power during the hours when it is experiencing or where is expecting to experience the peak batch load. It would be better be able to scale its CPU budget back to where its average load is, roughly just over 70 percent, and make use of the company's other free resources during off hours.

What happens if this picture does not set a goal of the day-to-day processing but of processing at month is end? What if this picture is only applicable for one week out of the month? Scaling an entire corporation's CPU usage and computing the budget for something that happens, at most, 25 percent of the time and allowing that CPU to go effectively unused for the other 75 percent of the time simply so that it does not run short during month end and close is overkill. Grid computing can increase the company's computing power while reducing its overall computing costs. Some companies have been able to cut their hardware purchases by nearly

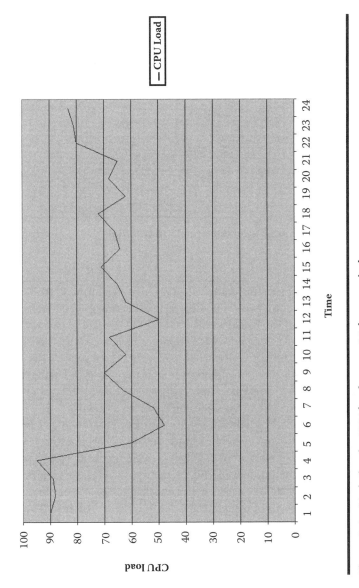

Figure 5.1   Variation in CPU load over a 24-hour period.

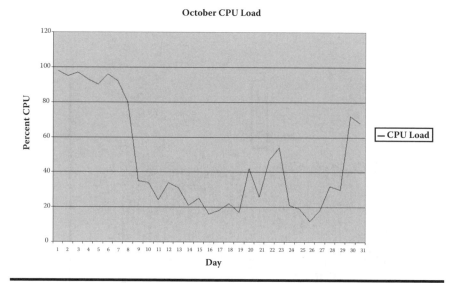

Figure 5.2 Variation in CPU load over a 31-day period.

90 percent by accessing existing computing power laying dormant. And the ability to distribute processing in a parallel processing architecture can cut costs by cutting the time it takes to perform calculations.

Purchasing computing power to have resources available for the times when the company has peaks in CPU usage is what is known as *peak provisioning*, meaning that the company is forced to buy enough computing power to handle its current biggest jobs, but with a little extra computing power in case the biggest jobs happen to grow. This is true even when these jobs only run occasionally.

In August of 2001, the National Science Foundation announced that, in the United States, its four computer centers would be linked together into one massive Grid-style virtualized computer. Then a distributed computing system was scheduled to go online in the summer of 2002. Scientists involved in that project said that the facility would help researchers better understand the origins of the Universe, help find cures for cancer, unlock secrets of the brain, and also help predict earthquakes and save lives.

A Grid environment is nothing more than several somewhat similar computers clustered loosely together. Internally, individual computers are connected through an ultra-fast network and share other devices such as disk drives, printers, storage systems, and memory with a controlling system that takes care of load balancing, and sharing in computing and other processing.

One major difference between supercomputers and a Grid environment is that a Grid is primarily built from a larger number of self-contained computers, often commodity systems or blade servers that have the ability at some level to work independently of the Grid.

Intel introduced a new chip set ideal for Grid servers and workstations in late 2002. The company started shipping the new Intel Xeon processors for two-way servers and workstations with speeds up to 2.8 GHz with 512-KB integrated cache (with support for faster), and a 533-MHz front-side bus to help speed the rate at which data can get to the processor. Intel also launched three additional new chip sets: (1) the E7501 chip set designed for two-way servers to help improve system performance and also to be used in embedded computing; (2) the E7505 chipset, formally named Placer, for two-ways; and (3) the Intel E7205 chipset formerly known as Granite, designed for single-processor, entry-level workstations and based on the Intel Pentium 4 processor.

The NCSA (National Center for Supercomputing Applications) is using Itanium®-based Linux servers to power its scientific computing system dubbed TeraGrid, allowing researchers to analyze, simulate, and help solve complex scientific problems. TeraGrid is a computing implementation that will serve as the underpinning for what has been called the world's first multi-site supercomputing system, the DTF (or distributed tera-scale facility). This system will perform 11.6 trillion calculations per second and store more than 450 trillion bytes of data via the comprehensive infrastructure of the tera grid, which will link computers' visualization systems and data at four sites through a 40-billion-bps optical network. This system will link more than 3300 Itanium processors and will have the ability to store, access, and share more than 450 TB of information. IBM Global Services will do the integration work for the system and will supply 1000 IBM E-servers running Linux. The cluster will use GPFS (general parallel file system).

While it is true that the Grid can be made up of inexpensive commodity-style hardware running Intel-based processors on commodity hardware, it is also true that mainframes and other large midrange systems are capable candidates to incorporate into a Grid system — saying that a mainframe cannot be part of Grid computing is like saying that everyone must drive a Ford in every NASCAR race. The Grid would not be the Grid without multiple computing platforms including the mainframe as part of the lineup, because Grid computing allows systems to take advantage of untapped resources across an enterprise and make them available where and when they are needed, thus eliminating the mainframe as a source of data and CPU resources would not be handling resources in an efficient manner. This especially makes sense in the data center. A data center typically has a mainframe and it should leverage what it has.

Because IBM is one of the companies at the frontier of the Grid and many business partners have also announced products aimed at delivering Grid computing capabilities to the Z series, specifically systems running on Linux. The mainframe appears to have been built for the grid. Virtualization is a key concept of the Grid and the series has inherent virtualization capabilities through the ZVM operating system virtualization allowing administrators to move workloads from one platform to another for better utilization and allow shops to manage spikes and lulls in demand. Blade servers allow for the addition of real engine hardware called capacity upgrade on demand if the customer needs additional hardware engine capacity on the Z series as these servers or external Linux Grids servers would communicate among themselves using an external TCP/IP network. The servers are actually operating as virtual Linux servers within the series mainframe hardware. The benefit of such hyper sockets is that they are faster media than an extra network because hyper sockets use the series memory bonus as media.

Blade Servers

One of the new technologies that will assist more companies in implementing a Grid environment is what is known as a *blade server*. Blade servers are narrow, hot swappable CPU units, several of which can fit into a single chassis that looks remarkably like a bookshelf. The resulting effect is similar to a library where one has several of these racks, each with several blade servers attached and each blade being an independent server with its own processors, its own memory storage network controllers, operating systems, and copies of applications. The servers simply slide into the bay and plug into the backplane. The backplane and chassis bring to the system shared power supplies, fans, floppy drives and CD drives, switches, and ports.

Because the blades share switches and power units, precious space is freed up and the blades are able to be placed with a far higher density within the cabinets with far more ease than has been possible historically. Moreover, because they will plug into a common backplane, one does not have the issues associated with stringing hundreds of cables through and around the racks. The two varieties are (1) server blades and (2) option blades.

A server blade is an independent server, containing one or more processors and associated memory, disk storage, and network controllers. It runs its own copy of both the operating system and applications.

Option blades may be shareable by several server blades. They provide those server blades with additional features such as controllers for external I/O or disk arrays, and additional power supplies. Option blades are mounted inside the chassis of the shared infrastructure features. Historically, these would have been externally attached to server arrays. By installing option modules containing gigabit Ethernet switches, KVM (keyboard, video, and mouse) switches, or Fibre Channel switches, one can save sidewall space in the racks. Because blades are powered by the chassis, the usual cascade of cabling used to connect each server to a power source is not required, thereby saving sidewall space and money.

Other types of option modules can contain systems management controllers, power supplies, advanced cooling systems, and additional redundancy and efficiency components.

Blade servers are highly efficient solutions for not only the Grid, but also for adding scalability capacity in any data center. Most blade server chassis use capacity added directly into a standard rack. These racks can be reused for blade servers as traditional server components are phased out. This means that blades can coexist alongside the existing traditional rack servers, and there is no need for special rack investments just to add the scalability of blade server chassis.

The addition of blade servers to a potential Grid environment allows for flexibility, scalability, and freedom from the limitations of the type of processor. With processors becoming increasingly faster, and thereby hotter, the ability to add extra fan units by simply plugging in an option server makes that server even more flexible.

Because they are hot swappable, if one server should fail, causing processing to be distributed over the other servers in the grid, the failed server can be swapped out simply by dismounting that one from the blade rack and snapping another into its place.

Blade servers will realize cost savings for the organization, partly because the purchase prices of individual servers may be lowered as a result of the reduction in duplication of components, the reduction of the need for KVM and cabling, and the sheer number of KVM switches that will be needed. Because fewer racks are needed to house the Morgan servers, savings will be realized on the cost of rack systems. And one of the greatest overall cost saving is the decreased cost associated with hundreds or thousands of cables. Furthermore, one will save on installation costs, and the cost of assembling. You'll also reduce the footprint and floor space required. Due to the increased density of blade servers, one might need only half the floor space required for traditional rack-optimized servers. That means fewer components to fail or replace in case of failure, and a reduction in the number of points of potential failure and the ultimate cost of servicing the server.

Blade servers eliminate the need to purchase excess processors up front to provide for expansion. They enable a company to right-size purchases and buy exactly what is needed today for the Grid system and as computing needs expand. This will allow one to spread the cost of capital expenditures over time.

Many companies today provide blade servers, including IBM, Sun, and HP. Even Apple has entered the blade server arena. Many companies that are starting to provide Grid solutions to companies (Sun and IBM) are providing blade servers as part of the total solution package.

Storage

Because to a great extent the Grid implies separating storage from memory from I/O, another component that should be addressed is storage. Because of the component nature of blade servers, people often make the choice to put an operating system on the blades only for emergency purposes or simply use diskless blades. With diskless blades, one simply points to a blade at the logical unit number (LUN) on an array, and that blade assumes the personality of the OS on that disk array. The operating system boots off the array and picks up the applications and personality of that array and of the application. This is also true for regular servers.

Current storage architecture needs to evolve and adapt to virtualization. Storage virtualization allows for separation of the on-disk physical storage from the logical view of that storage. The server's physical storage could reside anywhere within the company's storage network and could come from any vendor. While the virtualization layer would provide a logical view of all storage connected to it, individual storage systems would no longer remain separate but would rather be pulled into a single reservoir. This allows the description of storage needs in terms of simple capacity, response, time, cost, and backup frequency and also allows administrators to make best use of resources by dispersing that storage capacity only when it is needed. One would no longer have to worry about where a resource is located — only what that resource is called, be it a file or information, or a database.

When one considers the fact that with a Grid, data ordinarily is moved between servers over Ethernet, the date is taken off the disk, sent to the server, then off to another server or several other servers, and back to yet another disk array. It would be more efficient if a storage area network (SAN) could self-provision itself, creating a zone of specific Grid application for a specific time.

Storage virtualization is not a new concept; it has been around for decades on the mainframe (back when IBM transitioned its mainframes from System/360 to System/370 in the late 1960s), and nearly every storage vendor claims to have the ability to offer virtualization across at least some of its products. Virtualization creates a single view of multiple storage devices, and can simplify and thus lower the cost of storage management. Moreover, it can reduce the number of new arrays the company needs by combining the data from multiple servers for applications into a single shared pool of storage. This provides an alternative to buying more storage for one overtaxed server while huge amounts of disk space sit empty on servers beside it. However, because of the proprietary nature of the way much of the storage virtualization is created, it is important to remember that in many cases, a vendor's virtualization offerings work only — or at least, best — on that company's hardware. Most organizations own storage hardware from many vendors, and that storage is accessed by hardware servers from many other vendors. Some virtualization works only at the file level with the storage and retrieval of information as files, while other server virtualization works best at the level of blocks, the smallest form in which data can be stored and retrieved. It is important to remember that virtualization should not be seen as a product feature on its own, but rather as an enabling technology that will allow users, system administrators, and programmers alike to solve business problems.

Because of the heterogeneous nature of the Grid and of Grid computing, companies will likely want the flexibility that will allow them to move data among servers running different operating systems. These companies will likely opt for fabric-based virtualization, in which the intelligence needed to reformat data will be built into switches linking the storage devices.

Furthermore, fabric-based virtualization (or fabric-based intelligence) is not limited simply to the management of applications and allowing them to find a new home, but it also provides different types of administrators with their own views of data and varying levels and different views of storage infrastructure. Database administrators can view and manage the logical structure of the database and its data constructs on the same system that storage administrators view and manage the underlying resources, all through the same portal.

It also may become apparent that storage systems will need to become truly "open" equipment, much the same way that Linux is an open operating system. These open hardware systems will be available from multiple vendors and not only sit side by side but interoperate internally with one another. There will have to be server and software compatibility, as well as the ability of different server storage arrays to share information with centralized management functions. Administrators have been unable to integrate networks into a true heterogeneous patchwork of technology, partly because storage devices have been unable to share their information with one another. The result was an isolated data island.

Imagine that a supermarket chain kept its different departments in different stores in different parts of town. If one wanted bread, one would go to the southeast store. If one wanted dairy, one would go to the northeast store. The ability to centralize components becomes paramount in allowing heterogeneous servers to access required data equally as heterogeneous storage devices.

Storage virtualization is not really anything new with the Grid. It has been done for decades on mainframes. Nearly every storage vendor claims that it is offering virtualization across its products. By creating a single unified view of multiple storage devices, virtualization can simplify, and lower the cost of storage. Administrators just have to remember to check and double-check that the interoperability is supported on whatever product is ultimately chosen.

The Grid is a highly I/O-intensive system typically with large demands, such as satellite data processing, data warehousing, and data mining. The fact that such systems are increasingly relying on scalable computing architecture for their requirements means that it is critical that a wide range of scalable computer architectures form a cluster of workstations to provide sufficient support for these I/O-intensive applications.

I/O Subsystems

The required communication among different processors has traditionally created a bottleneck for the applications that are distributed across a network. In considering how distributed the Grid system could become, this bottleneck might become a preventative feature. With scalable computers and CPU sources becoming more available and less expensive, it may well be that in the very near future, the I/O subsystem will become the bottleneck in the equation.

Because of the continuing improvement in high-speed interconnects such as asynchronous transfer tode (ATM), Fibre Channel, and other high-speed technologies, these preventative bottlenecks will become less of an issue.

Underlying Network

Intelligent switches utilize externally defined policies to help decide when and how to establish connections between a server, a storage array, and other networking resources as they are required by each application. The switches shuffle application images from the storage array to servers and then link each server with the necessary amount of storage and network bandwidth. By automating the processes involved with resource connection, these switches can help remove many of the more tedious aspects of application provisioning.

It has historically been the case that database vendors have tried often to work closely with the switch vendors to help them to bring their expertise to the table to help form scalable database clusters across the network.

Operating Systems

Information on the operating systems combinations is available at http://www.cactuscode.org/Documentation/Architectures.html. While different compilers are suggested as being supported, the number of operating systems, compilers, and hardware platforms that are actually supportable is nearly endless. In keeping with the ideals of open systems and open sources, many Grids are operating on versions of the Linux operating system with Globus middleware.

Visualization Environments

Modern visual environments can allow more than simply viewing static data. It can allow for the dynamic and flexible user controls that are becoming a reality in several areas. Text-based interfaces and lists of data are quickly fading, forced into history by the requirements of the science, research, and business communities. There are different needs to see different data at different levels by different sets of users, and virtualization is an attempt to meet these varied needs.

Scientific visualization has had a tremendous impact on how science has been practiced over recent years, concentrating and making the best use of the human power of visual perception in working toward the identification of patterns found in complex data. Research focuses on finding ways to improve science education.

These environments will continue to be accessed by many of the high-capacity Grid environments to take advantage of the underlying computing power and provide a deeper and richer environment in which these experiences can be realized.

People

People can easily fall into the category of Grid hardware. Scientists, engineers, researchers, computer programmers, teachers, business leaders, subject matter experts, and people from many different parts of society are all working together and in parallel toward defining the Grid, its potential infrastructure, and its emerging standards. The interdisciplinary approach is extremely beneficial because with cross-cultural input, it will become something that everyone can take advantage of and more readily accept the changes it brings. If we look at how the Internet has impacted the lives of kindergarten students, grandparents, researchers, and game players, and we consider that the Grid is viewed by some as the next great leap in computing, the Grid will lead to tremendous leaps in research outcomes and provide new ways of working and planning in the coming decades.

Chapter 6

Metadata

I find that a great part of the information I have was acquired by looking up something and finding something else on the way.

—Franklin P. Adams (1881–1960)

I'm not dumb. I just have a command of thoroughly useless information.

—Calvin, of Calvin and Hobbes

If one looks at the Grid as a loosely coupled set of interfaces (both for humans and for applications), application logic, and resources (databases, devices, computational resources, remote instrumentation, and human capital and human knowledge), metadata can be thought of as the glue that holds them all together. The glue is easier to apply if all the pieces are resident inside the organization; but if some of them are located outside the control structure, additional information is needed for the glue to do its work.

Defining Metadata

Metadata is what is commonly known as data or information about the data. But this information is intended not necessarily for human use, but rather for use primarily by machines. Metadata can be used by search engines, and can give one a place to record what a document is for and about.

Typically, metadata is considered when talking about data warehouses and provides information relevant to the data as it is used in the industry in question. If one follows through with the insurance industry, metadata about claim numbers might include any idiosyncrasies connected with the assignment of numbers to claims based on claim type, the region of the country, the claimant, and the number of claims reported by a particular claimant, and all of these pieces of information would constitute data about the data.

A metadata service can provide the means for publishing, replicating, and accessing the metadata.

The Grid, by definition, is computationally and data intensive; therefore, metadata is absolutely necessary not only for the management of the data, but also for the management of the Grid itself. Metadata at the Grid environment level, unlike metadata at either the database or data warehouse level — where it is simply information about information — can take on many forms and many types.

Some of the important pieces of information connected with the Grid include:

- Computational resources, including computers and storage devices
- Data including databases, plain files, semi-structured documents, and unstructured data sources
- Tools and algorithms to extract, filter, mine, and manipulate data
- Knowledge that has been obtained as a result of computing processes (e.g., learned models or patterns).

Large sets of resources often require complex descriptions. Metadata should document the features of the application, allow for the effective search of existing resources, provide an efficient way to access these resources, be used by assisting software tools that support the user in building computation, and be easily accessible and updated.

There will no doubt evolve highly specialized Grid services for the collection and utilization of these different types of metadata. There are, and will continue to be, mechanisms for storing and accessing the metadata. These mechanisms allow for querying the metadata constructs based on attributes.

Scientists and business types alike strive to record information about the creation and transformation as well as the meaning of the data and also demand the ability to query the data in the metadata repository based on these and other attributes. Historically, many methods have been used, including descriptive directory names and filenames that carry information embedded within the naming conventions as well as notebooks and note cards. These diverse methods neither scale well to systems containing terabytes or petabytes of data nor do they necessarily work well together or have applications in heterogeneous environments. What is critical to this environment will be the extensible, reliable high-performance services that will be able to support the registration of enquiry of metadata information.

In a data warehouse environment or in any relational database system, the metadata can reside in the target database but would typically reside in a special metadata repository. This repository could be in a database of its own, or in a particular schema within the target database, separated from the data that it explains but relatively easily accessible to those who need to have such access. For programmers, metadata can explain much about the data that would assist them in better programming based on the data, the meaning of the data, and the business rules that the data portrays.

The metadata in a Grid environment will need to not only encompass the data about the meaning of the data stored within the Grid, but also information about the size of files, access permissions, and location of the files logically within the grid environment.

If one really considers what kind of information needs to be accessible and distributed across a Grid environment, one will see an awe-inspiring amount of data that needs to be corralled, stored, and distributed between and about the different Grid components. Along with data about the data, there also is information about work units and results (result sets from the work units and information about the processing and processes that took place in the work units) returning from the jobs.

Naturally, there is the typical metadata about the data, and also information about the activities and about jobs, tasks, and projects — in fact, about any and every piece of work and its associated data as it navigates through the Grid environment. For the Grid resources, there are catalogs, tables designed for looking up and determining the least taxed and most taxed resources in the Grid, and the location of resources that may be available. There should be information about the location of the pieces of information resident on any or all the servers available to the Grid.

All this information should be stored either directly with the objects being distributed (in the form of intelligent filenames or other keys directly associated with the physical data) within and throughout the Grid, or external to the information, independently in files or databases available to any and all nodes during the execution of the system. There also should be a mechanism for controlling the flow of information into and out of the metadata repository and further mechanisms to make that information reliably available to any requester or updater who needs it.

A lot of background information should be stored and distributed around a Grid. The reason one needs this information is that all the machines within the Grid need to know what they are involved in, whom they need to contact for different information, and whom to notify when something goes wrong. In short, there should be a centralized and distributed configuration repository.

Distributors need to know where to find providers; providers need to have information about any distributor and both entities need to have a place to go to get their information for processing their respective jobs.

At the distributor end of the process, one must have a basis on which to make decisions. These decisions should be made based on available space, CPU load on a given resource, and which storage node and storage device are available to provide or accept information from the proposed processes.

Servers that do not, or for some reason cannot, report on CPU load are either assumed unavailable or severely overtaxed and marked as such. This information is also stored for both active retrieval for deciding what resources to use, and as historic information to determine the reliability and predict the availability of any given resource going forward.

Looking at storage devices, their available storage is as important a piece of information as their current load status. If little or no storage capacity is available on a given device, it will not be practical to route an update or insertion task to that device; however, a retrieval job would be more than applicable on that resource.

What kind of information, in total, one captures and utilizes depends on the kind of Grid environment one is creating. A scavenging Grid needs different kinds of data than a data Grid does, for example.

For a computational Grid, one needs to store and access computational and parametric data that needs to be exchanged internally. A resource Grid will need application-based information, information about what applications are available, running and have run and the inputs, outputs, and jobs that have completed or are scheduled. Regardless of what kind of Grid one creates, one needs to store information about each unit of work history, the history about each node and component in the Grid, each and every source and destination, locations, and response times so that the organism can learn from history and be able to funnel jobs to where they are most likely to finish efficiently.

The negotiation among the different components will be critical to the ultimate success of any Grid system. If one component cannot describe what it is looking for, it cannot have it. If an application does not "know" what it needs to do its processing, nothing will achieve the application.

If a resource cannot describe what it has to offer, no one is going to be interested in using it. The CPU cycle provider needs to be able to tell the other Grid components that it has cycles at 2.8 GHz available for use for the time period starting at 7 p.m. If it cannot make its product known, it will not matter who needs it, as no user will know where to look or how to get there.

If a resource or a process or service cannot make its wants and needs known, it will never be able to get what it wants for the price it is willing to pay.

Information that would likely be necessary, regardless of the environment, would include the following:

- *Submitter data.* This is information about the user submitting the task or the job. This information might include, but is not be limited to, name, e-mail address, physical location, billing location, phone number, etc.
- *Priority data.* It might be important in your environment to store different users within the Grid with the ability to schedule their jobs and tasks at different priority levels.

■ *Date and time information.* Historically and for use in tuning and determining optimization features, it is useful to have a searchable record of when a given job was submitted, as well as the time taken to process the job and other timing information that can be attached to individual jobs, tasks, and projects.

■ *Transformation information.* Information coming back from processing will either need to return in the same format that it was sent, or be stored in a different format; the transformation information will need to be stored if it is relevant to processing. Further, if there is a need for a transformation due to heterogeneity in the database management systems, this information also should be stored in the repository. All of this information should be either pre-processed and sent to the providers for further processing or recovered from the providers and then placed into a result queue for post-processing before sending back to the requesting application.

■ *Central catalog (or metadata repository).* An index or catalog can be stored on a distributor server or a Grid data server. The index holds information about where data in the Grid system has been stored. The organization of this information depends on the type of data one is storing and the level of heterogeneity and distribution existent in the stored data. It is critical to find a balance, even a tenuous balance, between the storage of information for processing purposes and the data that one stores simply for cataloging purposes. If one stores enough information in the metadata repository, then one is defeating the purpose of distributing the data itself, and loses many of the advantages that a Grid database environment can provide.

The metadata required in a Grid environment can be broken down into three general types, as seen in Figure 6.1 and described as follows.

Grid Metadata

One of the basic pieces of machinery required for the management of information contained in and concerning the Grid is about the Grid itself. This includes information about the file instances the contents of the file instances and the various storage systems of the Grid. Grid metadata is data that deals directly with aspects of the Grid and the structure itself — the structure, the purpose, the components and resources connected to the Grid, and all the specifics of those pieces. Is this computer running Linux, Windows, or Z/OS? Does it have four processors or does it have six? Is that CPU available for processing access now?

While Grid metadata is not often thought of as important to processing, it is a vital part of the Grid system. It can be a determinant in finding proper protocols,

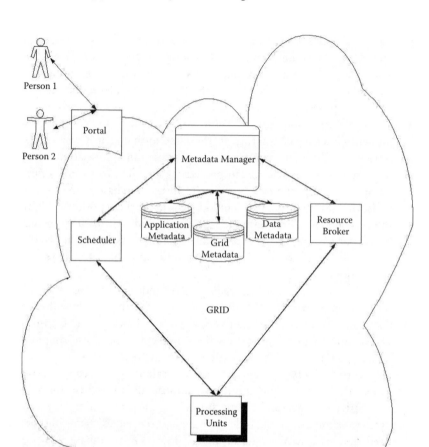

Figure 6.1   Metadata in a Grid environment.

formatting queries, and providing quicker, more elegant access to information and resources than might otherwise be possible.

Data Metadata

To a large extent, data metadata is what people typically think of as metadata. It is the data about the data. Data metadata can be further broken down into its own subcomponents of physical metadata, domain-independent metadata, domain-specific metadata, and user metadata.

Physical Metadata

Physical metadata encompasses the particulars about the storage of a file or about the data elements saved in a database. Attributes about files and database relations and attributes can encompass parameters such as file sizes, file locations, alteration dates, creation dates, and analysis dates, or the particulars about the storage of the given data.

Furthermore, physical metadata will need to include enough information about the data and its format and location to alter any processing, should it be needed to allow for retrieving the information from a heterogeneous environment. The structure of an Oracle query can differ somewhat from a query against DB2 or MySQL or Informix or SQL Server. The types of processing and joins can be different, as can the form that the data elements take within each environment. For this reason, the data elements' metadata needs to include what form they are in (varchar, character, numeric, or other format), the size of the data element, and in what kind of environment that data element can be found. To be truly fluid and flexible, this can also include the information that might be needed to construct the different types of queries in each environment. Moreover, there needs to be sufficient information to make the original transformation to access the required data and provide enough information to re-transform the data back into a consolidated response set to the calling program or calling user.

Domain-Independent Metadata

Domain-independent metadata includes the logical name of the file that maps to the physical names of the files. It deals with the structure and the physical characteristics of the item to be accessed. Document type definitions would be included in category at the data metadata level. Is the object in question a flat text file, an image, a sound clip, or a movie? Is the text document a .doc file, a .txt file, or a .log file?

Content-Dependent Metadata

Content-dependent metadata deals directly with the information about the information. Content-dependent information about data will include attributes such as color, size, and species. Resource information would include file system capacity, CPU speed, and telescope magnification or coordinates.

Content-Independent Metadata

Content-independent metadata will include information such as the creation date of a piece of information or file, last update ID, the type of sensor involved, or the location of the resource or information.

Domain-Specific Metadata

Domain-specific information would include concept descriptions sourced from the ontology data. Oracle and DB2 are relational database management systems, while flat files are not accessible via the same mechanisms and IMS is a hierarchical database management system. A Pentium 4 2.8 MHz PC is a potential CPU source; an electron microscope is a remote data source.

Ontology

Ontology can be considered the specification of relations that exist for an object, resource, or agent, or a community of these things. Pure logic and therefore computational logic are ontologically neutral; that is, they make no assumptions about what might exist or might not exist in any domain. One must deliberately place information about what might or might not exist in a given Grid domain into the repository; otherwise, it is not likely to be found.

At the ontology layer, metadata deals with general classifications of objects. Classification of data will be data- and topic-specific. Classifications of plants and animals would be far different from classifications of accident types or different drug interactions.

Ontological information dealing with the Grid itself would look at the types of resources or devices available to the Grid. Oracle, DB2, or MySQL databases; CPU sources; remote microscopes; telescopes or other data-collecting devices; and storage farms or other resources would be included in the metadata collected at this level.

User Metadata

User metadata includes user-provided annotations to the information about the information, ways the user uses the information, the way the information relates to other information, and the significance that is attached to those pieces of information.

Application Metadata

Applications can be viewed as being composed of application components. These components, along with their input and output files (and remember that "file" refers to any kind of information that the applications work on, files or database information) as identified by their logical names to the users and their physical names to the system as well as the order of execution in the system. These processes and their components are mapped to the appropriate grid resources for processing.

This means that the application metadata needs to include the components that each application can be broken into, as well as the input and output datasets and applicable resources on which each component can run. User permissions that can run each application can be carried in this location as well as the resources that the applications cannot utilize.

External Metadata

If portions of the Grid (components, resources) are located outside the organizational boundaries (outside the control of the organization), then extra metadata will be required. Additional relationships must be defined and determined, particularly one is connecting disparate items, and one has only indirect control over one's portion of those items.

Location information must be maintained for the resources located within the organization, and provide extended location information for the information located outside the organization. IP addresses for servers, access paths for the components, physical location of human resources in the world, and access paths (phone number, address, e-mail address) must be maintained.

Lifetime information for the data, for the accessibility of the resources (CPU resources and remote instrumentation resources) and for the URLs of the portals and the availability of those portals can be classified in this manner.

Access permissions and ownership information and privileges for others to access resources, must be maintained in the system. This will allow to access one's own portion of the Grid and to access someone else's portion of the Grid, and will assist in maintaining the security of the Grid environment.

Logical Metadata

Logical metadata is information about how a data item was created or modified, who modified it, when it was modified and the location of the modification, what resource created the data item, or the analysis software that operated on that piece of information.

User

A user is indeed part of the metadata chain. The user is the one who uses the data or the resources upon which the metadata is predicated, the one who ultimately creates the data and therefore the metadata, and the one who is most concerned with the correctness of the metadata.

Users bring their own conceptions or misconceptions to the system, regardless of what that system is. The only difference between a typical system and a Grid environment is the complexity of what is going on behind the scenes and often the interface through which the user interacts with the system.

Users must be taken into account in the Grid system. From their defined security to their implicit understanding of the underlying data and its meaning, certain data can be connected directly to the user using the Grid.

Data

While data is not usually considered as metadata about itself, it can contain relevant information to assist in the determination of its internal meaning and importance.

Resources

Finally, the lowest granularity comprises the resources involved in storing, creating, transporting, or analyzing the data.

Metadata Services

Metadata services provide a means to assist with the aggregate sum of metadata mappings into collections and also allow for the association of aggregation attributes with logical name attributes and storage related to the province of the information, such as creation transformation. These services should provide both good performance and extreme scalability.

It may be more accurate to think of metadata as the "big-picture" way of thinking about an information system object. It is the sum total of all the things that one can say about any information object. This total picture is true at any level of aggregation. It is typically considered that an object is any single or aggregate item that can be addressed or manipulated by a system, human, or any other discrete entity. It reflects context, content, and structure.

Context

Context refers to the who, what, where, when, why, and how of the information about the information. It is extrinsic to the information object.

Content

Content refers to what the object contains. It is the intrinsic information about an information object.

Structure

Structure is a formal set of associations within or among individual information objects. Structure can be either intrinsic or extrinsic to the information object.

While it is possible to store this information anywhere in the Grid environment and in nearly any format, it is also practical to store it in such a manner that it is easily updated as well as in a format that is accessible to any component that is likely to want access to it within the heterogeneous environment. It can be stored in a database such as Gadfly, MySQL, Oracle, DB2, or SQL server, either as typical data, or in XML stored in the database, or in flat files (ASCII text or XML).

However it is stored, decisions must be made when making that definition.

Defining Data Granularity

The more granular the data becomes, the better one must define the metadata. Ironically, the most important pieces of the Grid are typically some of the lowest on the radar of most businesses and are perceived to be of little value.

XML

Management of the extremely diverse nature of Grid components with metadata providing the information about the features of the resources and facilitating their effective use is critical. A user needs to know what resources are available, where these resources can be found, how these resources can be accessed, and when they will become available. Metadata will be able to provide easy answers to these questions and will therefore represent one key element to effective resource discovery and utilization.

And because of the heterogeneous nature of the Grid, one of the most promising media with which to manage the metadata appears to be XML (eXtensible markup language). XML is a simple, flexible text format derived from SGML (standard general markup language), and was originally designed by a committee of the World Wide Web Consortium in response to a need for a more generalized form of HTML. Where HTML was designed as a presentation language, XML was designed as a means to add consistent structure and to meet the challenges of large-scale electronic publishing. It is, however, also playing an increasingly important role in the platform-independent exchange of a wide variety of data via the Web and elsewhere. It has been enthusiastically embraced in many applications because many applications need to store data that is intended for human use but in a format that will be useful for the manipulation by machine. Ironically, when looking at XML as a metadata storage platform, it has even been referred to as a *meta-language*, or a language that is used to define other languages, and has in fact been used to define other languages such as WML (wireless markup language).

With XML one can define data structures and make these structures platform independent. One can process defined data automatically and quickly, and easily define one's own data types and tags. What one cannot do is define how one's data is shown; however, XML does provide an easy format that will allow parsers to more elegantly show the data.

While one can often do the same thing in XML that one can in HTML, HTML tells *how* the data should appear on a page, and XML tells *what* the data means. Basically, XML, provides metadata about whatever it contains.

The Grid can be designed as having a set of rules governing the contained components. Although all the components in the Grid have some resemblance to each other and some attributes that are common, they are all different in detail: different operating systems, different CPU speeds, different physical locations. Their commonalities include:

- Applications
- Rules (accounting rules, security rules, and usage rules)
- Implementation of primary processes

In HTML:

```
<p>Sony Vaio Laptop
<br>Best Buy
<br>$1438
```

In XML:

```
<product>
<model>Sony Vaio Laptop</model>
<dealer>Best Buy</dealer>
<price>$1438</price>
</product>
```

XML has the following characteristics:

- Provides a way to define infrastructure-independent representations of information
- Allows users to define data structures

- Allows the use of powerful query languages but does not require them
- Easily maps into data structures of object-oriented programming languages
- Is a simple way to start and is easily adaptable and extensible into relational databases.

Database

Traditionally, metadata, particularly metadata about data within or accessed through a database, has been stored in a database. While this also has historically meant that the data is stored in a flat text manner, it does not have to remain so. It is not only possible, but also it can be highly efficient to store data in XML in a database.

Access

In looking again at Figure 6.1, one can see where a client's queries access the metadata service manager with a list of attributes sought. That metadata service manager returns to the user (or the user process) a list of the logical names from the metadata repository addressing the location of the data to be used in the processes, retrieving the physical name of the data files and the logical names that the user understands. Using this information, the user process knows where to look for the data that is needed to complete its processing.

The user query also accesses the metadata repository to determine where to look for available and applicable resources on which to run the processes that the user seeks to run. This information is routed back to the job scheduler and the resource manager to adequately route the processing to the correct resources.

The application metadata is queried to determine what processes will be required for the user process to complete. The security requirements are examined to determine whether the user requesting the application has the authority to run the application, whether the application has adequate access to the data, and whether each of the pieces has adequate access to all the resources required for the processing.

Once the processing is completed, information is sent back to the metadata repository dealing with timing metrics, performance metrics, updates to the analysis, and update/insert/delete information associated with the data.

Metadata Formatting

We have an idea of what constitutes metadata, but what format should Grid metadata take? What does it take to make it work? It will take a standard syntax so that the metadata can be recognized as such and can be accessed by anything entering the Grid without the need for extended application programming to facilitate the access. It will mean using a standardized vocabulary to store the information in a central (but, again, distributed) location so that any resource or any service can access the information.

The representation and exploitation of centralized, standardized knowledge have always been primary challenges of *artificial intelligence* (AI), and at its heart, a well-designed Grid system has many of the features of a good AI system. If the Grid can store data, and make inferences based on the historic data to make determinations on what to do in the future, then it can be almost considered learning. A system that can learn from its history will be able to make better decisions about what to run where and when, and how to partition itself to make the overall product a more valuable system. Designing and conceptualizing is easy, but getting those concepts and designs to function and really work in the real world has always been a problem.

Ultimately, what needs to occur is the discovery of a new resource joining the system, and the registration of that resource with all of its idiosyncrasies and features within the metadata system.

The wonderful things about standards is that there are so many from which to choose. One of the most common options is to store the metadata in XML documents, either independently or within a database.

XML

What is XML?

XML is the acronym for eXtensible markup language. It is much like HTML in that it has standard formatting and has tags that make it look a lot like HTML. But XML is not a markup language; it is designed to be used to describe data, making it a prime choice for metadata storage and management. XML tags, unlike HTML, are not predefined, but allow for defining one's own tags (making it a prime choice for something as fluid and flexible as the Grid). XML uses a document type definition (DTD) or an XML schema to describe the data (either choice allowing the metadata to be self-descriptive).

While XML has found much more popularity in recent years, it has been around for several years. It has become increasingly popular as a medium for storing data for Web pages, separating the data layer there from the presentation layer, allowing for increased flexibility in coding, allowing for coding a page once, and changing the data for that page any number of times, adding to and taking away, without having to recode the page.

The primary difference between HTML and XML is that XML was designed to carry data and HTML was designed as a presentation media for data, including data that is located in an XML document. XML is not a replacement for HTML as each was designed with different goals in mind. XML is concerned with what the data is (describing the data), and HTML is concerned with how the data looks (that is, displaying the information).

It is difficult for some to get their hands on the fact that XML was not really designed to *do* anything; it structures, stores, and sends information. For example, take a look at Table 6.1 and see what might be presented in XML for Grid components.

Table 6.1   Grid Components Definitions in XML

```
<?xml version="1.0" encoding="UTF-8" ?>
 <dataroot xmlns:od="urn:schemas-microsoft-com:officedata"
xmlns:xsi="http://www.w3.org/2001/XMLSchema-instance"
xsi:noNamespaceSchemaLocation="component.xsd"
generated="2004-03-13T06:51:04">
 <component>
  <name>hagrid</name>
  <address>123.45.678</address>
  <type>Linux</type>
  <gridinfo>accounting</gridinfo>
  <communication_type>push</communication_type>
  <operation_mode>provider</operation_mode>
  <putmethod>file</putmethod>
  <getmethod>file</getmethod>
  </component>
<component>
  <name>wilbur</name>
  <address>234.56.789</address>
  <type>Windows</type>
  <gridinfo>HR</gridinfo>
  <communication_type>push</communication_type>
  <operation_mode>provider</operation_mode>
  <putmethod>file</putmethod>
  <getmethod>file</getmethod>
  </component>
<component>
  <name>kenny</name>
  <address>393.49.234</address>
  <type>UNIX</type>
  <gridinfo>reporting</gridinfo>
  <communication_type>push</communication_type>
  <operation_mode>provider</operation_mode>
  <putmethod>file</putmethod>
  <getmethod>file</getmethod>
  </component>
<component>
  <name>johnny5</name>
  <address>678.91.02</address>
  <type>linux</type>
  <gridinfo>purchasing</gridinfo>
  <communication_type>push</communication_type>
  <operation_mode>provider</operation_mode>
  <putmethod>file</putmethod>
  <getmethod>file</getmethod>
  </component>
  </dataroot>
```

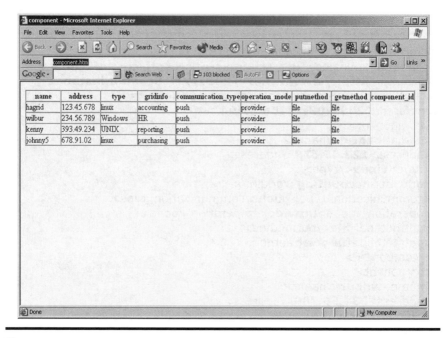

Figure 6.2

Figure 6.2 shows how this information defined in Table 6.1 might appear in a Web page. This means that the information on the servers in that document can be monitored (based on addition information maintained in the XML document, such as load or availability) from anywhere that the administrator has access to a browser.

In keeping with the ideals of the Grid, XML is both free and extensible, making it a highly flexible medium for storing and accessing Grid metadata. While many other ways use predefined structures, and the authors and those accessing those documents can work only within the predefined structures, XML does not have these limitations. The tags in XML are not standard and are, in fact, invented by the authors of the documents. The metadata for one Grid can be stored in the same kind of format as the metadata for another, and still be as customized as the implementation requires.

XML can store its information in either flat files, as is most common today, or in databases (growing in popularity because of added capability and flexibility). But storing the data in a database can add access complexities that might make it prohibitive for a Grid environment. To keep the environment as simple, open, and accessible as possible, it is typically still the case that the XML files are stored as flat files in secure areas of the Grid that allow for interface interaction with the data, but not deliberate human tampering.

Table 6.2   XML Definitions of Grid Databases

```
<?xml version="1.0" encoding="UTF-8" ?>
- <dataroot xmlns:od="urn:schemas-microsoft-com:officedata"
xmlns:xsi="http://www.w3.org/2001/XMLSchema-instance"
xsi:noNamespaceSchemaLocation="database.xsd"
generated="2004-05-07T04:01:53">
- <database>
  <database_type>Oracle</database_type>
  <database_version>9</database_version>
  <database_location>Bill's server</database_location>
  <formatting_information>Oracle docs</formatting_information>
  <owner>HR</owner>
  </database>
- <database>
  <database_type>Oracle</database_type>
  <database_version>10</database_version>
  <database_location>johnny5</database_location>
  <formatting_information>Oracle docs</formatting_information>
  <owner>Stephanie</owner>
  </database>
- <database>
  <database_type>DB2</database_type>
  <database_version>8</database_version>
  <database_location>Bill's ZOS</database_location>
  <formatting_information>DB2 docs</formatting_information>
  <owner>systems</owner>
  </database>
- <database>
  <database_type>MySql</database_type>
  <database_version>2</database_version>
  <database_location>webserver</database_location>
  <formatting_information>MySQL docs</formatting_information>
  <owner>web systems</owner>
  </database>
  </dataroot>
```

The definition and location of different brands and versions of databases can be stored in an XML file, (see Table 6.2 and Figure 6.3) allowing the Grid to make decisions based on the type of database involved in a query. Because databases have different features and different idiosyncrasies in their access methods, this kind of document can be extremely useful to the Grid in allowing it to make the correct decisions on how to format queries and how best to reformat the outputs.

XML, while extremely popular as a Web design tool, is also a very uniform and easily readable form. In the real worlds of business, science and academia, computer

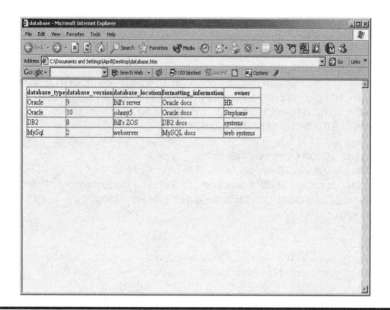

Figure 6.3

systems and databases contain data and are very useful for their owners. However, this data is usually stored in formats that may be incompatible from one company to the next. One of the most time-consuming functions for developers has historically been to find a means to exchange data between heterogeneous systems in an efficient and elegant manner. Often, this data is then exchanged either over a dedicated network link or, more often, over the Internet or an extranet link. Converting that data to XML (with tools readily available in whatever platform one can find) can reduce the complexity and create data that can be both read by different applications, and accessible and readable on whatever platform the sender and receiver find themselves using.

XML is becoming the language and means of choice for exchanging information (including financial information) between businesses over the Internet. Because, in effect, XML is plain text format, with tags added for extensibility, it provides hardware- and software-independent ways of sharing data. It is much easier to create data that nearly any application can work with, from Oracle to Access, from Internet Explorer to Netscape, from a single UNIX server to another server across the Grid.

Application

Storing metadata in an XML document allows languages that are specifically built to manipulate the data to access and update the information. Because of the nature (platform independence, extensibility, and accessibility) of XML, specialized tools do not necessarily need to be created to work with the documents. Generic metadata services can work on the documents, propagation tools for Grid and peer-to-peer can manipulate the documents for which they have manipulation permissions, and generic metadata registries can be created to allow for extensibility of the document by others for their own use.

Many of today's large databases have the added features of being able to store, access, and manipulate XML data within the DBMS (database management system) itself.

MCAT

It is often advantageous to find a solution to a metadata situation that does not depend on any given RDBMS (relational database management system) platform. This will remove the necessity for relying on knowing the specific access method to get to the data in the repository.

MCAT is a meta-information catalog system that has been implemented at the San Diego Super Computer Center (SDSC) as a critical part of the Data Intensive Computing Environment (DICE) project that is building a national digital library repository to help to facilitate the publication of scientific data. MCAT has requirements that are based mainly on the SDSC's storage resource broker (SRB) system (a middleware system that provides a unified interface for connecting users to heterogeneous data sources over a network, and allowing them to simply and elegantly access replicated datasets based on their attributes or on their logical names as opposed to accessing them via their literal names or physical locations).

Remember that metadata is defined as data about data. MCAT has determined that meta-information can be loosely defined as data about the entities in a system. There are four different types of elements of interest in a (DICE):

1. *Resources*: hardware systems, software systems, operating systems, file systems, and application systems. These hardware systems include computing platforms, communications networks, storage systems, and peripherals. Software systems include heterogeneous database management systems, and application systems include digital libraries, search engines, and extend to the logical groupings and extensions of these resources.
2. *Methods*: access methods for using standardized and non-standard APIs, system-defined and user-defined functions for manipulating datasets, data warehousing, data mining, data sub-setting and format-conversion routines, and composition of methods.
3. *Data objects*: individual datasets as wells as collections of datasets.
4. *Users and groups*: to create, update, or access any of the resources, methods, and datasets, and access any of the metadata on all four entities.

Conclusion

The unique challenge will be to efficiently determine means by which one can extract and filter relevant information as automatically as possible. However, one problem remains. Certain organization will insist on using different terms for different pieces of metadata. This means that there must be mappings nearly continuously taking place between what one system uses to refer to a piece of given information (for example, the *title* of a paper) and what another might used to refer to it as (for example, the *name* of a paper). There are complexities that exist in every language and every organization, and if the Grid expands to include other locations, other languages, and other cultures, then these complexities will only multiply.

Chapter 7

Drivers

I do not fear computers. I fear the lack of them.

—**Isaac Asimov (1920–1992)**

Any science or technology which is sufficiently advanced is indistinguishable from magic.

—**Arthur C. Clarke**

The Grid, as one might have noticed already, has been more of a matter of evolution than revolution. Many people believe it is the other way around. The Grid is seen as *the* ultimate "species" of computing to do. Computing has evolved from the vast refrigerated room-sized behemoths, through centralized computing, the World Wide Web, peer-to-peer computing, and the virtualization of underlying technologies.

Like the Web, and partly because much of the Grid's interface relies on the underpinnings of Web technology, the Grid goes a long way toward keeping the complexities behind the scenes hidden and yet allows all users to enjoy the same single, simplified, unified experience as if they are alone in the system. Unlike the Web that is basically a communication enabler), the Grid extends to full collaboration of all involved parties toward meeting of overall common business goals.

Like peer-to-peer (P2P) computing, the Grid allows for the free and open sharing of files across the network where appropriate. Unlike P2P, however, which provides the decentralized sharing of files and information, the Grid not only allows for the many-to-many sharing of files and information, but also the nearly unrestrained sharing of computing resources while allowing for the tightening of security where appropriate. This means that resources can be made selectively available, yet available when necessary.

Grid computing is an expanded form of a highly distributed system. When dealing with highly distributed environments, the network is critical. Computing resources are shared across networks, with the ultimate computing resource network being the Internet. The Grid promises to take the already emerging Web standards and Web technologies and create even more standards that enable universally transparent data access and access to virtually all computing resources.

The Grid will help enable the selection, virtualization, extreme aggregation, and information sharing for any resources that may currently reside on any of the servers in many different administrative domains; and the administrative domains can be located in many geographic areas. These information resources are shared based upon rules that govern their availability, capability, and accounting cost, as well as on user requirements.

Many commercial products are available today and more are becoming available to bring their customers the ability to "Grid-enable" their enterprises. Some of these products actually fulfill their claims. Others do not. Many products help organizations leverage open systems standards, including XML and Java. It is important to remember that the Grid is neither associated with any given hardware configuration nor any particular operating system. Rather, it allows organizations to leverage all the software configurations.

The Grid, like historic hardware clusters and other distributed computing genres, brings computing resources together to bear on large problems. The Grid, unlike clusters and distributed computing, which rely on both proximity and operating homogeneity to accomplish their goals, cannot only be widely geographically distributed, but also can be highly heterogeneous with respect to hardware and operating systems, data sources, and application designs.

Where the Grid meets other virtualization technologies (SAN [storage area network], NAS [network attached storage], clusters, and more), there is the virtualization of IT resources. Where the Grid goes beyond the others, beyond simple virtualization technologies that tend to virtualize a single system or a single system's view of the components, is in enabling the virtualization of a wide range of disparate IT resources.

While the Grid appears to be the one of the hottest new advances in IT today, Grid computing is not a completely new concept. It has gained renewed interest and increased activity for many reasons. One of the main reasons for this renewed interest is that IT budgets have been and continue to be cut. Grid computing offers a far less expensive alternative to purchasing larger new servers. Rather, it allows organizations to more fully leverage resources that they already have deployed and to bring in less expensive alternatives to replace what is already in place.

Another reason behind Grid computing's increasing popularity concerns the many problems involved in processing very large volumes of data and the problems that surround the performance of repetitive, often resource-intensive, computation on the same or similar sets of data. These computations are often intensive enough that they threaten to outstrip the capacity of the servers on which they perform these calculations.

Conceptually, Grid computing strives to build itself as the metaphor for treating computing and computational resources much the same way that the electric companies are the metaphor for the power grid. Grid computing users gain ubiquitous access to computing resources without having to worry about either the configuration or location of the hardware being used to run the applications, whether those applications are using a supercomputer, a mainframe, or a laptop somewhere.

This virtualization of computing resources may one day allow an organization's IT department to make the best use of not only its own on-site computing capacity, but also any of the computing capacity that can fall within its sphere of influence or that can be purchased or rented from other organizations. All this maximization and virtualization can be allowed to occur while at the same time enabling the rapid and efficient computationally intensive applications whenever necessary, but without the necessity of anyone (particularly users) seeking further computational capacity that is not needed.

Many of the bright visions of the virtualization concept have yet to be fully realized. Many others are conceptually possible but seem to have issues surrounding implementation on a broad scale. This is not to say that implementation and adoption are not possible. Small steps toward the leaps that we know are possible will go far in making the dream for even small and medium businesses a possibility. As time passes, those that have even limited implementations in place will find it easier to make incremental additions to these limited beginnings than to take the giant leap that would be required to radically change everything all at once. One server at a time, one application at a time, and a Grid will organically grow to fill the voids.

Business

The Grid can bring many advantages and features that can help a business to meet its goals and to excel in and expand its core competencies. It is important to understand that businesses typically do not rush out to join the newest and most cutting-edge technologies (with some obvious exceptions) but rather they wait until the technology has proven itself. In this case, it continues to prove itself and is allowing more organizations to leverage their computing potential.

Accelerated Time to Results

Because the Grid can not only run on any hardware and can span departments, entire organizations and inter-organizations, it also can greatly help with the improvement of productivity and collaboration between parties in the subject matter. This means that not only can projects benefit from the addition of the Grid environment, but also the entire society that is involved in that kind of project can benefit (in the case of a data-based Grid) from the openly shared available data. Projects can be brought to market (regardless of the market) sooner because the resources are available when and where needed to get past the hurdles without the necessity of purchase orders and requests for quotes on significant systems. In the ideal situation, one might need to invest only in the cycles that are necessary to get the job at hand done.

Not only can any new projects be implemented faster, but with a Grid infrastructure in place, and its increased power and flexibility, projects that were previously deemed impractical or too resource intensive or unsolvable, are now potentially possible. Projects that would have ordinarily required too much of an investment in hardware to implement can be reevaluated and considered in light of even a departmental or organizational Grid because spare cycles can be reallocated to where they are needed to solve the unsolvable problems.

This can mean advanced and expanded core competencies for those companies that choose to take a competitive advantage by implementing a Grid infrastructure because they are leveraging a new ability to solve unsolvable problems or pursuing innovative new ways of solving problems that were computationally prohibitive. This allows a company to more adequately meet internal or external needs.

Operational Flexibility

One of the key features that the Grid brings is flexibility. Previously, hardware resources either were siloed because of incompatibility of resources or because of the unwillingness of IT staff or business staff to have all processing for all departments entirely centralized with all the data co-mingled. Now, with the growth of the Grid-enabled middle layer, mainframes and PCs, and supercomputers and midrange systems can all work together toward a common business processing goal, regardless of where the resources are or what the processing demands might be.

While many systems may, not have sufficient power to contribute to the processing of an additional system, they likely have idle CPU cycles that have historically gone unused. This no longer has to be the case. These spare cycles (as well as the costs associated with the wasted processing) can now be used to solve problems where processing is tight.

With adequate rules set up in the system, one can almost effortlessly and automatically allow these adjustments to make themselves, allow for the harvesting of these CPU cycles by other systems, and become practical. The system, given an adequate supply of metadata with which to work, can become a sense-and-respond system (a system that notices that a given resource is becoming overtaxed and finds underutilized resources that might be candidates to ease the high utilization and spread out the processing).

This flexibility allows one to scale the overall system with respect to different operational loads during the day and also to shift resources from underutilized resources to overutilized ones. Moreover, it can also provide the ability to address rapid fluctuations in customer needs and demands.

One might have a customer that suddenly runs a query on a database that drags the system to its knees. With a highly flexible system, one can shift resources for the duration of the demand spike and just as quickly shift them back when the spike is finished.

This ability to shift resources from one area to another in the system allows for flexibility in the layout of the system, and also can assist with providing the organization with the security of having a far more resilient system. Many companies are looking for ways that will allow them to provide a nearly 24/7 system, that will provide maximum availability while providing the ability to perform maintenance and still maintain efficiency. While this is usually a tall order to fill, it is quite possible in a Grid environment.

This virtualization of all potential resources allows for untying workloads from the underlying hardware resources and the provisioning of resources with far more flexibility than can be found in a traditional environment. Because resources that have been utilized, are virtualized and can be allocated precisely and concisely to meet any and all needs of any given workload, administrators (either on the application end or anywhere within the Grid environment) can more efficiently allocate those resources based on rules, accounting demands, or other specifications that are in place for the given system.

Leverage Existing Capital Investments

Capital investments are important in business (obviously). Capital investments affect a company's bottom line and, by extension, its stock prices and its standing in the world market. They are dealt with in the accounting systems and they add complexity to all financial activities.

The Grid allows organizations to improve, the overall utilization of existing computing capabilities. Furthermore, they can then make capitalized investments later rather than sooner, making the time value of money and the net present value beneficial to the organization rather than to the computer company.

Moreover, one can avoid over-provisioning the overall system. The excess hardware, software, and licensing costs associated with over-provisioning also can therefore be avoided. This can help free up resources (financial as well as hardware and software) from the burden of administering more hardware, while that hardware is underutilized the majority of the time.

And because the Grid environment is typically maintained through a Web interface, some of the highest costs in a company (the people costs) also can be limited because fewer staff can administer the entire system through the single unified interface. This can allow even someone with expertise in UNIX to work on a Windows server at the operating system level (and vice versa) and the middleware level where it would have taken two people to do those jobs in a typically architected system.

Better Resource Utilization

Traditional processes that access that data and analyze, synthesize, and test that data are typically excessively time consuming and resource intensive. The growing amounts of data in organizations only tend to exacerbate the problems rather than help to eliminate them. Grid computing environments can manage and distribute resources more efficiently and work toward shortening analysis time and often time-to-market for many products than the individual resources could do on their own.

High-end, powerful servers could be replaced with lower-cost commodity servers, or blade servers that would meet or exceed the total output required. The combination of these lower-cost commodity servers with the distributed Grid systems can result in savings and efficiency.

No longer will an organization need to buy resources that are destined to be dedicated to individual applications or product lines. Rather, they will be able to instead buy resources for the organization that can be shared and distributed across the entire organization. These enterprise resources can be portioned out to individual applications and departments based on need, accounting rules, and policy decisions at the enterprise level. Management will, in a Grid environment, be able to decide how computing resources will be allocated in the organization, and can alter those decisions quicker and more efficiently than could be done if those companies were tied into the traditional purchasing and computing paradigm.

Enhanced Productivity

The Grid allows for extreme gains in productivity. Because jobs are able to run faster in a parallelized environment, and because one is able to give users nearly unlimited access to computing, data, and storage resources when and where they want them or need them, it is possible to make any given user (and by extension, all users) more productive. Because all systems have virtualized access to all the resources they need, different users with different levels of expertise in a given system and with different abilities and weaknesses can work together, building off each other's abilities far more easily and in a more ubiquitous environment. If everyone can see the system the same way, get to the data in the same way, experience the same responses at the same time in the same way, they can all contribute to provide overall productivity gains and the total is better than the sum of the parts.

Users are often far more productive in a Grid environment simply because they can be free to concentrate on their jobs without having to concern themselves with the need to locate resources and information in different systems and locations.

In a non-Grid environment, there is typically no central interface through which users can access their data that understands where the information is and how to go about getting it. This centralized interface — and with it the ability to centrally locate all information — will not only help with productivity, but will also add to the acceptance of the system by the end users.

Users more productive because of the unified interface and also because they have virtually unlimited resources at their command (within policy and reason), more jobs can run faster. Furthermore, an understanding of the overall view that one user has when used in discussion with other users can mean the difference between full understanding of sharing and productivity and only a simulated understanding.

Imagine what one could accomplish if one could define jobs, decide when they should run, and set them to run with the full expectation that running those jobs would occur without any intervention.

The Search for Extraterrestrial Intelligence (SETI) home computer screen saver is nothing more than a simple screen saver, right?

In SETI@home (now run through the Berkeley Open Infrastructure for Network Computing [BOINC] Grid and volunteer computing interface), large, computationally intensive jobs are broken down into manageable chunks and sent off for processing on any available CPUs during their otherwise idle time. Since SETI's beginning, well over 4,992,815 users (including 1100 new users in 24 hours) have dedicated more than 1,924,340 years of CPU time thus far (more than 1100 years in just one 24-hour period). Those CPUs have acted on nearly 62.31 teraflops per second of data in the same 24-hour period. The users are located in more than 225 countries; more than 150 types of CPUs and more than 165 different operating systems donate the cycles to analyze the data.

BOINC uses the idle time on a Windows, MAC, or Linux computer as a means to cure diseases, study global warming, discover pulsars, and run many other computationally intensive jobs in a safe, easy, secure, and attractive way. BOINC provides a singular interface (Figure 7.1) through which a user may different gridded and volunteer computing programs can be successfully run.

Consider acceptable performance in a data warehouse that is expected to have queries designed to mine data taking over a day (sometimes well over a day) to run. With a Grid environment, these same queries, running in parallel against a Grid-enabled database, will be able to run faster, providing answers faster with at least as much accuracy as was possible in a typical environment. This means a company is better able to adapt to the market, to meet the customer's needs, and to answer the questions that need to be answered, thus giving it a competitive advantage.

Better Collaboration

The Grid allows for collaboration among users (both technical and functional) in a variety of new ways. Not only can individuals involved in a project or a concept collaborate person to person, but different departments and even entire companies can collaborate to strive toward common business goals. With global businesses demands requiring intense problem-solving capabilities for more complex problems, the

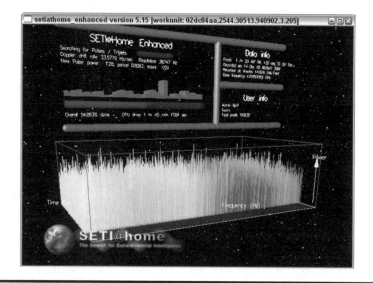

Figure 7.1 BOINC Seti@home interface.

requirement for allowing more collaboration of computing and human resources to become tighter and work together in an attempt to solve the problems facing business adds an additional component to the idea of collaboration. The Grid allows for the added complexity of collaboration among hardware platforms and other remote resources, making the problem solving more simple and elegant, and helping to facilitate the human collaboration that goes along with it.

Grid computing is fundamentally based on an open set of standards, and open protocols that enable free communication across homogeneous as well as heterogeneous environments that are both centralized an widely geographically dispersed. This means that organizations can optimize computing, data, storage, and other resources, pool those resources for use by large-capacity workloads and share those resources across networks (LANs [local area networks] and WANs [wide area networks] and eventually the Internet), and enable collaboration at entirely new levels.

A higher level of collaboration can be accomplished through the use of a Grid environment. Users can share data and resources in manageable and consistent fashions across the Grid environment, whether departmental sharing, enterprise sharing, or in the case of many of the research facilities that have already implemented Grid environments, across the country or around the world.

Scalability

Grid computing enables a company to maintain sufficient and even excess capacity to grow (with hundreds or thousands of processors at its disposal) while not needing to invest in significantly more servers. Because of the advent of blade servers and the ability to use PCs and other existing CPUs in the organization, one can utilize cycles that would otherwise go unused. By harnessing these available resources, one can solve highly computationally intensive problems. If one finds any part of the system becomes overloaded all the system needs to do is to find an existing available source that is already in that environment and add it to the system.

If tight spots are still present computationally the organization can invest incrementally in commodity hardware blade servers that are lower in cost and built for adaptability and scalability, snap them into a rack, and compute. No longer will an organization have to plan months in advance for a large outlay of capital to invest in excess capacity or need to justify the next outlay of capital. With a Grid environment, the growth can be incremental and minimal at any given time.

Return on Investment (ROI)

Executives and accountants often talk about a project's or an investment's ROI, or return on investment. Many companies, from some of the largest global organizations to smaller start-ups, currently claim to already have many corporate Grid computing clients trying to make efficient use of their existing assets and buying extra capacity where necessary, much like an application service provider (ASP) model. Utility-based computing has far broader intentions than simply being a glorified ASP model. Companies will be able to take advantage of shared infrastructure, resources, storage, databases, Web servers, and other in-demand resources.

This model will likely expand to fill existing and emerging needs. It will take application servers to higher levels, becoming a utility provider. Companies will be able to buy the needed extra cycles, thus allowing them to make better use of their own investments.

The academic community has been creating Grids using low-cost commodity computers (often, in fact, computers in university labs contribute significantly to the available resources of the Grid) to work together to attack complex and computationally intensive applications that require significant horsepower for several years. Applications that have successfully run on these Grids include complex research projects and applications that perform risk management computations or financial modeling processing. These are the same applications that many commercial companies starting to make inroads in Grid computing environment are finding they can run with great efficiency and reliability.

The advantages gained by turning to the Grid in many circumstances are compelling. Major business problems are parsed and distributed into bite-sized datasets and task sets to make efficient use of multiple computers for analysis. In this way, the problems are attacked more rapidly than ever simply by utilizing underused and idle resources that can be put to work to help to solve the existing problems in the organizations. Further, server purchases that may have been on the horizon before the reallocation of cycles can be put off possibly indefinitely.

Reallocation of Resources

Upper management has long recognized that computing cycles of thousands of machines are wasted on low-level, computationally nonintensive computing tasks such as reading e-mail, writing e-mail, word processing, interacting with co-workers on the phone or in meetings or in impromptu meetings.

Grid-enabling middleware has progressed to allowing the lowly desktop computer (that has all the power of the early computers and more) to wasted CPUs and contribute to complex tasks from remote locations. Computations that would have once required all the computing power of supercomputers or mainframes to execute now require an investment in inexpensive middleware that lies in a thin layer between a core set of servers and thousands of clients.

A small investment in new hardware can lead to enormous boons in productivity and a highly increased bottom line.

The financial services sector, insurance companies, and those that service the claims for those companies, as well as real estate and customer resource management-intensive companies where data mining plays an important role are likely to be high investors in the Grid as it adapts, emerges, and goes through its metamorphosis over the next few years. Initially, of course, it will not be utility computing at its finest; rather, many of the existing systems will be adapted to use Grid-enabled networks, workstations, servers, and clusters, and eventually cause the lowering of demand for high-performance mainframes and supercomputers. Higher-end servers will be replaced by the increased reliance and demand for high-performance Grid-enabled applications to run on these new flexible architectures.

It does not take true global utility computing, however, to make a company able to take advantage of computing-on-demand. It can be done internally or externally by a CPU utility model company. Internal utility computing services designed to provide CPU cycles for computationally intensive applications can meet the needs of internal clients while allowing an organization to better distribute and track the computing cost to the true users of the cycles and resources. Rather than dedicating resources to a department or to a specific line of business and its applications, the internal CPU utility division can provide all the lines of business associated with that organization with the processing power they need for applications that are computationally intensive, while also providing a virtual combined pool of resources from which to draw.

The goal of these CPU utility divisions is to improve the service levels that the internal customers can expect and cut their own costs by charging each business unit for the resources it uses. The internal CPU utility can even provide peak and off-peak pricing similar to what a typical utility company can provide.

In this way, many companies could allay their fears of security breaches that might arise from securing the required CPU cycles from a source outside the organization and can gain the efficiencies of scale and scope that can come from each individual department or line of business concentrating on its true core business strengths and then allowing those connected to the newly created intra-organizational utility company to become adept and efficient.

This symbiotic relationship could make for an overall stronger organization and an organization that can grow and flex with changing demands. Change will not have as great an impact if a company can provide the infrastructure on which to change easily and securely.

The concept of charging the cost of CPU usage may be foreign to many organizations, but it will provide information to the overall organization on how and where its resources are used. It also will provide more accurate information on what departments are truly more profitable than others. Moreover, not only could IT departments be seen as less of a money drain on an organization, if they were to adopt an internal utility company model for the Grid-enabled departments, these departments may even prove to be profitable from the perspective of the services they are really providing for the overall organization.

Total Cost of Ownership (TCO)

Total cost of ownership (TCO) is another accounting related term that business users consider. TCO takes into account all the costs and cash flows of a potential or active project and determines the effect of the project on the bottom line of the organization. Where many other means of determining profitability take into account obvious costs, TCO takes into account the costs of redesigning, the costs of training, and the costs of many of the components that would not otherwise make it into the mix. TCO is often applied to the purchase, lease agreement, or outsourcing of large manufacturing installations and to build-or-buy decisions. It has been applied, with mixed results, to technology decisions for more than a decade.

TCO essentially helps a company make quantitative determinations as to whether it wins or loses as a result of any specific technology implementation. TCO is typically used as a lens through which to look at the overall impact of a hardware or software implementation or at the decision to change the infrastructure of an organization. Cost is the numerator (usually broken into categories such as capital costs, technical support costs, licensing costs, additional software costs, training costs, and the marginal costs that can be associated with one decision, administration and end-user operations), and the denominator could be service level, customer satisfaction, quality levels or productivity levels, time-to-market, relative time to see results from a computation, or the overall success of answering inquiries in a reasonable amount of time — all with quantitative measures assigned even to the qualitative factors and weights given to each.

While it is true that there will be some added investment needed for the acquisition of software and training for the Grid middleware that ties together all of the disparate components, the overall cost of ownership for the Grid environment will prove to be lower than that of its traditional counterparts. And if one looks at the effects of the denominator as it applies to the Grid and the effects of the Grid environment on the organization, service level, customer satisfaction, quality levels or productivity levels, time-to-market, relative time to see results from a computation or the overall success of getting the correct answer back to the requester in a reasonable amount of time, one can see where the Grid can lower the overall cost to a fraction of what the alternatives would be.

Because one can more reliably meet service level agreements, both with internal customers and external clients, one can lower the costs incurred by penalties levied because of missed timelines and also can increase premiums charged because of the consistent meeting of timelines. Quality levels are met or exceeded by the Grid infrastructure, and productivity, as already seen, can be improved overall, allowing more jobs to run in a shorter amount of time and more answers to be gained from the same amount of processing power. Because users and customers do not have to wait as long for the answers to important questions, one can see an improvement because valuable time is not being spent waiting for answers, and computing time is not being wasted in wait mode for one process to finish and the next to begin.

In addition, if one adopts a pay-as-you-go model, the "cost of ownership" becomes completely minimized because one does not actually own anything and pays only for CPU capacity use. It becomes just another variable utility cost to the enterprise.

Technology

From a technology perspective, the Grid offers many advantages. When people look at the Grid and Grid computing, the first thing they think of is the technology that makes up the environment or the technology problems that the infrastructure can solve.

Infrastructure Optimization

Because one can consolidate workload management into the scheduler and the resource manager, and thereby distribute the workload over multiple, servers and CPU sources, one can optimize the utilization of resources and optimize workloads and job scheduling to take best advantage of the resources on hand. Because there is enough capacity in the CPU capacity pool, one can find the necessary supply of resources to throw at high-demand applications as they demand resources. This can reduce the overall cycle time that any single given job takes, and therefore the overall cycle time of a process and the overall time to answer computationally intensive questions.

Increase Access to Data and Collaboration

In a Grid environment, data is federated and distributed globally, providing extensive access to the data resources at any point in the Grid chain. This distribution and extended access can provide the underlying support for collaboration multi-departmentally, multi-organizationally, multi-nationally, and globally, depending on the type and security requirements for the data involved. This collaboration can lead to overall productivity gains because of the ability of many eyes to see a problem from different angles and different perspectives, making the problem easier to resolve .

Resilient, Highly Available Infrastructure

Grid computing provides the ability to distribute workloads and redistribute to balance the workloads on the network and on the individual servers in the system. Because the organization sees the resources as being shared equitably among the different users, the system fosters camaraderie with the users and allows for a more unified overall work environment where no one feels technologically slighted in favor of another department.

Just as important is the ability of a system to more quickly, elegantly, and automatically recover from the failures of servers, of the network, and of given resources in the system. Because there is no single point of failure in the system and jobs can be dynamically redirected in case a component becomes unreachable, the overall reliability of the system is increased, and the comfort level of the users in the system's availability is also increased.

Most Efficient Use of Resources

Maximized utilization of new and existing computing capabilities means that a few constraints need to be put into place on what a program can be allowed to do. Because administrators or the system itself can dynamically map and remap resources to highest-priority business (or technological) drivers, a system becomes more flexible and more adaptable to changing needs and changing demands. This can, naturally, be a mixed blessing. For anyone in the organization who finds a way to circumvent the governing measures put into place, it can be a tool to divert cycles from processes that are deemed more important to the business to processes that are less honorable. Again, this is a place where security is not only desirable, but also necessary.

There are many reasons why Grid computing has become such a hot new technology. There does not seem to be any one single major technological breakthrough that made Grid computing more applicable for corporate uses and more capable of meeting the widely diverse needs of universities and research organizations, and the far more complex and controlled needs of corporations and industry. Rather, subtle technical advances came together to make the modern Grid an enterprise-capable computing tool. Steady progress through all of the technological evolutions has brought technology to this point, to the place where business can leverage as much of the potentiality as science and academia have done thus far.

The Grid represents an almost unprecedented case of alignment of business and technology goals. Usually, business and technology are not so closely aligned. That the two such obviously disparate groups have so quickly come to a place where they begin to see eye to eye is encouraging.

Standards-based tools designed for creating Grid-enabled applications and connecting users to Grids, and Grids to Grids, are appearing on the market just as the need to increase server capacity and optimize utilization grows. These applications can help meet the needs of both business and technology.

The Globus Project and the Open Grid Services Architecture (OGSA) are interrelated efforts that are working independently to create the tools that are, and will continue to be, necessary to put the Grid to work in the wider corporate world.

The former need for more server capacity by all sorts of companies was typically solved by simply buying more servers. While this was exceptionally good for the server manufacturers, it led to corporate technical infrastructures that were segmented, highly dispersed, and running at a mere fraction of what their capabilities were. It has been widely suggested that many Linux, UNIX, and Microsoft-based servers continue to run at less than a quarter of their potential capacity.

Even with servers that have terabyte databases running and serving hundreds or thousands of concurrent users, all running ad hoc data-mining type queries, it is rare during a typical day to see the CPU on a server spike past 60 percent, and then drop almost immediately back down to 15 to 20 percent. But look at that same server during a daily or weekly bulk load, and one sees several CPUs running at 95 to 99 percent and the server unable to keep up with the demand. This implies that the servers have processing to spare at some times and that they are resource starved at other times. If we can alter the processing stream, move some of the batch processing to the "off" hours without impacting the real-time processing, then we can better utilize these resources.

In addition to this server, its brother server is sitting with half as many CPUs because it is a test server that only sees real demand when there are load tests to be performed before a major system move-up. This server is utilized only by developers and program testers. It uses 5 to 10 percent at its most taxed. Although it is sized significantly smaller, computing cycles are computing cycles.

With the Grid, the capacity that sits wasted in the test server could be used by its overtaxed brother to distribute the processing and the load during the batch load process and allow the jobs to finish faster.

Many IT departments, particularly in recent years, have been called upon to provide more computing power than ever before; however, they are no longer able to buy servers on a whim, without proving to upper management that the job can simply not be done with the existing capacity. Making do with less is the solution: make better use of what already is owned. The adoption of Grid technology relies on the simple premise that it makes better sense to provide the required capacity without resorting to buying of servers that would sit mostly idle or be underused most of the time.

While one needs to be able to alter the use of processing power on a task-by-task, job-by-job basis, this is what schedulers and resource brokers accomplish. This means that servers and server technology do not have to change because of the Grid. The tools simply must have an understanding of how the various pieces react on their own and extrapolate on how they can react when combined.

How computation is accomplished will change; it will necessarily have to change, as will the way that applications as a whole perform their work. The ubiquitous underlying framework will simply run whatever is sent to it.

Lower budgets, lower staff numbers, and more demand all work to drive technology to this new paradigm. Moreover, the more computing can do on its own will mean the less we have to rely on human resources and the more computing will be asked to do on its own.

Services-Oriented Approach

The basic inner workings of the Grid are a series of interrelated or totally unrelated services that cooperate to make the whole bigger than the parts. Together, these services process the jobs that users submit, determine where and when those jobs should run, find interdependencies between those jobs, and return results to the user who called them

This is one of the interesting differences between the paradigms that typically accompany computing as it has always been and computing as it is in the Grid. The users make suggestions as to how and where they would choose to run their given program, query, or job; however, the services that make up the Grid have the ability to override many of these suggestions, with their decisions based on past history and the understanding of what could be right or wrong in reference to the operation. While, to a great extent, on many operating systems, administrators and often certain services have the ability to override what the user suggests, with the Grid, many of the decisions are made solely by the services.

Batch-Oriented Approach

The batch-oriented approach is based on job scheduling paradigms similar to other distributed workload management systems. Through simple interfaces, one can describe parallel workflows, node requirements, pre-job and post-job instructions, special conditions, and other job- and environment-specific requirements. Batch-oriented approaches are extremely well suited for precompiled, predefined programs that can be launched many times with different input parameters. This is called parametric parallelism, meaning that it is parallelized based on parameters that are passed into it, or based on input datasets that it is set to work on. Batch-oriented applications can easily integrate into the Grid with little or no alteration to the underlying source code.

Object-Oriented Approach

The Grid makes extensive use of object-oriented concepts and models. Virtually everything in the Grid is an object, or can be expressed in object-oriented terms. A server, a CPU, a program — everything can be assigned methods and attributes. This feature of the Grid environment makes the Grid extensible and flexible, and conceptually far easier for many programmers to deal with. Administration is a major component in the Grid, but programming and building applications, interfaces and components that take advantage of that underlying structure are just as important as the administration of the services and the maintenance of the hardware and software that make up the infrastructure.

Supply and Demand

Technologists understand that usually the CPU is not one of the overtaxed elements of the existing structure and infrastructure of the environment. They understand that spare capacity exists in nearly every environment and know that the waste is customary.

There is often an excess of demand in other places, demand that means that jobs run slower and need to be paged in and out to share the existing resources (meaning that efficiency is lowered even further due to the paging).

If 10 percent of the time, there is insufficient capacity, two different tracks can be taken. One can ignore it and deal with the slowdowns. This would be the solution if the processing window for these processes is big enough to contain them. The other option, historically, would be to buy more capacity, adding to the supply and adding to the overcapacity.

The Grid can allow one to divert capacity from other computers to assist with keeping the processing within the available window. No more having to answer the questions on why a process did not finish on time, no more missed SLAs (service level agreements), no more difficult upper management justifications and explanations.

Open Standards

The siren call of many technologists is the call to open standards and open systems. The broad adoption of open standards is an essential key to the utility computing model for e-business on-demand, regardless of the size or distribution of the model. Without the open standards working together, the enabling of all kinds of different computing platforms to communicate and work effectively with one another would be much more difficult. Without open standards, the integration of a company's internal systems, applications, and processes would remain a difficult, impractical, and expensive task. Without open standards, the Grid would be both unpractical, and nearly impossible.

The broad-based acceptance of open standards, rather than the typical adoptions of historic, closed, proprietary architectures, allows the computing infrastructure and the departments surrounding that infrastructure to more easily absorb and adapt to new technical innovations.

Corporate IT Spending Budgets

How many IT organizations have made the statement that the cost or the justification does not matter? In almost every organization, there is a long and rigorous justification process for any additional capacity, and that was the case when the economy was booming, before the dot.com crash. Today, such purchase requests are scrutinized even more closely, and the decisions are even more difficult.

Having to make do with what they have has driven many organizations, starting naturally with universities and research institutions, to devise the creative solution known as the Grid. This solution now provides the opportunity for other companies to adopt those creative solutions.

Cost, Complexity, and Opportunity

Cost is a tremendous driver in today's market. Many companies find it challenging to keep revenues up and costs down. Companies are looking far more closely at expenditures and typically technology expenditures are among the first to be cut. Prior to the year 2000, these expenditures were rising at amazing rates. Now there is great deal of scrutiny of expenditures. Because many software and application purchases are tied very closely with the underlying hardware (operating systems, storage infrastructure, CPU source), this scrutinizing is occurring at the application level.

Because utilization does increase, and there is required overhead for any utilization of resources, the incremental cost of scaling existing applications to work on existing large computers can tend to escalate almost logarithmically. This is particularly true as the cost of adding components increases, often nonproportionally to the increased number of CPUs. Licensing fees are often calculated by the number of CPUs regardless of their dedication to one specific application, and the costs of making the newly scaled applications function efficiently in the scaled-up boxes can add even more cost to the venture. While these fees must be based on some tangible resource, the fact that CPUs can be partitioned off does not always make it into these calculations.

For this reason, many organizations are feeling the need to move away from mainframes and large-scale UNIX or VMS cluster machines to lower-cost Intel processor-based clusters that can be scaled up incrementally instead of relying on the need to add more expensive nodes to existing clusters or upgrading an entire mainframe. Add Linux into the equation and even more cost-effective solutions can enter the mix.

The Grid and its underlying technologies promise to keep existing infrastructures, limiting the cost of migration or redesign of existing systems, and at the same time linking the other, often widely disparate technologies and Intel-and UNIX-based clusters together. This means that the existing technology can be reevaluated and put to work on new problems. This will also mean that, because Grid-adopting companies can simply add to existing infrastructure, they can therefore reduce the overall purchase of hardware to only adding the necessary additional capacity. Not only will this limit the cost of hardware, but it also will increase the scalability of existing applications without having to radically redesign everything to take advantage of the new hardware.

The increasing complexity of many firms' technology infrastructures partly because of changing needs and software decisions that affect the hardware decisions that have to be made, is another solid argument for the drive toward implementing a Grid environment that will allow the existing heterogeneity to work efficiently to meet the common goals. This allows applications to take advantage of the underlying infrastructure through a virtual portal interface and also allows, through similar virtual portals, the infrastructure to be managed with a smaller set of tools (limiting the learning curve and often the siloed maintenance and administrative capacity that exists in many organizations). Lower training costs, less time to efficiency, reduced frequency of mistakes due to the user (or the administrator) having to remember commands are all additional reasons that a Grid environment is making inroads into some unlikely organizations.

Many Firms have discovered tasks that they have determined to be advantageous to their business, but have also determined to be too computationally impractical to perform without the addition of massive computational infrastructure.

The Grid enables these firms to better utilize their current resources and expedite the desired, computationally intensive analytics they desire, along with the already complex and time- and resource-intensive analysis that they already perform on a regular basis and those that are run on an ad hoc basis. The companies using a Grid computing environment can take advantage of the opportunity to leap ahead of their competitors.

Better, Stronger, Faster

Users and technologists naturally want bigger and better computers that meet their computing needs fast enough to allow them to keep up with what they believe to be their abilities. In some cases, computer programmers, developers, administrators consider these high-end computers a necessity. However, for most users, the latest and greatest is for the most part a waste.

How much is necessary to run PowerPoint, Word, e-mail, or browse the Internet? Most of these applications have a far greater need for memory than they will ever have for CPU cycles. Even in financial markets, it takes limited capacity to actually enter a trade or update a customer file. It is often necessary to get bigger and better computers to meet the minimum required amounts of memory or CPU speed to run many of the applications in the market today. But many of these same applications could be Web enabled, and by extension Grid enabled and run on a server, allowing the Grid to manage the load rather than having to scale the PCs to manage the load.

Companies often look on these increased requirements at the end-user level as a waste of money and resources. They look long and hard at who wants a bigger better workstation, what that user will ultimately do with that workstation, and to what extent will the newer and greater capacity be utilized.

If one looks at it from the Grid perspective, those investments in user desktop computing can be viewed more as an enterprise investment in capacity rather than as an end-user cost of work.

The Grid can help a company utilize all of the existing excess capacity without ever running short on cycles, even during 100 billion days of share trading, or when a risk management company tries to analyze enterprise risk on a global basis. It can take a company's existing heterogeneous hardware, its multiple operating systems and applications written for and optimized to run on a particular platform, and make them perform more elegantly together. Fortunately, many applications and application suites, similar to Oracle E-Business suite, are becoming more component based and more Internet (or intranet) enabled. The programming languages and protocols that these more flexible applications run efficiently (Java, SOAP, XML) mean that the applications are more robust and more able to be hosted on nearly any server in the network. While they are capable, with the Grid they have the ability to prove that they have the staying power to run effectively as well as to deploy themselves in active locations to access the appropriate data, execute the proper programs and protocols on that data, and return the results to the requesting location in an efficient and dependable manner. For those processes that are bound to a particular operating system, the Grid will be able to determine the operating system and direct the processing necessary to that operating system. This all is the promise and the challenge for Grid technology and for the companies that are willing to cut their operating costs while allowing the network and the infrastructure to do the job that they were designed to do.

Efficiency Initiatives

Along with the requirement to make do with as many of the existing resources as possible, the necessity for these organizations is to increase the efficiency of resource utilization. There was a time when efficiency did not matter as long as a program ran and finished in the allotted window of time. This is no longer necessarily true.

Now that programs and applications are having more efficiency demands put on them, they are required to do the same work in a smaller time window, and often more work in a smaller time window than previously.

These new demands mean that programmers, administrators, and developers are having to find ways to do more with less and the Grid is one optimal way to do that. Jobs that are deemed independent, not reliant on the output of one application as the input to the next, can be broken out and run in parallel, allowing for faster execution on existing resources. However, those resources must have the ability to be totally independent while being orchestrated to work in such a way that all results are both correct and timely.

The programming paradigm needs to change slightly to take advantage of potential efficiencies and to enable the jobs to run in parallel. The Grid will then take these more efficient versions and launch them independently to achieve the total desired outcome for the end user.

APPLICATIONS IN THE GRID

Computers are magnificent tools for the realization of our dreams, but no machine can replace the human spark of spirit, compassion, love, and understanding.

—Louis Gerstner, CEO, IBM

Data and databases in existing Grid projects and Grid environments have traditionally been simply extensions of what had been in place before the Grid was introduced. This means that the database is typically centralized, with the software and data residing and accessible through that one server. The location becomes a bottleneck, and often a single point of failure. This will not be able to support the Grid environment and access patterns for the duration. This section looks at means by which one can adapt existing database management styles to the new conceptual model of the Grid.

Section III discusses what databases will look like in a Grid environment and what considerations should be taken into account when determining how to place data into the new environment. To start out, let us look at relational databases, because these are the databases that will be primarily impacted in the Grid environment. This introduction to databases will present the vocabulary used through the final section of the book.

The chapters in this section tend to focus on relational database management systems (RDBMSs) because they are the most prevalent today. Hierarchical still exists and thrives, but for the purpose of simplicity, the author targets one model. In a relational database, data is represented as a collection of relations with each relation depicted as a table structure. The columns in the tables are considered to be the relation's attributes and rows (or tuples) represent entities, instances of the relation or records for backgrounds in flat file processing. Every row in the table (record) has a set of attributes (at the RDBMS level and hidden even if at the logical level they are allowed to be duplicated).

Chapter 8

Virtualization

> Computer Science is no more about computers than astronomy is about telescopes.
>
> **—Edsger W. Dijkstra**

Virtualization, loosely translated, means an abstraction of computer resources. It is a technique used for hiding the physical characteristics of computing resources or a way of making multiple physical resources (storage devices or servers) appear as a single logical resource.

Virtualization, however, is not necessarily a Grid-related concept. Far from it, in fact. Virtualization has been used extensively since at least the early 1960s and has been applied to many different aspects of computing. It has been used in entire computer systems component and components.

Virtualization technologies are usually employed through the hiding of technical details of the underlying components through encapsulation that creates an external interface to the underlying implementation. Recent developments in Grid technologies have renewed development in these technologies and refocused attention on the concept.

Platform virtualization is used to simulate virtual machines. Resource virtualization is used to simulate combined, fragmented, and simplified resources.

In Grid-related information technology, virtualization can take on several meanings, depending on what is being virtualized.

If computer hardware is what we are visualizing, then virtualization implies that we will use software to emulate either the hardware or an entire computer system environment other than the one on which the software is actually running. This virtualization of hardware is often referred to as a *virtual machine*. The term "virtual machine" has been connected directly with Sun Microsystems' Java programming language. That context defines an abstracted or conceptual machine rather than a real machine. Virtual machines can also be multi-user, shared resource operating systems that allow users to be under the impression that they have singular control over an entire system. The latter is the case in the Grid environment and also in the case of IBM mainframe environments.

In the Grid, all computing resources are virtualized. They are all combined until they appear to be one unified resource, generic in type and description. In this way, the user appears to have control over an infinitely large machine that has no noticeable operating system and no other application save the one in which the user is interested.

Not only is the hardware virtualized. The memory of the individual computers is virtualized as it relates to the way that the software programs are able to address more physical memory than the computers actually have (even as swap space).

How does one virtualize memory? Typically, this is done by swapping address space back and forth between storage devices and physical memory. This is one of the intrinsic features of UNIX and Linux operating systems and is typically referred to as paging. Data is read into and out of memory in units called pages. These pages can range in size anywhere from 1024 bytes to several megabytes. With the increase in size of available physical memory on a machine, the available space has increased accordingly, as has the efficiency of paging. Ordinarily, the process of paging actually speeds up the overall system performance despite the fact that data must be written to and retrieved from hard disks. The only issue is when paging is caused by an application on that system that makes poor use of memory and paging, causing the overall system to begin thrashing, and this can result in performance degradation.

Virtualization of memory can be combined with the virtualization of storage management to provide even greater advantage to an organization. In terms of storage, virtualization is the pooling of the stored data from multiple network-accessible storage devices into what can appear as a single, nearly limitless storage device which can be managed from a single console.

Storage virtualization is typically used in storage area networks (SANs), network attached storage (NAS), and even NetApp Filer systems. The management of these devices can often become tedious and time consuming for system administrators, but can also be beneficial to the administrative tasks of backups, data archiving, and post-failure recovery.

Virtualization in a Grid environment, rather than taking one machine and allowing it to behave as if it were many machines, takes many vastly disparate resources and melds them together so that they appear to the system and to the users of the system as a single entity. In this way, companies can balance the supply and demand for computing cycles and other resources by providing users with a single transparent and highly aggregated source of computing power, ultimately reducing the total cost of computing by providing reliable and transparent access, on demand.

Benefits of virtualization include:

- The ability to leverage existing investments in heterogeneous resources
- The chance to increase both return on assets (ROA) and return on investment (ROI) by enabling organizations to do more with less
- The ability to reduce both operational and infrastructure costs within the organization, including, but not limited to, hardware and software resources
- Improved user productivity due to the single unified interface to through which the user can simply do his job without having to concern himself with the mechanics of where things are located
- Faster time-to-market with higher quality and often more reliable results (getting to market faster with the end product, regardless of what the end product is, to achieve increased revenues and profits for the organization

Virtualization is nothing new. Distributed computing has been around for decades and has grown into what we now call Grid computing. The newer paradigms have allowed all IT components to work together (databases, applications, storage, and servers) without constriction or rigidity in the system. Components can react more quickly to changing loads or to altered user requirements.

In the late 1960s, IBM was home to what was then known as the M44/44X Project whose goal was to evaluate the concept of time-sharing that was only then becoming a viable concept. The architecture in this case was based on virtual machines. The primary machine was the IBM 7044 (M44). Each virtual machine was an experimental image of the primary machine (or the 44X). The address space of each 44X was resident on the M44's memory hierarchy and implemented via virtualized memory and multi-programming.

Originally, virtual machines were developed to correct some of the shortcomings that third-generation architectures and multi-programming operating systems brought with them. These hardware resources had dual state organization — privileged and non-privileged. In privileged mode, all machine instructions are available for the various software products running in that space, while in non-privileged they are not. User programs can execute in non-privileged space and make system calls to the privileged space and can expect that privileged functions will be run on their behalf.

Only one kernel can run at a given time. Anything else running on that machine or on another machine that requires action from that machine needs to "talk" to that machine's kernel. It "talks" to the kernel but it does not run with the kernel. No activity can run without disrupting the running system (no upgrade or debugging, no actively running system or any program that needs to access resources associated with the operating system). By the same account, no untrusted application can run on that resource in a secure manner. It is not simple to create the illusion of hardware configuration that is not physical. The creation of virtual multiple processors, arbitrary and virtual memory, and storage configurations comes at a price.

Definition

If one looks at what can be included in virtualization, it can be as all-encompassing or as narrow as one would like it. In general, it can be thought of as the framework used for dividing the resources of one computer into multiple environments for execution of programs or the unification of multiple resources into what appears to be a single entity. Virtualization is the partitioning or unification of hardware, software, time-sharing, machine simulation and emulation, as well as the quality of service rendered by those resources and the effect on the overall environment gained by the virtualization of these resources.

Grid environments tend to extend traditional definitions and begin to create their own definitions. SAN and NAS technologies virtualized many disks to make them appear to the systems accessing them as other than what they were. They might appear to be a single unified disk or a conglomeration of multiple disks, but they do not have to appear to be configured in the way that the underlying hardware is actually configured. This is accomplished through a virtualization layer that obfuscates the true nature of the disks from the users and the applications that access those disks.

The Grid enables virtualization of distributed computing and along with it the provisioning, deployment, and decentralization of applications and resources, storage, memory, CPU, and bandwidth. Virtualization allows a Windows computer to be utilized through the network by a Linux computer or a UNIX computer, or even a mainframe if need be, to access the resources on that computer. In this way, through the network, all resources appear to act as a single parallel processing computer and there is little to differentiate those resources from each other. Virtualization is little more than abstraction of one resource from many or many resources from one.

Why Virtualization Matters

Virtual machines can be used to consolidate the workloads of a number of underutilized servers to fewer but better utilized machines or even a single, more powerful machine. This is known as server consolidation. One related benefit, whether real or perceived, is savings on hardware and other environmental costs and server management system administration of the infrastructure. If an organization can cut down on the number of servers, then it is a benefit. However, those savings may be outweighed by other costs.

Often, an organization needs to run a legacy application because it has no viable alternative. These legacy applications often will not run or will not run efficiently on alternative hardware or on newer hardware and operating systems. The cost of changing platforms may be prohibitive. For this reason, if one virtualizes the resources, one can utilize the platform on which the application will run while adding additional resources to aid in speeding up applications processing. Frequently, multiple applications are not written in such a way that they can coexist in a single environment; but if one can extrapolate the environment and allow it to appear as multiple platforms (for example, with logical partitioning of a larger machine into smaller logical machines), then one can utilize a larger machine for multiple applications that would otherwise have required dedicated hardware of their own.

One can use virtual machines as a means to provide what appear to be isolated and secure sandboxes on which one can run untrusted applications without fearing that they might corrupt other applications or that they might leave the system in a vulnerable state. These sandboxes can be created permanently or dynamically whenever an untrusted program presents itself to the system for processing. Many of these untrusted applications are user-created applications that will not jeopardize the overall environment; but until they are proven trustworthy, the ability to segregate them into their own virtual machine will benefit overall system integrity. These miniature machines can even have their IP addresses obfuscated so that any attempt by a truly nefarious application will not yield any data that may be of value either directly or by inference.

If one uses virtual machines, one can create one's own operating environment in which one sets one's own operational limits, resource limits, and schedules with defined resource limits and guarantees. In this way, one can create specialized quality-of-service environments to tightly control all aspects of the environment and assure that those jobs running within those specialized environments will not have any competition for resources.

Because virtual machines can provide illusory hardware resources, one can obfuscate the actual hardware environments so that users and unwanted eavesdroppers will not be able to easily realize what the actual resources are and will therefore have a much more difficult time leveraging vulnerability that might exist in the resources. Moreover, in this same way, one can give the illusion of hardware resources that one actually does not have (devices, processors, memory, etc.), or give the illusion of entire networks of computers.

Through the use of virtualized machines one can run multiple operating systems simultaneously or different versions of a single operating system or entirely different systems simultaneously. It is possible test changes in systems on new versions of operating systems simultaneously with the old versions and test them on the same hardware to take as many variables as possible out of the mix.

Virtualization allows one to take advantage of far more robust debugging and performance monitoring while in a nearly production environment and add monitoring tools to one virtual environment while allowing others to run without the additional overhead. In this way, not only software, but also operating systems and environmental changes can be implemented, tested, and debugged in parallel without losing productivity and without the need to set up complex and complicated debugging scenarios and without investing in additional hardware that will be relegated simply for this purpose, thereby again reducing wasted CPU and memory cycles.

One can use virtual machines to help isolate what is running in one environment from what is running in another environment and thus provide fault containment and error containment that might not be possible otherwise. One can use this to determine what is going wrong with a program or application or provide a case study for an application vendor to prove a scenario that might otherwise harm production environments. Further, with a virtual system, one can introduce deliberate faults into a nearly production-ready software product to proactively determine what behavior may be expected from this new software in the environment and protect the rest of the environment from unanticipated side effects. Because of the ease of allocation of these environments and the limited impact that the addition of another environment might have on an organization, more robust testing scenarios can be created without fear of impacting a production environment, and more production-like test environments can be created as a system against which to test changes. Furthermore, because of the flexibility that can be created for this purpose, more creative testing scenarios can be created and more reliable results can be gathered based on those scenarios. "What-if" scenarios can be encouraged where simple canned system tests would have sufficed in other environments. This can allow programmers and developers to bring a higher-quality product to production than might otherwise occur.

Through the use of virtualization, software migration through different environments can be easier and more seamless. By making one environment appear to be test and another production, the movement of this software through the on-boarding process can appear as if it is truly moving from one environment to another. Testing is occurring in what amounts to a secure and separate environment but still allows the software to be migrated without ever having to be truly moved from one physical system to another.

Research and Development (R&D) departments can use virtualized machines as tools. These machines can provide both the expanded computing power to assist researchers in their hypotheses, coupled with isolated segmentation that can allow for safer and more secure work on the unproven hypotheses. One can encapsulate the entire state of a running system by combining many systems together to mimic what would amount to a supercomputer while it remains necessary to provide that level of computing power and then allow R&D researchers to save the state of the system that they create, examine it, modify and recreate it as necessary, modify the workloads being run against the system, and then add or take resources away to more closely mimic what would be anticipated in an ultimate production environment. In this way, computer models of proposed changes can be allowed to take the place of other mock-ups as a means to meet the demands of a production-like environment.

One can introduce shared memory multiprocessor operating systems into the environment and allow currently running applications to run on these virtual machines and virtual operating systems to investigate what effect these changes would have on the system without having to undergo the outlay of extra capital for this purpose or be saddled with nonproductive hardware if the experiment fails. In this way, one can freely propose changes to the environment while providing proof of concepts and more quantitative result sets to back up the suggestions.

One can retrofit new features into existing applications and systems without the need to completely retool the application from the ground up. By adding incrementally more hardware (CPU and memory) to the system, one can add pieces to the edges of existing applications in parallel with redeployment of a fully integrated application. This will allow the organization to benefit from the new services that can run as a semi-stand-alone services while development is adding this same functionality into a future full release or upgrade of the application.

Because of virtualization, one can more easily test changes to and manage existing systems of migration, backup, and recovery, and even disaster recovery situations within the existing environment. This can provide additional savings to the organization if one can virtualize multiple physical data centers to appear as a single data center the majority of the time, but break that level of virtualization when it becomes necessary or advantageous to meet audit requirements for the organizations. By breaking one level of virtualization, one can back up an entire system in a consistent state without having any undue impact on the running portion of the system. By a similar break of the virtualization, one can restore a system as if a disaster had occurred and verify that restoration is correct and timely without having to interrupt the running production system or add the cost of needing to relocate a subset of the organization's human capital as a means to do that verification. By allowing for rolling maintenance of the system, one can further limit the impact of downtime on the production system because one can upgrade a portion of the system, move the running application space to the newly upgraded areas, and roll the upgrade into additional areas and bring those areas online to the remainder of the Grid with minimal impact to performance and virtually no downtime necessary.

How to Virtualize

In general, to virtualize resources in an environment, one uses a software layer that gives the illusion of one huge, real resource or many virtual resources from a pool. It is possible to think of several, often intersecting and intertwined different ways that hardware and software can be virtualized in a system's architecture. One can virtualize a single hardware resource and virtualize that resource without requiring a host operating system. VMware is this kind of virtualization and can help one operating system pretend to be another operating system or another version of the same operating system.

One can allow the virtualization software to ride entirely on top of a host operating system and use that operating system's API (application programming interface) to perform all tasks. Emulation of another operating system may or may not come into place. Depending on whether or not the host and the virtual machine's architecture are the same instruction set, emulation may or may not be achievable.

One can handle all the instructions that would execute on a virtual machine in the software, have most of the instructions (including privileged instructions) executed in the software, or have the majority of all the instructions execute directly on the underlying machine or machines. Much architecture has been designed with virtualization uppermost in mind; however, it is not the case that these are the only architectures that can be included in and involved with virtualization. One can virtualize nearly any operating system and hardware platform.

Recall that many architectures have privileged and non-privileged instructions. If the programs to be run on a virtual machine are native to the architecture in question and no emulation is necessary, the virtual machine can often be allowed to run in non-privileged mode. Any privileged instructions would be caught by the virtualization software, and appropriate actions could be taken by that software. It is important to note, however, that even unprivileged instructions may rely on sensitive or privileged instructions to run "under the covers" and therefore problems can arise and must be dealt with as one of the effects of virtualization. How these are dealt with is virtualization layer software-specific.

Problems

Whenever a process on a hosted virtual machine invokes a system call, the call must be executed on the virtual system, but not necessarily on the host system on which the virtual machine is resting. The underlying operating system must have the facility to notify the virtual operating system of the requested call and allow that system to handle the call appropriately. It is possible to allow trace processes to reside in memory, identify system calls, and convert those direct system calls to indirect system calls to the virtual systems or convert to an invalid system call that faults, depending on what the call is and what the end result would be. The same is true of page faults that might occur based on instructions run. Page faults should be caught and directed to the virtualized operating system rather than causing issues on the underlying operating system; faults directed to the underlying operating system have the potential to disrupt the operation of the system and applications in question and of any other virtualized systems that may be riding on the same underlying architecture.

Whenever the kernel of a typical operating system is running on physical hardware and it has nothing to do, it runs as an idle thread. When a similar kernel runs on a virtualized machine, the same behavior can cause issues because the virtual machine is seen as wasting processor time during these periods. Optimally, a virtualized machine could have a mechanism in place to suspend itself in situations such as this, or brokers and schedulers could perform a similar task. Ideally, this situation would not be allowed to present itself; rather, the system would dynamically allocate and de-allocate virtual environments as they are needed or not needed any longer. In a true Grid environment that has been integrated into an organization, this should be allowed to occur (within limits). However, whenever a new environment is in process, the administration needs to be more manual and less automatic — if for no other reason than the learning curve.

Virtualization makes use of emulation and OS (operating system) simulation, often because the underlying host computer and the virtualized system are architected differently. An emulator reproduces the behavior of one system on another system and allows it to execute the same programs as would have been executed on the original system in hopes of producing the same results for the same inputs. What is most important in an emulator is that the user does not need to understand or care how it is working and only needs to know that is working correctly. It is easy to find software emulators that mimic old and new computer hardware architectures. Ironically, some of the emulators that are most rapidly accepted in the marketplace are gaming interfaces.

Simulations, on the other hand, are imitations of real systems, and can be considered accurate emulators.

Most often, virtualization provides for multiple execution environments (typically referred to by administrators as virtual machines). Each of these virtual machines is frequently similar to the underlying computer architecture and operating system. Each of these virtual machines looks decidedly like a real machine to the user while, in reality, each virtual machine is isolated from every other virtual machine running on the real underlying machine. One of the most common connotations of virtual machines is the Java Virtual Machine (JVM).

ABI/API Emulation

Rather than creating virtual machines as a means to create entire operating systems, an API emulator can create an execution environment that can be used to run alien programs on a platform. CYGWIN and MKSToolkit are two such ways that enable a Windows computer to run UNIX or Linux commands as if it were nearly native UNIX. Sun used Windows Application Binary Interface (WABI) to allow Solaris to appeal more to Windows users and Windows applications. WABI sits between the native Windows applications, and the operating system intercepts the Windows calls generated by the applications and translates them to their rough equivalent in the UNIX environment. Were these applications run on a true Windows box, these instructions would be run directly by the processor. To add even more flexibility, WABI can also provide optional DOS emulation on Solaris to allow the Solaris to run native DOS-based applications. This can mean that, because on the Grid one has virtualized such a platform, one can extend the useful life of the software investments that have proven useful.

Later, Sun used SunPC software emulation to ape PC hardware equipment on a SPARC system. This software emulator emulates a 286 nearly natively; but with the addition of a SunPC accelerator card with a coprocessor, Windows 3.1 or Windows 95 programs will run successfully, although only one session at a time will run due to the fact that the accelerator card is the hardware that must be used to run the Windows programs.

A later configuration used the SunPCi III, along with a coprocessor card, 1 GB of RAM, and a 10/100 Base-T Ethernet and FireWire port on the optional daughterboard, a physical floppy drive, and a virtual C and D emulated drive. Other drives can be mapped to local or networked file systems. This allows for the addition of DOS and early Windows programming, and also for later versions of native Windows programs running on a Solaris hardware platform.

Lxrun is a software emulator that allows one to execute Linux and ELF binaries on any x86 UNIX systems (such as SCO OpenServer, SCO UnixWare, or Solaris). This feat is achieved by allowing the emulator to remap Linux system calls to UNIX proper calls dynamically. The Linux shared libraries that the natively running application requires, as well as a Linux dynamic loader, must be available on the system for use by the applications. Lxrun is thus a system call emulator. There are, naturally, applications that will not run in this manner; but for a wide array of these applications, this will be a viable alternative. More recent versions of LunxOS even have Linux ABI compatibility. Wine, on the other hand, allows one to run Windows applications on Linux, FreeBSD, or Solaris. Wine, however, emulates only the operating system and not the processor.

Bochs is an open source x86 emulator that was written in C++ and provides user-space emulators that can be used to emulate the x86 processor, several I/O devices, and custom BIOS. Because it is open source, Bochs is highly portable but does not perform overly well because every instruction and every I/O is emulated rather than the overall instructions. In fact, this emulator is rather slow and is not used where performance is critical. However, while it is not a tremendously high performer, it is highly flexible and customizable. The Chorus system's kernel provides a low-level framework on top of which distributed operating systems can be implemented (such as System V UNIX assist code in the Chorus kernel).

FreeBSD provides binary compatibility with some UNIX and UNIX-like systems (including Linux). This product has evolved over time to include a process file system that emulates a subset of the Linux commands on other operating systems. FreeBSD also brings with it a jail-like concept, which allows one to create an isolated environment via software that allows each system to have its own virtual root, and processes running within this virtualized system would not have access to or visibility from any other files, processes, or network services (including IP addresses) that are used in any other jail-like environment. This jail-like environment can be implemented by making the various FreeBSD components in the kernel jail-aware.

Virtual partitions (VPARs) or logical partitions (LPARs) can provide operating systems and applications (complete with namespaces) with isolation. Each VPAR or LPAR runs its own copy of an operating system (potentially even different versions).

These partitions can often be dynamically created, and each can have its own set of resources assigned to it. Within each partition, one can further granularize and create resource partitions that can be used in different ways by that partition. LPARs allow one to run multiple independent operating system images of AIX or Linux on a single server.

Mac-on-Linux (MOL) is a virtual machine implemented on the Linux operating system and allows the Mac OS to (versions 7.5.2 to 9.2.2), Mac OS X, and Linux all on the same system. MOL's functional virtualization is implemented as a kernel module. A user process takes care of the input and output. There is a limited open firmware implementation within MOL.

Microsoft has had its own achievements in the area of virtualization. Windows NT had several subsystems and execution environments (including the virtual DOS machine or VDM, Windows on Win32 or WOW, OS/2, POSIX, and Win32 subsystems). It is true that OS/2 and POSIX, as well as Win32 are server processes, and the DOS and Win16 subsystems operate within the context of a virtual machine process. VDM is essentially virtual DOS and derives from the MS-DOS 5.0 code base running on a virtual x86 system. A trap handler was present to handle the privileged instructions. Windows NT also ran MIPS, so an x86 emulator had to be there in the MIPS version.

In a similar manner, Windows 95 used virtual machines as a method to run older applications (Windows 3.x and DOS native applications). The system virtual machine that ran the kernel had an address space that was shared by all 16-bit Windows programs and a separate address space for any 32-bit Windows applications. With the advent of the 64-bit Windows operating systems, the same will likely be true as for 32-bit applications.

Microsoft included this virtualization as one of the key components of its offerings for the enterprise with the acquisition of Connectix early in 2003. As with Virtual PC, the concept of running multiple operating systems simultaneously on one machine provided flexibility to each additional operating system. As a result, many software vendors that target Microsoft operating systems also have made their applications virtualized. Microsoft has built its own applications (SQL Server 2000, for example) with the multiple instance virtualized instance capability. Its exchange server, file/print servers, IIS servers, and terminal servers do not necessarily need virtualization support in the operating system.

Programming languages also are often implemented using virtual machines. There are many benefits to doing this, including isolation (the virtualized environment as a sandbox) and portability. The UCSD P-System was a bright spot in the 1970s and 1980s, a virtual machine running p-code (something nearly like byte code). In this environment, one of the most popular programming languages was the UCSD PASCAL language. The operating system itself was written in PASCAL.

Arguably the most famous innovation is the Java Virtual Machine (JVM). JVM is an abstract computer with a virtual machine specification that describes the machine in terms of register sets, stacks, heaps, a method area, instruction sets, etc.

JVMs are typically implemented for a particular platform (for example, x86 Linux, x86 Windows, SPARC/Solaris, AIX, and even ZOS) and represent software implementation of the specification. It is possible to implement JVM in microcode or directly on the silicon. JVM allows one to compile a Java program on any platform and run that compiled program on any other platform — such is the advantage of virtualization.

Ultimately, through virtualization, each instance of an environment can be managed independently of all others. These instances can be administered, configured, rebooted, shut down, started up, upgraded, and maintained as a unit unto themselves. Each instance should be allowed to have its own system calls, its own root user (or whatever concept parallels a root user in the given operating system), its own network scheduler and brokers to maintain itself within the broader scope of the Grid, and its own underlying OS resource limits on memory, CPU, disk utilization, and bandwidth. Each environment can have its own virtual sockets and ports, its own virtualized network file system, and its own IP address space. Disk drivers and enhanced virtual file systems must be accessible where each instance sees its own physical disks that can be resized dynastically on which it can create its own disk partitions.

The Grid will require virtualized inter-process communication (IPC), wherein each instance gets its own IPC namespace. IPC is a set of techniques for the exchange of data between two or more threads in one or more processes. This protocol will allow the processes within the virtualized environment itself and with those applications running in their own namespaces. Moreover, the Grid will mean that each virtual environment will need its own process file system where running information on running processes will appear. Each environment will have its own syslog facility and virtual device file system.

It may be to the organization's benefit to virtualize not only the local network stack, but rather an entire system with isolated individual network stacks, each with its own port space, routing table, packet filters, and parameters. These isolated stacks could be provided either within the kernel or running as individualized user processes, with each stack given its own resource limits or guarantees. This is the approach that has been used in academic projects, as well as by virtualization companies in their software.

UML (User Mode Linux) is a port of the Linux kernel to an abstract architecture; UML is a Linux kernel that is created to run on itself (on Linux) as a set of Linux user processes that will run normally unless they are trapped by the underlying system's kernel. UML was originally created to run in what is known as trace thread (tt) mode in which a special trace thread is notified whenever a system call occurs and an entry or exit nullifies the original call. The trace notifies the UML kernel to execute the intended system call locally to the virtualized environment. Because of the way that the UML kernel runs within an external version of the similar operating system, the UML processes and the underlying processes both run in the real user space, and these processes can read from and write to the kernel's memory. UML makes relevant memory temporarily read-only, which hampers performance greatly. Modifications to the underlying Linux kernel addresses many of these issues. Further, one can layer one version of UML inside another version of UML inside the external underlying version of Linux.

VMware was founded in 1998 and its first product was the VMware Workstation. Soon after, the GSX server and the ESX server products were introduced. VMware Workstation and GSX both have a hosted architecture (each needs a host operating system, typically Windows or Linux, on which to ride). As a means to optimize the complex mix of performance, portability, and ease of implementation, the product acts both as a virtual machine monitor (by talking directly to the hardware) and as an application that runs on top of a host operating system. This means that it is free from having to deal with the large number of devices available on the PC. VMware Workstation's architecture includes a user-level application, a device driver for the host system, and a virtual machine monitor created by the driver as it loads. The execution context in which the Workstation runs can be either native (the context of the host) or virtual (belonging to the virtual machine). The driver is responsible for switching contexts. Any I/O operations initiated by a guest system are trapped by the application and then forwarded to the application, which then executes the request in the host's context and performs the I/O using regular rather than trusted system calls. VMware now employs numerous optimizations that reduce various virtualization overheads. VMware Workstation is targeted toward client machines. GSX is also a hosted application, but it is targeted toward server deployments and server applications.

VMware's ESX server enables a physical computer to be made available as a pool of secure virtual servers on which operating systems can run. In this way, dynamic and logical partitioning can occur. ESX does not need a host operating system but runs directly on hardware and in that sense it is the host operating system. ESX was inspired by work on other systems, which were experiments in virtualized shared memory multiprocessor servers to run multiple instances of alternative operating systems. Sensitive instructions that cannot be run in non-privileged mode (for fear of causing general protection faults) are typically handled by the virtual machine monitor. ESX solves this issue by dynamically rewriting those portions of the operating system's kernels code such that it inserts traps at appropriate places to catch such sensitive instructions. ESX can be allowed to run multiple virtual CPUs per each physical CPU. With the addition of physical network interface cards inserted logically into a single high-capacity virtual network device, the ESX can be allowed to extend the reach of a virtualized system.

Chapter 9

Strategy and Planning

However beautiful the strategy, you should occasionally look at the results.

—Winston Churchill

Answers.com (http://www.answers.com/system&r=67) defines a system as it relates to technology in the following manner:

System:
1. A group of related components that interact to perform a task.
2. A computer system is made up of the CPU, operating system, and peripheral devices. All desktop computers, laptop computers, network servers, minicomputers, and mainframes are computer systems. Most references to computer imply a computer system.
3. An information system is a business application made up of the database, the data entry, update, query, and report programs as well as manual and machine procedures. Order processing systems, payroll systems, inventory systems, and accounts payable systems are examples of information systems.

Introduction

No system evaluation, either existing or proposed, happens spontaneously. A systems analysis typically happens because someone requests it.

1. *Department managers* will request that a system be analyzed either because they have an awareness of changing business needs or because they know of changing technology and market conditions that mean that the organization should leverage changes if possible.
2. *Senior executives* often make a recommendation of systems analysis because they are aware of changing market conditions surrounding the organization, less because they have a fundamental knowledge of the technology, and more because they have an understanding of future trend that will impact the company, either requiring the organization to be more flexible or requiring more capacity.
3. *System analysts* will suggest an analysis because they are aware of what is changing in the world of technology and they want to make the organization aware and see how those changes fit into the organization.
4. *Outside groups*, including stockholders, partners, and the competition, will suggest (either directly or indirectly) that it may be time to perform an analysis to meet market conditions.

The first step is figure out exactly what problem one is trying to solve. This is important because it is often true that systems are forced into a company because someone found a new technology that could work really well or that would make the company stand out as a leader in technology. Several problems that are potential reasons for systems analysis follow:

1. The *problem of reliability* rears its head when an existing system either has gone out of compliance or because it no longer meets the needs of the organization. If an existing system begins to fault or fail, and support is having difficulty determining what the problems are, it is time to consider a new system particularly if the existing system is starting to cause data issues (corruption) or begins to not be able to process sufficient data in the window that is available to do the processing.
2. The *problem of validity and accuracy* is encountered when data validity comes into question. When data changes and systems do not change, the validity of data and the accuracy of processing may require review.
3. The *problem of economy* can occur when the computer systems on which the applications reside are no longer able to keep up with processing. This is one of the optimal times when systems can be migrated to a Grid environment to take advantage of the infrastructure architecture.
4. The *problem of timeliness* goes hand in hand with problems of economy. If the current system does not have sufficient processing power or if the process of going through the steps that make up the system can no longer be accomplished in the given processing window, then the system is ripe for systems analysis, and possibly for processing on the Grid infrastructure.
5. The *problem of capacity* is another place where systems analysis is a good place to start and a good time to consider the Grid environment. Capacity can mean

storage space, computing capacity, human processing capacity, or time. By distributing the processing and storage over multiple resources in the environment, it is simple to spread the application over additional capacity.

6. The *problem of throughput* is yet another place where systems analysis optimally occurs and also where the Grid can help with the analysis and with the application so that additional analysis will not likely have to recur in the near future.

The first step in an analysis of a potential system must be the evaluation of current business procedures and problems. Analysts typically begin the exercise by talking with managers and subject matter experts (SMEs) to determine the precise nature of the problem that the organization hopes to solve and to break down the problem into its component parts. This overall task can involve several interviews with different members of the organization to identify what information is currently processed, where that information comes from, and where it goes.

In addition to the interviews, it is common practice to employ written surveys and personal observations of workers performing tasks. Occasionally, those doing the analysis may step into the user's role for a period of time and perform duties in the current system to better understand and document the processes performed.

After collecting sufficient data and information, the analyst or analysis team prepares charts and diagrams that provide a general representation of the existing system and the proposed new system. These documents are created in business terms rather than in technical terms. They are designed to be presented to and used by managers and users and therefore should be written in terms they can understand.

The analysis team stays in close contact with management and users throughout this part of the analysis phase to make sure that team members understand the current system thoroughly and to make sure that the analysis team and management and users agree on the overall principles and processing of the current system.

In addition to the documents generated from of this step in the exercise, another document generated in this phase is a cost-benefit analysis for the new system. This analysis must take into account the cost of migrating the data from whatever system is currently in place, as well as the cost of training users on the new system and the time cost that would be lost while users are overcoming the learning curve of moving from the old system to the proposed system. This will likely be an iterative process. It is nearly impossible to gather all the information in one iteration.

A system typically has inputs and outputs. One natural way to characterize a system is to separate the system definition by number of inputs and outputs and how those inputs and outputs are configured.

- ■ SISO (single input, single output)
- ■ SIMO (single input, multiple outputs)
- ■ MISO (multiple inputs, single output)
- ■ MIMO (multiple inputs, multiple outputs)

However, this is not the only manner of characterization and it is nearly always necessary to break any system into smaller pieces or sub-systems for further analysis and later configuration. This means that anywhere one sees an "M" in the input/output list, one can consider that to be a series of "S" statements. Single input/multiple outputs (SIMO) can simply be broken down into a larger system of single input/single output (SISO) systems. Once a complex system of inputs and outputs has been broken down into singles, they are as granular as they can get.

Design

All computer systems consist of the series of input → processing → output → storage pieces. Outputs are typically either reports or inputs to other systems. The purpose of the design step of systems analysis and design is to figure out how those pieces work together, how they will look at completion and what the outputs will look like when they are done.

Inputs and Outputs

One of the most common design methodologies is to start with the end in mind. If the analysis starts with the end result he can back into what the other steps should be. If one knows, for example, what the output should be and in what manner it will be stored (for how long, in what format, and with what access capabilities), it is possible to craft the system around that information to make it a reality.

Looking at the outputs in a Grid environment adds an extra layer of complexity. Where will the outputs reside, what nodes should and should not be able to access the information, what programs should and should not be able to access the information once it resides as output? Are there any special security concerns surrounding those outputs or any communication issues that might have to be taken into consideration?

Once one realizes that the most important part of the project is the end product and all of the issues that surround that product, the rest is simple.

After the decisions are made concerning what the outputs should be and how best to get those outputs from the inputs, it is time to start building. The initial product that the team builds will be a prototype or a proof of concept. This will be a small-scale model of the ultimate product, incomplete but able run in the Grid environment and leverage the fluidity of the Grid. It must be a working sample of the end product system. Some of the features might be scaled down, but it needs to be robust enough to allow for the addition or subtraction of available nodes, failover from one node to another, or whatever other action is defined should one node in the active Grid fail, to prove that the access paths are applicable.

The output from a prototype should be a scale model of the desired output from the finished system stored in the same manner (if not necessarily on the same hardware location) as the end system will be.

Screens into which information will be entered should be representative and should gather the information that is necessary to achieve the desired outputs. Any additional data that is collected should be handled in a representative fashion. These screens should have the look and feel of the end product screens and should be able to scale and flex with the environment. It is important for the designer to keep in mind that the application must be nearly stateless, and none of the application should fail simply because of a change in hardware that may or may not take place. If automatic data gathering takes place as a part of the end system (for example, input from sensors, from cameras, or other automatic data gathering devices), representative data may be substituted from a file or from user at a terminal keyboard rather than from the actual devices themselves.

One of the considerations for the screens, as well as for the input and output data, should include an understanding of how the data is arranged. In a Grid environment, the layout of the data can be critical. The systems analyst may be called on to make decisions or recommendations concerning this layout. Whether the data is resident in a database or it resides in flat files, these are considerations.

Parallelism versus Fragmentation

Parallelism and fragmentation are similar, and fragmentation can even be used to increase parallelism. This typically is designed to occur when the data is much larger than the programs. Programs should be, as much as possible, executed where the data resides. However, with parallelism, there is no need to attempt to maximize local processing because users are not associated with any particular node, and load balancing is often difficult with fragmentation when one starts dealing with a large number of nodes. Maximizing response time or inter-query parallelism leads logically to portioning. Maximizing the total amount of work throughput typically leads to clustering. Full partitioning versus clustering often leads to variable partitioning.

Data partitioning of a relation involves the distribution of its tuples across several disks, regardless of architecture, and provides high I/O bandwidth access without the necessity of relying on specialized hardware. Partitioning is accomplished, typically by several methods: round-robin partitioning, hash partitioning, and range partitioning. These partitioning methods are used in conjunction with any database-specific partitioning methods that are implemented by different vendors. They are complementary, but often not the same kinds of applications.

Round-Robin Partitioning

Round-robin partitioning maps the ith tuple to disk I mod n. It places the tuples equally among the disks, regardless of the given partitioning attribute's uniformity. It is the most simple of the partitioning strategies; however, it does not typically lend itself to support an associated search. This type of partitioning is excellent for sequential scans of full relations (either for a point query, returning a single value or a single set of data; or for a range query, returning all data fitting into a given range) but is poor for associative access. One of the primary reasons why people adopt this partitioning methodology is that the load is fairly evenly distributed.

Hash Partitioning

Hash partitioning maps each tuple to a disk location based on a hash function. The hash partition's distribution however may or may not be uniform if the partition attribute is not uniform. Hash partitioning offers associative access to the data tuples with a specific attribute value accomplished by directing the access to a single disk. The algorithm is excellent for exact matches. It does tend to randomize the data rather than clustering it for logical accessibility.

Range Partitioning

Range partitioning maps contiguous attribute ranges of a relation to the same sets of disks. The range partition's distribution may or may not be uniform if the partition attribute is not uniform. Range partitioning has the added feature of being able to keep the tuples in some sorted order. It also has the advantage of being very good for an associative search and for clustering data for logical accessibility, but risks execution skew by directing all the execution, to a single partition. If, for example, one assumes a relation that has client_id as a partitioning key, and all client_ids <1000 are found in one partition, all client_ids greater than or equal to 2000 and less than 3000 are located on another partition, and all client_ids greater than or equal to 3000 are located on a third partition (and so forth), and a query attempts to find client_ids between 2100 and 2500, then the query would be sent exclusively to the third partition, leaving the others to run other queries independently. Range partitioning is particularly good for equijoins, range queries, and group-by statements.

Horizontal Data Partitioning

As with fragmentation, one has the option of partitioning data horizontally. The rows or tuples are fragmented across devices in such a way that the tuples all stay together and are distributed by value across the devices.

Keep in mind that data allocation strategy is simply an optimal usage strategy with respect to any given query type if the execution of those queries can always use all the processing nodes available to the system. It is an optimal balance strategy with respect to any given query type if the execution of the queries always results in a balanced workload for all the processing nodes involved.

Primarily, it remains important to not only understand storage strategies, but also it is vital to understand what the data is and how the users typically access the data.

An allocation scheme that is very good for row and column queries is often not optimal for all queries. Equijoins perform especially well on hash partitions.

Replicated Data Partitioning

High-availability requirements mean that data replication is required. Simple hardware replication can be accomplished with RAID solutions that allow for mirrored disks or mirroring with parity. There are load-balancing impacts on the system, however, when one node fails. More elaborate solutions can achieve load balancing. Interleaved partitioning and chained partitioning can accomplish this without having to rely on hardware replication.

Interleaved partitioning allocates a primary copy of a relation on each node. It then provides a backup copy of a part of a different relation to that same node.

Placement Directory

A placement directory performs two functions. It allows the relation name and the placement attribute to be associated with a logical node. It then allows the logical node to be associated with a physical node. It also requires that the data structures in either case should be available whenever they are needed at each node.

Index Partitioning

Index partitioning uses the index as the means to determine *how* to partition the data. Hash indexes would be partitioned by hash, and b-tree indexes would be partitioned as a forest of tress, with one tree per range.

Disk Partitioning

For range partitioning, a sample of the load on the disks is taken. Hot disks are cooled by making the range smaller. For hash partitioning, one would cool host disks by mapping some of the buckets to other disks.

River Partitioning

In river partitioning, one uses hashing algorithms and assumes a uniform distribution of data. If using range partitioning with this data distribution method, the data would be sampled and a histogram is used to level the bulk.

Data-Based Parallelism

A database management system (DBMS) typically hides parallelism. This can make a systems analyst's job more simple and makes the application's data access more transparent. DBMS automates system management via tools that assist with data placement, data organizations (usually using through indexing), and periodic maintenance tasks (such as data dumping, recovery, and reorganization). DBMSs also provide venues for fault tolerance with duplex and fault failover for data and transactions. Furthermore, DBMSs provide an avenue for automatic parallelism with maintenance among transactions accomplished through locking and within a transaction through parallel execution.

Interoperational Parallelism

In interoperations parallelism, a set of P operations, all pieces of the same query, run in parallel.

Intra-Operation

The same operation runs in parallel on different data partitions. There are three ways of exploiting high-performance, multi-processor systems:

1. Automatically detect parallelism in sequential programs as in FORTRAN.
2. Augment an existing language with parallel constructs as in Fortran90 or C.
3. Offer a new language in which the parallelism can be expressed or automatically inferred.

Processing

The processing step of the systems analysis and design is often one of the places where less consideration is given to the building of the application. With applications resident on the Grid that will be taking advantage of the power and flexibility of the key features of a Grid environment, more thought should be given to how these processes are designed.

Processes in a Grid environment should have the ability to easily modularize and break down into sub-components so they can process in parallel. Care must be given to this design step to make sure that each piece determined to be parallel processing-capable does not rely directly on the output of another step or the output of one step needs to be made available to steps that rely on that data to complete their processing. Some applications will decompose more easily than others, and some of the decomposition will depend directly on the underlying data structures.

Data Storage

Once the analyst determines what the inputs and outputs are and creates a prototype model of the end system, it is important to think about the storage that will be necessary for not only the end results, but also any interim results. Furthermore, it is important to estimate the hardware resources that will be necessary to support the system.

The system should be sufficiently scalable to be able to run on a single machine if necessary, yet flexible enough to scale to many nodes to take advantage of economies of scale to assist in the production of output for the end user.

Realistic estimations should be made as to how much data will be generated with each iteration of the application, how long that data needs to be stored, and what the anticipated growth rate is based on anticipated organizational need changes.

How often and in what manner will the data items be accessed? Who will be able to access the data and from where (application, geography, other systems) will it be accessed? How will access to the data be controlled, and how many different levels of access control will be necessary?

Is there sufficient hardware available for the storage solution chosen? Will there be sufficient storage dedicated for the beginning stages of the application implementation, and also for the reasonable future of the application. If additional storage hardware is necessary, will that hardware be easily acquirable and readily available when it is necessary to expand? Can the required hardware be acquired as necessary?

Signoff

Once the design is complete users and management need to sign off on the acceptability of the proposed new system. This should be done early enough in the process that the users can reject design elements without having invested too much time, effort, and money in the system. There needs to be enough detail (even if it is theoretical detail) to allow everyone to get an overview of the system while permitting rework if necessary.

Once the system is accepted, the analysis team prepares specifications for programmers to follow. These specifications should include detailed descriptions of the records, files, and documents used in both the current and proposed processing, and data flow charts describing the interrelationship of the data elements to be considered by the programmers. The team also should be able to coordinate the development of test problems and scenarios to be used to debug the system and participate in trial runs of the systems.

This team should be aware of the computer hardware platforms involved in the Grid and any additional software needed to set up the system. The analysis team will work closely with the programming team to help make sure that programming conforms to the proposed system, to make sure that both teams are working toward the same design end and that the flexibility stays within the specifications.

Implementation

After the input, storage, and output have been analyzed and designed, it may appear that the natural next step would simply be to create the software.

One of the most important steps that anyone can do in the creation of a software program or an entire system is testing that entails determining each component to test for functionality and then testing it. Each component should be tested individually and then as part of a units. Each unit then should be tested and then, finally, the complete system.

Once testing for functionality, often called system integration testing (SIT) is complete the next step is to give the system to the users for user acceptance testing (UAT).

Allowing users to work with the system early and often in the iterative creation phase will allow them to exorcise the bugs that will doubtless show up in the system. It also gives users a chance to determine what works from a usability perspective and from a business needs perspective — and what does not work. If users have a say in a system that system will be more of a success. They will adopt it more easily and more willingly because they will have a vested interest in seeing that it works.

One of the key ingredients in testing is, without a doubt, the test plan. Draw up a test plan that includes what tests will be done and what data will be used in the tests. Include what the anticipated outcomes will be and what performance is anticipated (user load, response time). The overall testing strategy will normally include testing of all the different parts of the software.

Launching Solution

Now that the system has been planned and created, documented and tested, it finally is ready for implementation.

If the system is completely new and not a replacement, it must be put into place and turned on (literally or metaphorically).

Most systems, however, are built as replacements or upgrades for an existing system and implementation is a bit more involved. One must change over from one system to another system and often run both in parallel (or limited parallel) for a period of time. The first thing to do is install any new hardware that is necessary. In the case of launching on the Grid, the only hardware one has to worry about is that proprietary hardware that may be necessary. Once this has been taken care of, data, if necessary, should be loaded into the system. Often, this data will need to be transformed into the format the new system expects. This might mean moving from flat files to a database or from one database system or one database format to another. It will be even more difficult if the data currently resides only in paper format and must be typed in or scanned into the system.

Once the new system is installed, users must be trained. If it is a new system, there will be a learning curve while the users learn the new system. The learning curve will be even bigger if one has to unlearn another system while learning the new system.

One way to accomplish the implementation of the new system is a direct or straight changeover. This kind of implementation happens with a complete replacement of the old system by a new or a totally rebuilt one all at once. This kind of implementation usually takes place during a slack business time. Implementation in this case is simple and clear-cut, but there is the risk of undetected bugs or data-introduced errors in the new system. The new system will be used if users are confident that the system meets their needs and if they are well trained on it. Optimally, the new system will not be directly comparable with the old, but issues may occur if there is little money left in the budget for extra staff to fill in or if the system is large. Implementation takes considerable planning and testing. An inadequate approach may lead to data loss or attempts to circumvent issues or errors that may arise in the new system.

Another method is phased implementation. This approach involves migrating from the old system to the new system in a staged approach rather than all at once. The way the application is staged may be based on location (for example, bringing England and Ireland on board first, then Japan and Asia Pacific at a somewhat later date, and finally to the Americas. This could be based on number of users or amount of data involved). It might be based on implementation of a sub-system (first for hardware, later for women's department, after that men's and later home and garden). Advantages of this kind of implementation include the fact that the implementation team and the developers can learn lessons from one location to the next. Problems are encountered in the implementation; errors or bugs are uncovered in real-life use that were not uncovered by testing. Another advantage of this approach is that the organization is never in any serious danger of failing because only a limited number of groups are using the new system; and during the time when different groups are active on the system, others can be using their time to learn the system in parallel. The primary disadvantage is that it takes considerable time to implement. It is also difficult to control a system when it is running in parallel. Different customers may be treated differently based on the system handling their data. Different customers' data may be in different locations, or worse, one customer's data may be in multiple locations. This could mean having to combine data from the different systems to ensure that all the data is in the same location and in the same format.

A third method of implementation is parallel running. This method is the logical opposite of direct or straight change-over. It includes a period of time when both the old system and the new system are allowed to run in parallel until every one is satisfied that the new system is running successfully. Once the determination is made, the old system can be turned off. This is the least risky method of changing over from one system to the other. It allows users to get thoroughly used to the new system before they have to give up the system with which they have become comfortable. Bugs and data errors can be worked out of the system, and users can be completely trained on the new system. Unfortunately, it is also the most expensive alternative, as it is costly to run two systems at the same time and parallel running requires extra staff or existing staff working overtime. It will likely be difficult to make direct comparisons between the results provided by the two systems. Furthermore, there will be the necessity to migrate data, from one system to the other, often several times between the two systems so that users can accomplish their jobs regardless of what system they are using.

Regardless of which implementation method is used, full implementation notes must be kept about each problem encountered and how each problem was solved, complete with instructions on how to fix the issues. This information should be added to the documentation provided on how to use the new system. However, test plans, results, and problem resolution documents should be added as a separate set of technical documents whereas the system documentation is considered *user* documents).

It is important to note that problem resolution documentation should be created early, before issues occur, and maintained continuously. One should not rely on memory. With a Grid implementation, this is even more critical because issues that arise on implementation may arise whenever a new blade is snapped into the Grid; and having that knowledge either in a hardcopy document or online where it is easily accessed will be beneficial over time. Further, as more applications are created for the Grid, sharing information in the organization on issues and resolutions will make implementations run much more smoothly.

Technical Documentation

One of the most important pieces of information that should come out of the implementation or re-implementation of a system onto the Grid environment must be the technical documentation describing bits and bytes and hardware requirements for the system. This documentation is designed to allow a technician or administrator to update the system in the future, either by adding components additional hardware. It will allow the reader to better understand how the system works and include details on the programming (assumptions, distribution algorithms used for the Grid environment, and pseudo-code and flowcharts or other programming diagrams). Also helpful in this documentation will be annotated changes or customizations that were made to any commercial off-the-shelf (COTS) products included in the application, along with annotations on what each change and each alteration in code does as well as the business reason that may have made the change necessary. The documentation will likely need to show which pieces of the application can be spawned into their own nodes in the Grid.

System flowcharts (diagrams that show how the different hardware components fit together and where all the data is stored as well as access paths) must be included. To provide adequate metadata information to the schedulers and the resource brokers, hardware requirements must include file access, processor capabilities, and memory recommendations for the machines on which the application is likely to be launched. Also required is documentation of software on which the new system relies, software that will need to be brought in or changed to allow the solution system to operate effectively. This will also be important for the resource broker as it will need to be aware of what software should be resident on any given node to assist with processing applications.

User Documentation

User documentation is geared toward people who will be using the system. This person does not need to care where the data is located or how it is stored; she just needs to know what question she wants to answer. For this reason, user documentation should be much less detailed than technical documentation. User documentation needs to include information on what kind of hardware will be necessary for the user to use to access the system.

If there is a supported version of the browser that must be used to access the system, it should be noted in this documentation. Inputs, their type, and how those inputs will get into the system should be noted in this documentation. Anticipated outputs, their format, and where those outputs are supposed to go should also be noted, as should screen shots of successful operations and, if possible, failed operation so that users know what to expect should they experience a failure, and so they know that they have successfully submitted a job. It would also be helpful to include the meaning of any error messages that might appear on the user's screen and what to do if and when those error messages appear. This way, users will be better prepared should errors occur and will have realistic expectations of the system so they will not become frustrated when those errors occur.

Evaluation and Maintenance

Once the system has been implemented, the next important step is evaluation of its performance and maintenance.

The performance of the system must be evaluated for efficacy and compared to objective. Objectives or business needs should have been collected before considering any system — before writing a single line of code. The systems analyst, in conjunction with subject matter experts (SMEs) from the organization, will have agreed on all the things that the end product needed to do. These specifications will have been captured on paper and signoff will have been achieved. This document is the basis for the evaluation of the system against the specifications.

This evaluation step is important whenever the solution is completed and implemented because agreement of all parties on the successful delivery of the product. How successful the project and the ultimate system is a requirement should be measured and a determination should be made of how well the problem was solved. The solution system will be considered a success if all objectives are met and performance is adequate for the target users.

Once this comparison is performed, it is easy to see gaps (whether anticipated or not) in the system. It is also the starting point for the people involved in the project to accept the fact that it is not always possible to have thought of everything they wanted the end system to do. Once everyone sees what the system is capable of and what can be expected from the system, they will be better able to see where the system misses the ideal. Most of these will be places that no one ever considered in the early design phases, and likely never even considered in the testing phases.

People should approach the exercise with the understanding that the system they now have is not the ultimate single solution but rather a point on a continuum. It is always possible to find better ways to help users do their jobs better and more effectively, and better ways to leverage the flexibility of the Grid as the organization learns more about it.

This shows why the technical documentation is so important. It will be the basis for this evaluation and maintenance step. With this documentation, anyone should be able to see what has been done and how the system is put together and know where to build on the additional modules and make the necessary changes to existing functionality.

Services

Services are unique as they apply to a Grid environment and how that environment deals with them. They must be taken into account when considering applications that will be resident on the Grid environment and that will leverage the Grid's flexibility. Services are nothing more than loosely coupled software programs designed to support the requirements of business processes and software users. Resources are typically made available on the network through the use of independent services that those applications require. Services are rarely tied directly to any one given technology but, rather, are usually implemented using a wide array of technologies.

Remote procedure calls (RPCs) allow computer programs to cause a procedure or subroutine to execute in another hardware space (usually another computer, but often resident on the same computer as the calling program) without the programmer of the calling program necessarily having to write the same code. An RPC is often used for implementation of client/server models or distributed computing. The programmer of the calling or client, application would need to write some kind of similar code to the subroutine that sends a request message to the remote server service to execute the specific procedure using supplied parameters. A response is returned to the client, where the application continues along with its process, but there are many variations and subtleties in the implementation, resulting in different protocols. When the software components are written in object-oriented programming principles, the RPC can be referred to as remote invocation or remote method invocation.

Another implementation of these services can be created using the Distributed Component Object Model (DCOM), which is a Microsoft proprietary technology for components distributed across multiple networked computers. DCOM extends the Microsoft COM technology and provides a communication substrate for the Microsoft application server infrastructure but has been deprecated in deference to the .NET technology.

Object Request Broker (ORB) is another service component used in distributed computing. It is a piece of middleware that allows programmers to make program calls from one computer to another through the network, regardless of the size or complexity of the network. ORBs transform the in-process data structure to and from the byte sequence, which is transmitted over the network. This is what is often referred to as serialization. Some ORBs are CORBA-compliant and use interface description language (IDL) as the means to describe the data that is to transmit on remote calls. Before OOP (object-oriented programming) became quite so mainstream, RPC was the most popular service broker. ORBs often expose many features to calling programs such as distributed transactions, directory services, or real-time scheduling.

Finally, Web services are software systems designed to support interoperability from machine to machine over a network. These services are often implemented simply as application programming interfaces (APIs) that are used to access over a network executing procedures on a remote system hosting the requested services. It is important to note, however, Web services can also refer to those services that use SOAP-formatted XML envelopes and have their interfaces described by WSDL (Web service definition language).

SOA (service oriented architecture) can be implemented through any of these protocols or through the use of file system mechanisms as the communication media for data conforming to a defined interface specification between processes. The overriding feature is independent services with defined interfaces that can be called to perform any tasks in a standard way without the service having foreknowledge of the calling application. The application does not have to have to know how the services actually perform the tasks. The interface definition hides the implementation of any language-specific service, and this means that the SOA interfaces are independent of development technologies.

A key feature of these services is that they should, particularly in a Grid environment, be independently upgradeable. Versioning and compatibility of services must be managed and expressed in such a way that clients can discover not only the specific service versions, but also any available compatible services. These services need to be alterable without disrupting overall environment.

While an environmental change may change a set of network protocols used to communicate with the service, an upgrade to the service may correct the errors or enhance the overall interface. The service definition or specification indicates the protocol bindings that can be used to communicate with the service.

Analysis of a System

- A system has many characteristics. Some characteristics are universal while others are unique to a Grid system.
- All systems have structure or organization.
- All systems function in this case, handling the flow and transfer of information and require the presence of the driving force or source of information as well as a destination.
- All systems show some degree of integration. Components of the system act together to form the integral whole.
- Changes in the value of one or more variables (or reservoir) are detected throughout the system. This results in the regulation of variables.

- Systems tend to interact with each other, either in a causal relationship or as procedures in which the components interact.
- Systems tend to have interdependence if only in that they exchange data. Very few systems are totally independent and not reliant on information that is fed to them from other systems or that feed on information from other systems. They are often integrated tightly with the other systems on which they depend.

Every system has a central objective. It is always critical that, when determining how to design the application, the team remembers what that central objective is. When looking to design a system for a Grid environment, it is of paramount importance that the central objective fit with the design of the overall Grid.

One of the primary features of systems analysis is the output of the system. Reports are critical to the operation of most organizations. Anyone looking to design a new system (regardless of whether or not it is a Grid system) must consider these same features. The location, type, and format of the outputs in a Grid environment are more complex to design than is often the case in other environments.

After the outputs, the next components to account for are the inputs. In the case of the Grid environment, the inputs are even more difficult to nail down in many cases. This is typically due to the fact that the inputs are as fluid and flexible as the Grid itself. Data input must be accurate, and the system in question must be able to ensure the accuracy of the data. If many systems access (as inputs or as outputs) this data, accuracy needs to be even further guaranteed. The system in question also must not introduce any inaccuracies into the data. Timeliness of the inputs is critical to take into account because there are likely many different applications accessing this data nearly simultaneously. The timing of these inputs must be assured whenever the application in question initiates. The input data format should be understood so that the application is assured of processing the inputs accurately.

Files used as inputs, outputs, and throughputs for the system in question or are used to drive the application that the systems analysts are designing should be identified and specifications for these files should be recorded in the design documents.

Once all these pieces are considered, the processes that make up the way the tasks are done in the system and the way we anticipate doing it in the future should be identified. It is often optimal at this point to sit with the users and watch what they do. It is even better if those doing the analysis are able to carry out the processes, but this is not always possible. Extensive notes are important at this step because these notes will be translated into the new processes that will make up the new system. All the processes in the current system will need to be mapped into the new system.

Types of Systems

Having mapped out the inputs, outputs, and processes, it is time to determine what kind of system is most appropriate for a particular situation. Manual systems are still almost entirely paper based. While these systems are no longer the norm, they are not completely out of the ordinary. Many smaller organizations rely on manual systems for accounting, bookkeeping, marketing, and various other processes that are intrinsic to the organization. While, as systems analysts and computer professionals, we typically attempt to solve most of the world's problems with technology, there are still organizations and situations where manual efforts continue to be used.

The most common system is the combination. Such systems are partly computerized while other parts of the system are manual.

Finally, there are completely automated systems. These systems using human input as their source of information performance of their processing automatically. They have flat files and databases behind them, and the processes and the computational power reside in the computer rather than in someone's head or in a desk calculator. These are typically the most optimal systems to migrate to a Grid infrastructure.

One of the most common computer-based systems, is an online transaction processing (OLTP) system. OLTP systems respond immediately to user input or requests. Each user request is considered a transaction. An automatic teller machine (ATM) is an example of an OLTP system. OLTP systems typically handle high numbers of transactions, but each transaction is typically low in processing resources requested, and these transactions often are fast and not resource or computationally intensive. Exceptions in a transaction processing system that may be optimally and intimately related to Grid environments are front-end applications that take user input through the Web interface and, based on that input, proceed to back-end processing on the Grid.

Batch processing systems often handle the back-end processing that drives the information that is initially processed by OLTP systems. Historically, when people hear the term "batch processing," they automatically think of mainframe processing. While many mainframes actually perform online transaction processing very well, most people think of batch processing when they think of mainframes. There is often a great deal of batch processing that must go on to support OLTP systems. It is also true that batch processing does not always mean mainframe processing. Midrange and even small systems can contribute to batch processing. ATMs have, batch processing in the bank to process the payments and the withdrawals to the relevant accounts, credit card transactions, and the associated fees and interest. Batch processing is often very resource intensive due to the amount of data that must be processed and the amount of computation that must be done to get to the end of the batches. Batch jobs are typically set up so that they can run to completion with absolutely no interaction from human hands or minds. All input data is preselected through scripts or through passed-in command-line parameters. Batch processing allows sharing of limited computer resources among many users. It shifts the background processing to times when the data is available and when other processing is not occurring (when the resources are less busy). Batch processing allows the computing resources to not remain idle, but allows the processing to occur without continuous interaction by humans. How do organizations typically help provide for batch processing? By providing expensive computers (mainframes, midranges, and banks of minimally used servers) and attempting to amortize the by increasing the utilization of these expensive resources, organizations attempt to meet what they believe are their computing needs.

Management information systems (MIS) are computer systems designed with the express purpose of helping managers plan and direct business and organizational operations. These systems are typically the precursors to decision support systems. Often resource intensive, long running, and critical to the overall business, these systems compete with the other systems for resources. Organizations frequently do not spend the money on resources to dedicate to these systems because the systems do not contribute to the obvious bottom line of an organization. These systems are optimal systems to run on the spare CPU cycles of the organization — the same spare CPU cycles that the Grid environment can help harness.

Office automation systems provide integrated information handling tools and methods that are geared toward improving the productivity of employees. Typically, the handling of information by office people is the focus of this newer technology; the effects stretch beyond this area. Organization of functions, lines of reporting, training for new methodologies for getting tasks accomplished, and workspace design and travel patterns are often included in this kind of system. Frequently, these systems stretch to include the design of branch office locations, home offices, hours of working, and employee morale. One of the most important things to consider in this kind of system is that not only should technological changes be taken into account, but also that change is difficult for many people to deal with and these systems introduce a tremendous amount of change. These systems may, at times, be resource intensive; however, they do not typically run routinely or for extended periods of time. They may reside in the Grid and leverage the power of the Grid but they are not likely to need to be designed specifically for the Grid.

Data warehouses and decision support systems (DSS) comprise a class of computer-based information- and knowledge-based systems that support decision-making activities. There is no single glorious approach to the creation of DSS, any more than there is any single approach to decision making. Basically, a DSS is a computerized system to assist in making decisions. A decision is a choice of a number of alternatives. A DSS uses estimation, evaluation, and a comparison of alternatives based on an analysis of data as it exists in the organization. Features of DSS include interactivity in defining the "what-if" analysis, flexibility in defining the variables, and adaptability in that the scenarios and the parameters must be able to be changed by whoever needs to run these scenarios. These systems are specifically developed for the thought processes that go into the decision makers' decisions and capture as many of their insights as possible. DSS couples the intellectual resources of managers with computer system capabilities to improve the value of decisions. DSS does more than just analyze the data that has connections that are known to exist (like time of year correlates to sales, or income bracket correlates to the amount of discretionary income).

- Model-driven DSS look at statistical, financial, optimization, or simulation data. These systems are not necessarily data intensive but are often computationally intensive.
- Communication-driven DSS work to support more than one person working on a shared task. These systems tend to virtualize organizations.
- Data-driven DSS emphasize access to and manipulation of time series sets of internal company data, typically vast amounts of company data often coupled with external data.
- Document-driven DSS manage, retrieve, and manipulate unstructured information in electronic format. Because the nature of the data is unstructured, the majority of the processing is computationally intensive.
- Knowledge-driven DSS support problem-solving expertise that is stored as facts, rules, procedures, or other electronic structures.

Investigations

When looking through an analysis, it is often beneficial to conduct a feasibility study (a preliminary study undertaken before the critical phase of a project begins). The concept behind a feasibility study is to determine the likelihood that the project will succeed. One looks at possible alternative solutions, determines the best possible alternative, and then attempts to determine whether the new system will be more efficient than its predecessor. A feasibility study can be used to determine whether a current system still suits its purpose or to determine whether a technological advancement has improved or made redundant the current system. It can be used to determine whether the current system is able to cope with the expanding workload and can meet the increasingly astute needs of customers' demands for speed and quality. Feasibility studies can whether determine technology is changing to such a degree that competition is gaining on the organization's market share. Based on the answers to these questions, one can determine whether a new system can meet the increased need. During feasibility studies, one looks at the following areas:

- *Economic feasibility* concerns financial ability to build a new system, or maintain the current system over time. The benefits should outweigh the costs. The system should be compared to any other projects that are slated for the same period of time.
- *Technical feasibility* answers questions regarding the actual need for the new system, how difficult it will be to build, whether a commercial-off-the-shelf product would meet the need, and whether there are any compelling reasons to use new technology to meet the new need.
- *Schedule feasibility* determines to whether the system can be built in the given time period and whether it can be implemented during periods of low activity to minimize any impact on the organization.

- *Organizational feasibility* concerns ample organizational support for the new system to be implemented successfully, whether the organization can withstand the changes that the new system will entail, and whether the organization is changing too rapidly to master the new system.
- *Cultural feasibility* looks at the project's alternatives, and all the impacts are evaluated on the organization's local and organizational culture and environmental factors.
- *Legal feasibility* addresses any legal, ethical, or security issues that surround the implementation of the newly proposed systems or their existing alternatives.

Regardless of the outcome of the study, several steps should be followed:

1. Form a project team and appoint a project lead. While the overall project probably has a plan, the feasibility study must have its own sub-project that must also be planned. This means that it needs its own team and a project leader or manager. It is often useful to have a different project manager for the feasibility study than for the overall project, simply to keep one person from becoming overloaded with tasks.
2. Prepare system flowcharts. Ideally, they should include as much detail on the existing system as possible. Note wherever there is branching in work-flows and anywhere that a decision needs to be made in the process. If possible, flowchart as many of the proposed system changes as possible so that one can compare differences on as many characteristics as possible.
3. Enumerate potential proposed systems.
4. Define and identify the characteristics of the proposed system.
5. Determine and evaluate the performance and cost effectiveness of each proposed system.
6. Weight system performance and cost data.
7. Select the best proposed system. Selection of the system depends on several features:
   a. *Capability* (the ability of the system to allow or disallow access to the system and its data for specific users, uses, or purposes). This feature can be particularly important when looking at a Grid environment because the nature of the Grid allows for more lax access rules on the system in general and relies to a greater extent on the applications to do their own limiting of users and uses.
   b. *Control.* This includes flow control as well as control over the application. Be sure to have control over the flow of information in the programs, as well as control over the way that the application performs in and interacts with the environment in which it will run.
   c. *Communication.* This factor must be addressed because these Grid-enabled applications will have associated network costs and will need to communicate with all related systems as well as access those resources

(computing, human, and data resources) that are necessary for its successful implementation.

d. *Cost.* Cost constraints relate, naturally, not only to the creation of the application in general, but also to the cost of running the application (performance and learning curve) and the cost of maintaining the application.

e. *Competitiveness.* The organization must know what the commercial off-the-shelf (COTS) alternatives are to the given application and at least infer what it means to the organization to customize the COTS application to make it fit the organization's needs. If the cost, the features, or the functionality of the application do not compete favorably with any of the readily available alternatives, then the application will never come to fruition.

8. Prepare and report final project directive to management.

More questions will arise during the feasibility study; and when they do, clarification should be requested and, if necessary, additional cycles of face-to-face question and answer sessions or other analysis should be conducted.

Once the feasibility study is complete and the documentation compiled has been presented, the next step is to request approval for the new system and make a determination of requirements for the new system that should in turn, should be presented to the stakeholders and agreement from all relevant parties should be gained.

After accomplishing all these steps, one can begin to design the final system. Story boards can be employed at this step, as can flowcharts and process charts. The design process should include as many possible details on the process flows noted in the analysis of the existing system. The more detail that one can put into this section, the easier the remainder of the project will be and the better the end product is likely to be. A good approach is to include screen design descriptions or pictorial representations of the screens and an explanation of what those screens will do and how users will make use of them.

After the design phase is complete, one can progress to working on the development of the software. It is important at this point to meet software expectations while building in the functionality of the specifications and keeping in mind the flexibility one is trying to leverage for the Grid environment. Wherever one can build in the potential for parallel threads of application, that should be the target. While programmers and designers are working through all the issues of coding and development, they need to be thinking about and working on documentation and development notes so that they will be better able to provide the appropriate level of documentation to all the stakeholders. This step is even more important in a Grid environment than in a conventional platform because anyone running the system must have an understanding of where the parallelism and multi-threading can be leveraged, to what level one can anticipate that the data will be distributed, and where and how to input information on where to find relevant data and parameters.

Periodically, as different pieces of the system are finished, it is important to test the system or components for functionality and performance. Then, when it comes time to do an overall system test of the application, the majority of the functionality will have been tested and the bugs are already fixed.

Having completed the programming and system testing, one can then proceed to the implementation, evaluation, and maintenance phase of the project.

Chapter 10

Programming

There are 10 types of people in the world: those who understand binary and those who don't

Select count(*) from users where clue > 0;

No Rows Returned

—Seen on technology T-shirts

Grid Programming

Several concerns arise with regard to programming applications for the Grid environment. Not every program is destined to be a Grid-aware program or an application that leverages the power of the Grid. Those that are not can reside comfortably alongside those that are and can leverage many of the virtualization changes that come as a part of the new environment.

It is important to understand that to be able to truly leverage the Grid's power and flexibility, an application must be able to be broken into pieces, and those pieces must run in parallel and have their output brought together and returned to the end user as a single unified output set. There are many ways to accomplish this, and the decision on how to get there is a great part of the adventure.

Parallel Programming

Parallelism is the process of performing large, complex tasks faster and more elegantly than might otherwise be possible. Larger tasks can either be performed serially, with one step following the previous one, or it can be decomposed into smaller independent tasks that can be performed simultaneously.

This is accomplished by breaking up a larger task into smaller tasks, assigning the smaller tasks to multiple workers to be acted upon simultaneously, and having the workers work independently and coordinate with each other. Solving problems in this way is common in building construction, conducting business in large organizations, and manufacturing large products.

Sequential processing executes one instruction at a time using one processor in the server. The processing speed of that application depends on how fast the data can physically move through the hardware. Even the fastest computer can only execute one instruction in nine to twelve billionths of a second, and most organizations do not have the fastest servers on which to run all their applications. However, there are applications that need more intensive, faster application processing than that. Simulation problems and modeling problems based on successive approximations that use more and more calculations and that demand more precise computations require more processing power than may be available.

Many business problems depend on computations and the manipulation of large amounts of data. These businesses process images or other digital signals that render images or other media, or store and utilize these data elements as a means of doing business. Many organizations are starting to process images of invoices and those images need to be stored, utilized, and processed. Other businesses process vast amounts of data in data warehouses and data mining. Still others process weather information and seismic data. All these businesses and applications need more processing capability than is likely available in conventional serial processing.

Processing that handles climate modeling, fluid turbulence, pollution or population dispersion, the human genome project, ocean circulation, semiconductor or superconductor modeling, combustion systems and vision processing, or cognition requires vast quantities of computing power — and all these applications require a better response time than nine billionths of a second per application.

A traditional supercomputer only has a single processor, although an extremely fast processor with peak performance achieved with optimal memory bandwidth. These supercomputers support sequential programming, which is the kind of programming most developers understand best. This is supported by more than 30 years of compiler, language, and tool development. I/O is handled in a relatively simple way. Two limitations of supercomputers are that each contains single processor and they are extremely expensive. The computing power that is harnessed creates a significant amount of heat and therefore a significant amount of cooling is required to keep it running. It is important to note, however, that performance is reaching its theoretical limit of how fast it can process data.

Parallel supercomputers as a single unit apply smaller, more cost-effective processors to the same task, thereby capitalizing on work being done in the microprocessor markets and networking advances. Using these advancements, it is possible to put a supercomputer to work on problems that are impossible with traditional computers and traditional supercomputers. It is possible to scale a problem to fit the hardware and scale the hardware to fit the problem.

Parallel supercomputers are very much like the Grid, and the concepts that work in parallel supercomputers work in Grid programming.

It is important to understand that, whether they work with parallel supercomputers or the Grid, programmers need to learn parallel programming approaches; they need to learn to compartmentalize the applications that they create and the processing that is involved. Standard sequential code will not run as efficiently as a similar program with parallel code on the same set of hardware. Different concepts involved in these kinds of programs do not ever have to be taken into account in traditional programming.

Message passing, for example, should be understood because the different components must have the ability to communicate the processing program. The message passing interface (PI) is the *de facto* standard protocol used for this language-independent computer communication interface. It does not define the protocol by which the communication is performed, but rather only provides a productivity interface that is callable from any computer language capable of interfacing with routine libraries.

Parallel programming involves the decomposition of a programming algorithm or data into parts, then distributing the parts and their tasks to be worked on by multiple processors simultaneously. One of the difficult problems is the coordination of work and communication among the processors. Another is the need to determine what kind of parallel architecture is being used. Parallel programming is more likely to have these issues than a Grid.

One of the most optimal places where parallel programming can be leveraged to its best is a single set of instructions that need to be performed on multiple data sets. When one has applications that have a single instruction set, each of the sets of data can have its own processor and have its processing handled by that machine. In this case, the data and its processing should not have to be synchronized at any point in the process (other than perhaps the last step, depending on what the processing is). All the processors operate at the same time, or in their own time, and the processing finishes quicker overall. This kind of processing is very good for data feeds from several locations that consist of receipts that need to be processed into a system, or orders or inventories from a large number of stores that need to be processed, filed, and calculated and orders filled or inventories adjusted. It is important to remember that this can even be a part of the overall process stream. Many applications process, for example, invoices, and that processing would be optimal for this kind of parallel processing and a report on the overall process is created. This could be easily incorporated in the process described here if one pulls all the information (maybe from interim files) into a single process that can rapidly combine the data into a single output report. Typically, this kind of processing deals with a finite and known number of processors or machines and can leverage much of the flexibility of the Grid but would need adaptation to be able to leverage adding blades to the system.

Certain problems that have a single instruction set that needs to be processed on a single set of data. It is important to realize that many of the programs and processes that exist in the environment are not conducive to being parallelized. While a system may be flexible, having all of these programs leverage the full power, the full ability of the Grid is neither practical nor is it likely. This is not a bad thing. Try to figure out what features of the Grid one can leverage and leave the other features to more appropriate applications.

In a single computer with multiple processors that can be put to use in this way, the processors communicate through the memory architecture. This affects how one writes a parallel program. In looking at multiple processors on multiple servers in a Grid environment, one needs to create the facilities (or have the facilities created already on the environment) that will allow one to do this interprocess communication across the LAN (local area network) or other interconnect. Multiple processes running on the same computer either use a shared memory architecture or a distributed memory architecture.

In *shared memory architecture*, multiple processors on a single server operate independently but they all have to share the same memory resources on that server. Only one processor at any given time can access the shared memory location. Synchronization is achieved by controlling the tasks reading from and writing to the shared memory location. This means that data sharing among the tasks is fast (depending on the speed of the memory). It also means, however, that because bandwidth is limited, increases in processor speed without a corresponding increase in bandwidth can cause severe bottlenecks and that the user programs are responsible for specification of synchronization and locks.

In *distributed memory architecture*, multiple processors operate independently, with each having its own private memory. Data is shared across a communication network using message passing (this is what can be made to be applicable in a Grid environment). User programs are responsible for the synchronization using message passing but not necessarily having to get to the level of manual lock manipulation. Distributed memory architecture allows one to scale memory to the number of processors. If one increases the number of processors, one can increase the memory and bandwidth. It is, however, difficult to map existing data structures to this memory organization; the user is responsible for sending and receiving the data among the processors. It is necessary, to minimize overhead and latency, to block data in as large a chunk size as possible and ship to the relevant node that needs it before it is actually needed.

There are several different kinds of memory/processor arrangements that can be used in this kind of architecture. One can see distributed memory architecture in massively parallel processor (MPP) configurations. Shared memory can be seen in either symmetric multiprocessor (SMP) or non-uniform memory access (NUMA) configurations. SMP systems make use of identical processors, each with equal access to memory (sometimes this is called UMA or uniform memory access). The cache coherence of this model means that if one processor updates a shared memory location, all the other processors know about the update. The NUMA model is actually often accomplished by linking multiple SMPs, one of which can directly access the memory of the other. Not all processors in NUMA necessarily have equal access to all memories on all machines.

Is this the only possible set of combinations? Of course not. And as the combinations become more complex, the more the system resemble a Grid environment. Multiple SMPs can be connected via a network. All the processors within a local SMP communicate with brother processors via memory interconnect, but messaging is employed when one has to map between processors on one SMP and the memory of another one. One SMP cannot directly access the memory of another SMP.

Multiple distributed memory processor machines connected together over a network are applicable for blade servers. One uses small, fast memory to supply data to processors and larger slower memory to backfill the smaller memory where it does not fit all needs. Transfer from main, high-speed memory to shared memory is transparent to users. This model is becoming more and more feasible because now one can more easily couple several processors and their local memory with surrounding larger shared memory all on a single board or a single backplane.

But how does one write programs for these parallel processing paradigms? There are two primary methods: (1) message passing (where the user makes calls to libraries with the specific purpose of sharing information between the processors), and (2) data parallel (where the partitioning of the data determines the parallelism of the processing). There are, however, several other models, including:

- Shared memory allowing processors to share common memory space.
- Remote memory operation permitting sets of processors to access the memory of other processes without deliberate participation.
- Threads allowing a single process with multiple concurrent paths to execute.
- Combined methods composed of any two or more of these models.

In message passing, the model is defined as a set of processes using only local memory; the processes communicate by sending and receiving messages between running processes. Data transfer between processes requires that cooperative operations be performed by each process. This means that for every send event, there must be a corresponding receive event. Programming with message passing is accomplished by linking with and making calls to the libraries that manage the data exchange between the processors. Message passing libraries are available for nearly every modern programming language.

Data parallel paradigms work by allowing each process to work on a different part of the same data structure or by allowing the same process to work on different sets of the same format of data. This is commonly accomplished with a single program/multiple data (SPMD) approach. Data is distributed across processors or is accessible centrally across multiple processors. All message passing is done invisibly to the programmer. These models are commonly built on top of the common message passing libraries. Programming, in the case of data parallel, is accomplished by writing a program with data parallel constructs and having to compile the programs with a data parallel compiler. The compiler converts the program into standard code and calls the message passing libraries to distribute the data to all the processes.

If one is starting to create a parallel program with an existing serial program, debug the code completely. If one is not starting with an existing program, determine exactly what flows need to be accomplished in the program and, if possible, flowchart the program showing the decision paths that are needed in the program. Once one has an idea of what the processes are required, identify the parts of the program that can be executed concurrently. This requires a thorough understanding of the program's algorithm and determines where exploitation of any inherent parallelism may exist. This may require restructuring the program or completely rethinking the algorithm.

Now decompose the problem into functional parallelism, data parallelism, and parts of the program that can be accomplished by the combination of functional and data parallelism. Functional decomposition is accomplished when one decomposes the problem into a series of different tasks that can be distributed to the multiple processors for simultaneous execution. This is particularly effective when there is no static structure of fixed determination of number of calculations that must be performed. Data parallelism (or domain decomposition) partitions the problem's data domain into discrete partitions and distributes those sets (either literally or virtually) to the multiple processors for simultaneous execution. This is particularly good for problems where the data is static (factoring and solving large matrix or finite difference calculations); where dynamic data structures are tied to a single entity and that entity can be broken into subsets (some processes come into the overall application at some point after other parts of the application have completed processing a portion of the data and feed those outputs into other processes as inputs); and where the domain is fixed but computations within the various regions of the domain are dynamic, either over the duration of the run or over time.

Only now can one start to develop the new code. Code may be influenced (or even determined) by the machine architecture used. If there are multiple AIX boxes, one may need to consider the programming differently from multiple VMS boxes or even a series of mainframe programs. Then choose a programming paradigm, determine the intra-program and inter-program communication methodology, and create the code necessary to accomplish task control and communication.

It is important that to understand inter-processor communication for programs in this model to perform effectively. Message passing in these programs must be programmed explicitly. The programmers must understand the process and code the communication appropriately. Data parallel compilers and runtime systems do all their communications behind the scenes, and the programmer does not need to understand all the underlying communication. To get optimal performance from code written for data parallel compilers, programmers should write their algorithms with the best communication possible. Communication in these kinds of processes includes (1) point-to-point (one processor sends to another and that one receives); (2) one-to-all broadcast (a node has information that other nodes need, and a broadcast message is sent to many other nodes); (3) all-to-all broadcast (all nodes broadcast messages to all other nodes); (4) one-to-all personalized (one node sends a unique message to all the other nodes); (5) all-to-all personalized (each node sends unique messages to each other processor); (6) shifts (information is exchanged in one logical direction with each processor passing information to the next); and (7) collective computation (one member of the Grid group collects all the data from all the other members using mathematical operators such as min, max, or add).

Once all these steps have been completed, one can then compile, test, and debug the program. One needs to measure performance (this likely happens sometime after the application is implemented), locate any problem areas and improve them. There are many different optimization methodologies for any given application and any given environment. What is most important to remember is that, in practice, performance tuning is at least as much art as science, and usually more art than science.

One way to improve performance is to load-balance tasks (distribute them in such a way as to ensure the most time-efficient parallel execution). If tasks are not distributed in a balanced way, one ends up waiting for one task to complete while others are idle. It does not necessarily mean that this should be avoided, only taken into consideration when designing and implementing. Performance, however, can be increased if the workload is more evenly distributed. This can be accomplished if there are many tasks of varying sizes and one maintains a task pool to distribute to processors as each finishes. In this way one can more efficiently complete each job and utilize the infrastructure. One needs to consider the heterogeneity of the machines in the environment; machines can vary widely in power and user load versus a homogeneous environment and identical processors running one job per processor.

Other performance considerations include the granularity of the problem. To coordinate different processors working on the same problem, they should communicate. The ratio between computation and communication is the granularity needed to optimize performance. If using fine-grained parallelism, all tasks execute in a small number of instructions between communication cycles. This means a low computation-to-communication ratio, and also that one can optimize load balancing. However, it implies a higher communication overhead and a smaller opportunity for incremental performance gains. Taken to its extreme, granularity that is too fine can mean that the overhead required for the communication and synchronization of tasks actually begins to take longer and become a bigger bottleneck than the computations themselves. In course-grained parallelism, one deals more often with long computations consisting of large numbers of instructions that occur among communication synchronization points. There is a high computation-to-communication ration, which implies significant room for performance increases. It also implies, unfortunately, that it is more difficult to load-balance efficiently.

The most efficient granularity depends on the algorithm and the hardware environment. In most cases, the overhead associated with this communication and synchronization is high relative to the execution speed that can be expected, so it is typically more advantageous to have coarse granularity unless there is a compelling reason to have a finer granularity.

For some problems it is possible to decrease execution time that is directly attributable to computational execution but this will increase the execution time that is directly attributable to the communication. In this case, the time required for communication is not attributable to granularity, but is attributable to bandwidth parameters. Communication patterns will also affect the computation-to-communication ratio and optimizing bandwidth will optimize the communication.

I/O patterns are also potential roadblocks to optimizing a parallel processing application. Parallel I/O systems are largely undefined and minimally available, but multiple paths to a virtual storage device allow this to be nearly approximated. In an environment where all processors access the same file space, write operations will often mean that files get overwritten or incorrect versions of files will be processed. Read operations will be impacted by the infrastructure's ability to handle multiple reads at the same time from the same location. A reduction in the number of I/O operations that need to occur (often by larger block sizes) will allow for fewer I/O operations. Also, if one can confine the majority of the I/O operations to a discrete portion or each process, then one can minimize the impact. To minimize the chances that files will be overwritten, one can create unique file names for each task's input and output files. Another way to minimize impact is to utilize temporary files in distributed locations can minimize the impact even further.

One final performance bottleneck that must be taken into account is data dependency that exists where data for multiple uses exists in the same data storage location. A single path to a single data location can be a large inhibitor to parallel execution.

Multi-Threaded Programming

Threads are nothing more than semi-processes, each of which has its own stack and each of which executes a given piece of code. Each thread typically shares its memory with other threads, but this need not necessarily be the case. A thread group is a set of threads all executing inside the same processes and all of which can access any global variables, the same heap memory, and the same file descriptors. All these threads execute in parallel using either time slices or literally in parallel across multiple processors. Using thread groups instead of normal serial programs means that events can be handled immediately as they arrive (user interfaces, database queries, or error processing). With thread groups, one can switch contexts (one thread to the next) quickly, and communication among threads and processes can be accomplished much more elegantly. However, a thread that corrupts its memory means that other threads are also likely to suffer. While the operating system usually protects against this, the potential is always there.

Web Services

"Web services" describes a vital, emerging computing paradigm that will help the Grid in its adoption. In recent years it has become more imperative to connect people to resources; information and processes have changed the way that software is developed. IT systems increasingly require interoperability across platforms and flexible services that can easily evolve over time. This has led to the prevalence of open source solutions such as XML and other universal languages used for representation and transmitting structured data that is independent of programming languages, software platforms, and hardware. Many Web services build on the broad acceptance of XML. These are applications that use standard transports, encodings, and protocols to assist with the exchange of data and information. Because of the increasingly broad support across vendors and businesses, Web services can enable entire computer systems on virtually every platform to communicate over intranets, extranets, and the Internet (with the support of end-to-end security and reliable messaging). Distributed transactions are making the Grid a reality.

Web services are based on a core set of standards that describe the syntax and semantics of software communication, and these standards are pivotal to the interconnectivity of the Grid. Typically speaking, XML provides the common syntax for representing data to the applications in the system. The simple object access protocol (SOAP) provides the semantics for data exchanges, and web services description language (WSDL) provides mechanisms that can be used to describe the capabilities of a Web service. With Web services the issue is less about describing *that* resource (a Dell E1705 laptop, and more about describing classes of objects and the way that one needs to interact with those classes of objects. Additional specifications define functionality for Web service discovery, events, attachments, security, reliable messaging, transactions, and management.

Web services will become more critical to the Grid's success in any organization. By creating these services, more applications can be built to take advantage of the services themselves and incrementally grow as the organization grows. As the market for Web services rapidly expands, the need for advanced standards to govern security, reliability, and transactions becomes more apparent. Vendors across industries respond to the need by authoring sets of specifications, the goals of which are to provide a blueprint for advanced functionality while retaining the simplicity of basic Web services. In isolation, each requirement (security, reliable messaging, attachability, discovery, etc.) meets an elemental need of the system and when combined they address higher level functionalities required by distributed applications. With the right combination, one can eliminate the complexity and overhead associated with specifications that attempt to define multiple capabilities that are tightly coupled with other specifications and at the same time enable developers to apply only the necessary functionality needed to solve the immediate and longer-term needs as they arise. As more applications arise and needs change, new specifications can be created without concern with backward compatibility.

This paradigm differs from all other approaches. It focuses on simple Internet- (or intranet-) based standards (such as XML) as a way to address the heterogeneity of the Grid and other such broadly distributed computing. It is a technique for describing software components that need to be accessed, methods that are to be used to access components, and methods that can be used to discover and enable identification of relevant resources and service providers. These services are, ideally, programming language-independent, programming model-independent, and operating system-neutral.

Web services are becoming so important and so widely adopted that standards are being adopted and defined within the W3C (World Wide Web Consortium) and other standards organizations. There are three primary standards of particular interest.

A Web services framework has many advantages. Two are primary to our needs. The first is due to the need for dynamic discovery and composition of services in heterogeneous environments. This means mechanisms for registering and discovering interface definitions and endpoint implementation descriptions and for the dynamic generation of proxies based on bindings (potentially multiple bindings depending on the size and complexity of the interconnected resources) for specific interfaces. To some, Web services are synonymous with SOAP for all communication. This need not be true. Alternative transports can be and often are used to achieve higher performance or to run over specialized network protocols that SOAP does not work well with.

SOAP

Simple object access protocol (SOAP) provides a way to handle messaging between a service provider and a service requestor. It has a simple enveloping mechanism for the platform-independent XML document that will hold the remote procedure calls (RPCs) and messaging mechanisms. It is totally independent of the underlying transport protocols used in the system, and its messages can be carried over HTTP, FTP, Java messaging, or any other transport mechanism within the system and can describe multiple access mechanisms to the software components. Its primary purpose is to format a Web service invocation.

WSDL

Web Services Description Language (WSDL) is an XML document whose purpose is to describe Web services as a set of endpoints that operate on messages containing either messaging (document oriented) or RPC messages. Service interfaces are defined abstractly and the definition is in terms of message structure or sequences of simple message exchanges and operations. These are then bound to a concrete network protocol and data encoding format that defines an endpoint. All related endpoints are bundled together to define abstract endpoints and services. WSDL allows one to create descriptions of the endpoints and representations of their message payloads for a variety of message formats and network protocols, and provides binding protocols for using WSDL along with SOAP, HTTP, and MIME, among others.

WS-Inspection

WS-Inspection uses XML and related conventions as a means for locating service descriptions that are published by service providers. A WS-Inspection language document can contain a collection of service descriptions and links to other sources of service descriptions, making it flexible and extensible. Service descriptions are usually URLs to WSDL documents but can also be a reference to an entity within a universal description, discovery and integration (UDDI) registry. Links are usually URLs to other WS-Inspection documents. Service providers create WS-Inspection language documents and make those documents network accessible. Service requestors use standard Web access mechanisms such as HTTP GET or Java to retrieve these documents and discover the services that the provider is making available.

There are, of course, other Web service standards that address service orchestration, building sophisticated Web services by combining simpler services together to form more complex ones, and to create more flexible services to meet more needs.

It is critical to remember that the ability to virtualize and compose services depends almost directly on standard interface definitions. These standards include the semantics for service interactions so different services follow the same conventions for critical interactions such as error notification and completion notification. For this purpose, one can define a Grid service as an extension of Web services that can provide a set of well-defined and structurally sound interfaces that follow given sets of specific conventions. These interfaces will address discovery of resources, dynamic service creation, lifetime job management, notification, and manageability. The necessary conventions address naming and dynamic upgrades, even including rolling upgrades where possible. Authorization, authentication, reliable invocation, and concurrency also should be included in the specifications of these Grid services. These services will bind protocols and services and can remain external to the core Grid service definition. In this way, one can increase the generality of the architecture while not having to compromise functionality. Services in a Grid environment are transient, and it is critical to take into account the behaviors related to the management of these services. Because of the transient nature of the environment, services must be created and modified dynamically. When a service's activity is no longer needed, one can destroy the service.

Service instances might need to be instantiated dynamically to provide for consistent user response time. This can be accomplished by managing workload through dynamically adding capacity (additional blades, for example). These transient services might be responsible for instantiating a database query or a data mining operation. Another set might be responsible for bandwidth allocation or a data transfer between two distributed resources. Still more may need to be allocated to pre-reserve processing capability that is anticipated based on anticipated computing requirements. This transience is extremely significant because of the implications on how these services need to be managed, named, discovered, and used. Discovery will doubtless be a big issue as the transient nature itself makes discovery difficult at times; this also means that the ability to spawn new services will be key.

Building in the ability to allow for self-determination of characteristics of the services will provide the necessary flexibility to allow the Grid programs to thrive. This self-determination means that services should be able to configure themselves and the requests against them appropriately. They need a way to understand a standard representation for data services, including the representation of the controlling metadata. To accomplish this, one often uses named and typed XML elements encapsulated in standard container format and couples these elements with access modes such as push and pull.

Even in the Grid, it is important to remember that failure is inevitable as it is in any system. For this reason, there need to be mechanisms to provide for the reclamation of services, and the state associated with the failed services, and the failed operations.

Distributed services must be able to notify each other asynchronously of interesting changes in their state. There should be service interfaces for the subscription to and delivery of notification so that services can be constructed through the composition of smaller and simpler services and still deal with notifications in the same standard ways.

Other service interfaces should be created and enhanced to better handle authorization, management of policies, control of concurrency, and the monitoring and management of larger sets of Grid services.

Chapter 11

Wrapping It Up

In the end, whether an application gets to be a member of the Grid depends to a great degree on how the analysts and programmers determine whether the application can be created in a way to take advantage of all that the Grid has to offer or to leverage all of the virtual resources that make up the entire organization.

The bigger question, by far, is how one structures the Grid to allow the applications that can be brought into the environment to take advantage of as many of the Grid's features as possible. One needs to give thought to how one puts together the pieces of the applications and look carefully at how the users really use the data and how they expect the results to return to them. Is there any way that one can leverage breaking down the application into smaller pieces and allow those pieces to be used in as many ways as possible by as many other applications as possible.

One needs to ask questions when analyzing the applications that are in place that lead one to look outside the box. That may sound trite, but it is true. The problems are likely to be the same problems (maybe with a larger problem space or data space than has historically been the case), but the potential solutions to those problems now have been expanded almost logarithmically. Ironically, this means that solutions that would likely have been considered too costly or too computationally prohibitive may now be practical and applicable if one can leverage the newer architecture.

The first time one makes the recommendation to change the way that one's business does something so radically, so completely different from the way things were done previously, it feels a lot like standing on the edge of a raft waiting to take the plunge into the icy Colorado River. One takes the chance with one's application: put the raft into the water of the Grid environment, watch it float, and hope it does not sink.

So have faith in your abilities and at the end you can look back and realize that you did it. You are one of the adventurers who took the chance, who made the leap and pushed the boundaries, and know that it makes you one of the leaders of the pack.

Index